BLOOD ROYAL
The Story of the Spencers and the Royals

John Pearson is the author of several novels and biographies, including *Gone to Timbuctoo* (Author's Club Award for best first novel of the year), *The Life of Ian Fleming*, *The Life of James Bond*, *The Kindness of Dr Avicenna*, *The Profession of Violence: The Rise and Fall of the Kray Twins*, *Stags and Serpents: The History of the Dukes of Devonshire* and *The Ultimate Family*, a collective biography of the British Royal Family.

The Profession of Violence was awarded the Edgar Allan Poe Special Award by the Mystery Writers of America.

Also by John Pearson

BLOOD ROYAL

The Story of the Spencers and the Royals

JOHN PEARSON

HarperCollins*Publishers*

HarperCollins*Publishers*
77–85 Fulham Palace Road,
Hammersmith, London W6 8JB

www.fireandwater.com

This paperback edition 2000
1 3 5 7 9 8 6 4 2

First published in Great Britain by
HarperCollins*Publishers* 1999

ISBN 0 00 653054 0

Set in Linotype Sabon
by Rowland Phototypesetting Ltd,
Bury St Edmunds, Suffolk

Printed and bound in Great Britain by
Clays Ltd, St Ives plc

A catalogue record for this book is
available from the British Library

Contents

For Jane and Charles Cullum
and my wife Lynette

The author and publishers are grateful to the following
for permission to reproduce photographic material:

3, 7, 11, 12, 14 15, 16 courtesy Althorp; 4, 5 Photograph by Chris Andrews
and reproduced by kind permission of His Grace the Duke of Marlborough; 6
Photograph © National Trust Photographic Library/Tim Stephens; 8 courtesy
The Trustees of the Chatsworth Settlement; 17, 18, 19 courtesy Mary Roche;
20, 23 Photograph © PA News; 21, 24, 25, 29 Photograph © Rex Features; 22,
26 Photograph © Tim Rooke/Rex Features; 27 Photograph © Duncan Raban/
All Action; 28 Photograph © Peter Nicholls/Rex Features

Illustrations

16 Albert Edward John, seventh Earl Spencer. Painting by Augustus John.

17 & 18 Frances Burke-Roche and her first husband, James Burke-Roche.

19 Maurice Burke-Roche, fourth Baron Fermoy.

20 Edward John, Viscount Althorp (later eighth Earl Spencer) and the Hon. Frances Roche.

21 The teenage Diana Spencer.

22 Prince William.

23 Edward John, eighth Earl Spencer with his second wife, Raine.

24 The Prince and Princess of Wales on their wedding day.

25 The Princess of Wales with Raine Spencer.

26 The Princess of Wales in Bosnia.

27 The Windsors at the funeral of Diana, Princess of Wales.

28 Prince William, Prince Harry, Prince Charles and Earl Spencer at the funeral of Diana, Princess of Wales.

29 Charles Edward Maurice, ninth Earl Spencer.

Introduction

On the July morning in 1981 when Diana Spencer married Charles Windsor, Prince of Wales, the bride's father left his flat in Grosvenor Square before being driven off to Clarence House, from where he would accompany the twenty-year-old virgin bride in the Royal Glass Coach to St Paul's Cathedral.

A tall, rather shaky figure in his pale grey morning coat, Edward John, eighth Earl Spencer, had never entirely recovered from the cerebral haemorrhage he had suffered three years earlier, and there were fears as to how he would cope walking his daughter up the aisle before the assembled royal family, the massed cathedral congregation and nearly a billion television viewers round the world. (In fact he did it rather well.)

Just before leaving home, he managed to read out to the journalists waiting by his doorstep a carefully prepared statement of three short sentences specially composed for the occasion with the help of his second wife, Raine, Countess Spencer, daughter of the romantic historical novelist Barbara Cartland.

'The Spencers have through the centuries fought for their king and country. Today Diana is vowing to help her country for the rest of her life. She will be following the tradition of her ancestors, and will have at her side the man she loves.'

History was clearly on Johnnie Spencer's mind around this time, for not long before, also in front of journalists, he had mused aloud, as was his wont, about the forthcoming royal marriage.

'Honestly, what do I get out of it? You'll say the glory, but is glory the word? My family go back to the Saxons, so that sort of thing's not a bit new to me.'

Even allowing for the fact that history had never been the eighth Earl's strongest suit, remarks like these appear distinctly odd, revealing as they do an extraordinary depth of ignorance about his own family. For except in the sense that all our families go back somewhere, the Spencers simply don't 'go back' to the Saxons, and if there were any Saxon Spencers, no one knows if they kept pigs, tilled the fields or were hanged for cattle-stealing.

Nor do the great majority of Spencers whose lives we do know about in detail seem to have been over eager to 'fight for king and country through the centuries'. Of the nineteen individuals who have headed the Spencer family from the days of its founder, Sir John Spencer, back in the reign of King Henry VIII, only four saw any service for what might be broadly termed their 'King and Country'. The only one actually slain on the battlefield was a reluctant cavalier who thoroughly disliked his king and entertained grave doubts about the royal cause he died for. Of the other three, one, the future fourth Earl, fought bravely in the Royal Navy in alliance with the French and Russians in a naval battle with the Turks and the Egyptians; the second, Johnnie's father, 'Jolly Jack', seventh Earl Spencer, received a German bullet in the knee in Flanders and Johnnie himself saw active service with the Royal Scots Greys in the last two years of World War Two.

The rest of the Spencers range from more than half who could be described as calmly indifferent to the fortunes of their King if not their Country, to one avowed republican and several who, as dedicated Whigs, had little time for royalty in any form, except when they were milking the royal exchequer or doing their best to crop the powers of the king still further. One Spencer courtier seriously advised King George III to have the Prince of Wales murdered.

It was only on the subject of his daughter, Diana, that Johnnie Spencer spoke truer than he knew, when promising that she would 'follow the traditions of her ancestors'. Indeed, back in 1980, when the idea of her marriage to Prince Charles was first mooted, had the royal family and their advisers known just how closely she would end up doing this, they might have paused before welcoming her so warmly to their bosom. But again, at the time of the royal wedding, no one was very interested in the history of the Spencers, or particularly aware of the extraordinary tribe that Diana sprang from.

Certainly no one even half aware of her ancestry would have regarded 'shy Di', the demure ex-nursery-school teacher, as a malleable and harmless Cinderella figure who would bring painless glamour and romance to a lacklustre Royal Family, however badly she was treated. Indeed, they would probably have guessed that a direct descendant of Sarah Marlborough, who was also a distant kinswoman of Sir Winston Churchill, was unlikely to put up with being pushed around for ever – and that she would more than likely shake the throne if slighted. It was also conceivable that this girl from a family which boasted a nineteenth-century monk who died in the service of the poor and is currently a candidate for sainthood, might herself attempt to help the sick and needy. Nor should anyone have been entirely surprised when this distant niece of Georgiana Spencer, later Duchess of Devonshire, and undisputed queen of late eighteenth-century fashionable London society, suddenly turned herself, with such instinctive magic, into one of the most glamorous women in the world.

The most striking thing about the history of the Spencers is the range and richness of the individual characters involved, along with the diversity of their achievements. They really are a most unusual family, and it is this that makes their rise and continuity across so many generations such a fascinating story, culminating as it does in the tragic story of Diana Spencer.

Towards the end of her life Diana told a friend that she was prouder to have been a Spencer than a member of the House of Windsor, and her Spencer heredity must, in part at least, explain the mystery of how she found the strength to cope with a situation few others could have handled. Similarly her heredity must have also played its part in that startling transformation from the most naive and unsophisticated of child-brides into the most famous woman in the world.

Ironically, it is only following her death that one realises just how much she really was a Spencer. And now that her most important legacy rests in the two young princes that she leaves behind, the history of the family appears more relevant than ever. For while one cannot be too dogmatic about the often contradictory workings of heredity, already those dominant Spencer genes have brought a startling change to the future appearance of the British monarchy. Both boys are very much Spencers, and William in particular bears a startling resemblance to his mother, having the same classic profile and even the same wary glance which Diana so often gave the world. At sixteen, six foot two and still growing, Prince William promises to be the first very tall English king since Charles II. Following more than a century of distinctly short British monarchs, this in turn suggests that with the Royal Family the Spencer genes have overridden those of tiny Queen Victoria, and that something new and unexpected will succeed them.

At the moment it is still impossible to predict the result of this Spencer presence upon the future character of the monarchy, but one could make some interesting guesses after learning more about the rich and revealing history of the House of Spencer.

BLOOD ROYAL

The Story of the Spencers and the Royals

CHAPTER 1

The Rise and Rise of the Spencers

For several years before he died in 1522 Sir John Spencer had been pondering his tomb for the church of St Mary in the Northampton-shire village of Great Brington. It had to be as dignified and grand as possible, with life-sized alabaster effigies of himself and his wife, Isabella, lying dutifully beside him. He would be wearing armour, with a dagger at his hip, and Isabella was to wear her favourite cloak, with the three gold chains that he had given her around her neck, and two of her favourite puppies at her feet.

No one knows how much he paid the sculptor, but Sir John could clearly afford it. For, having planned his tomb, his thoughts did not rest there. He was not concerned solely with his own memorial, but was already making preparations for the future glory of his family. What better way than to build a sanctuary where he and his as yet unborn descendants could lie together and proclaim in death the splendour of the living?

Sir John must have discussed all this with Thomas Heritage, the rector of Great Brington, for Thomas was a clever man who would later move to London and become Surveyor of the King's Works, a post involving him in the building of a far grander sepulchre – the great renaissance tomb, by the Florentine sculptor Torrigiano, for the king's father, Henry VII, in his magnificent chapel in West-minster Abbey.

But the Spencer chapel in Great Brington Church has a touch of magnificence all its own. Here, in this unassuming country church, Sir John's chapel, with its pillars and elaborate stone tracery, forms what the omniscient Professor Nikolaus Pevsner – not one for unnecessary praise – described as one of the county's 'great storehouses of costly and self-confident monuments'.

Note the word 'self-confident'. For when he built his chapel it was as if Sir John foresaw the future splendours of his line, and was willing his descendants to be worthy of this splendid resting place he was creating for them all.

This was remarkable enough, but what makes the Spencer chapel extraordinary is that the tomb he built for himself is not exactly what it seems. The heraldic shields, the knightly posture, and the other trappings of chivalry proclaim the presence of a great medieval noble.

But Sir John was nothing of the kind. He was a prosperous farmer who had moved to Northamptonshire from the nearby Warwickshire village of Wormleighton some years earlier. And the money for his tomb and chapel did not come from knightly deeds in foreign parts or courage in battle or the service of a royal master. It came from sheep.

If the 'green and pleasant land' of Diana, Princess of Wales's favourite hymn exists, it has to be in the gentle fields and fertile valleys of Northamptonshire. Together with its next-door neighbour, Warwickshire, this whole area of the Southern Midlands forms the rich green heart of England, large areas of which were once a royal forest.

Northamptonshire remains a secret county. Tucked beneath the industrial Midlands, which barely touch it, it has stayed far enough away from London to avoid the suburban fate of the Home Counties, while keeping contact with the capital. Northampton itself is not a graceful city. In the last century it found fame as 'the footwear capital of England': but the countryside is never far away, and large areas of this county of 'spires and squires' remain unspoiled. With fine hunting country, it has attracted the fox-hunting gentry and nobility, and supposedly boasts more of their 'magnificent and elegant seats' than any comparable county in Britain. Here they have tended to stay put across the centuries and still survive as nowhere else in England.

The sheep have also stayed put in the fields around Great Brington, black faced, mysterious creatures with their stiff disdainful gait and their alchemist's ability to turn green fields into meat and wool and money – in the days of the Tudor Spencers, very large amounts of money.

When Henry VIII was crowned, the demand for English wool was starting to produce a boom in sheep production not unlike the twentieth century's boom in the demand for oil. Sheep-farming was already big business and the great 'sheep walks' of the Cotswolds, Derbyshire and Romney Marsh dedicated solely to enormous flocks of sheep, amazed the foreign visitors to Tudor England.

What was good for sheep was not so good for human beings, and the creation of sheep walks caused widespread suffering. But what became a social problem for Tudor governments was a golden opportunity for great 'sheep masters' like Sir John Spencer, who realised that turning large tracts of fertile land to sheep was the surest way to make a fortune.

Spencers had been farming in Warwickshire for generations, but it was only with Sir John's arrival on the scene that their lives began to change appreciably. It was he who brought the family to Northamptonshire by purchasing the loam-rich pasturage round Althorp, and in 1508 he followed this by building there a timber and redbrick manor house, probably on the site of an earlier medieval structure, set in a hollow to protect it from the elements. He had only recently enlarged the family home at Wormleighton, but he needed Althorp as a centre of operations for the seven hundred acre sheep-run he had bought and in 1512 he was licensed to create a deer park round his house – proof of his new gentlemanly status.

As founder of the family, Sir John was clearly a remarkable man – not least because of the way that in his youth he seems to have avoided the temptation of taking a swifter but far riskier path to riches in the service of the crown. His maternal uncle was the notorious Richard Empson, who together with his partner Edmund

Dudley, became Henry VII's richest and most extortionate tax gatherer. Following the practice of the day, the young John Spencer could almost certainly have made a career working for this powerful relation. But Empson's extortions made him widely hated, and when Henry VIII executed him as a scapegoat in 1510, it must have been a fearsome lesson to his nephew and to his descendants on the hazards of the court and royal service. Unlike many rising Tudor families, the Spencers would carefully avoid the court as a source of enrichment for many years to come, and although John Spencer proved extremely sharp at making money, he also showed unusual concern for the future of his family in the care he took never to create unnecessary enemies.

Allowing for the flattery of a later generation, his description by an eighteenth-century genealogist as a 'noble spirit tempered with the greatest humanity', may well have had some basis in reality. Certainly Sir John took his social and religious obligations very seriously, being 'liberal to his poor neighbours', and rebuilding several local churches, including Great Brington and Wormleighton. Since the land round Althorp had already been cleared for sheep, so the peaceable Sir John was able to avoid arousing anyone's enmity through evictions. His anxiety to avoid feuds against the family even extended to his will, where he charged his executors after his death to 'recompense anyone who could prove that he had done him damage'.

During the last years of his life, John Spencer advanced unspectacularly but surely, becoming sheriff for Northampton in 1511, and being knighted by King Henry VIII soon after. This also established his family as being of knightly rank, and all his successors would receive the same honour. At the same time, although Wormleighton remained his principal residence, something must have told him that Althorp was the place where the future of the Spencers really lay.

Like the shrewd countryman he was, at Althorp he had selected some of the finest pasturage in England, and since it was purchased out of capital, he left no debts behind to plague his children. He also knew what he was doing when he chose this land so close to the territory the Spencers already farmed in Warwickshire, which meant that their two great sheep walks could be run with maximum efficiency and the whole be 'treated as a vast single flock'.

There is something very up-to-date about his insistence on cutting labour costs and rationalising activities into this single large-scale holding. Before he came to Althorp he had run the entire Wormleighton sheep walk with nine skilled shepherds managing upwards of 10,000 sheep, which meant that he could check his employees' honesty and personally supervise the way they did their work. Now he could do the same at Althorp.

As a good businessman he was also unusually responsive to the demands of the market. According to Trevelyan the one defect of English sheep was that, being bred exclusively for wool, they tended to be 'pitifully small and thin'. Knowing the Englishman's love of meat, Sir John bred his sheep not only for their wool but for their flesh, and was soon selling them to the area around Northampton and 'when it was fatt to the Citie of London and other places yerely'.

But in spite of his self-confidence, the fact remains that however rich he was, Sir John was gambling on the longest odds when he built his chapel for the future glory of the Spencers. As he must have known, it was rare for farming families to stay prosperous over several generations, and local gentry like the Spencers were particularly vulnerable.

According to J.H. Plumb, 'Throughout the centuries . . . landed families had risen only to fall again. For one that survived a score were destroyed, overtaken by those natural disasters which beset families – failure of heirs, wanton extravagance, reckless loyalty, sheer bad luck. But debt, the crushing, inexorable burden of debt, extinguished most.'

Even for Sir John, the thought of debt must have been a constant nightmare for the future, worse than the smallpox or the wasting flux or death in childbirth. There was one sure shield against it – money; and he taught his children by his own example to acquire it and invest it, and never, never waste it.

Apart from the profits from his sheep, there was another method of enrichment which Sir John bequeathed to his descendants. As a sheep-breeder he had learned that money spent on stock to improve the strain was rarely wasted. The same applied to sons and daughters, and Sir John was the first of the Spencers who seriously concerned himself with hyperogamy – the art of marrying above one's station.

A good marriage, particularly for a son and heir, was a wonderful investment, since it produced not only useful family connections but also whatever dowry or inheritance the bride brought with her. As with everything in money-conscious Tudor England, it could be expensive to provide a son with an adequate settlement to win an heiress. But just as the Spencers put their money into breeding better sheep, so Sir John began the practice of investing in fine marriages to enrich the family.

Long before he built his tomb he had achieved this with his son and heir, young William Spencer, when he married him to Susan Knightley, daughter of one of the richest families in Northamptonshire. When it was Susan and William's turn to find their son a wife they were more ambitious still, moving outside the county to tap into the wealth of the City of London by marrying John Spencer II to Katherine Kitson, daughter of the 'merchant prince of London', Sir Thomas Kitson. Sir John Spencer II was the first member of the family to become a local MP, and he and his wife had ten surviving children, six of whom were daughters. But they were rich enough to provide sufficient dowries to marry all the girls but one into the landed aristocracy. One daughter, Anne, was widowed twice, becoming successively Lady Mounteagle, then Lady Compton and ending up as the Countess of Dorset. Her sister, Alice, became Countess of Derby.

However, when John and Katherine came to choose a wife for their son and heir, John Spencer III, they avoided both the aristocracy and the City, and picked on an area of conspicuous wealth – that of the flourishing rich Tudor lawyers. John was married to the great heiress Mary Caitlin, daughter of Chief Justice Sir Robert

Caitlin, and when she died the bulk of the great Bedfordshire estates of the Caitlins descended to her son Robert, thus enriching further still the fortunate and fertile breed of Spencers.

Throughout the reign of Elizabeth I the Spencers continued to advance, for these were serious people following their life's essential purpose. They had found no problem in embracing the new religion after the Reformation and the Protestant work ethic clearly suited them. Since they had succeeded, God was clearly with them and, despite their wealth, they dressed soberly, lived righteously and continued to invest extremely shrewdly. They never borrowed. Surplus capital was spent on further purchases of land, and the family domain grew accordingly.

They were not miserly so much as careful, even in their hospitality, and although Althorp was considerably enlarged in 1577 with Caitlin money, it was widely said that 'the Spencers always tempered ostentation with frugality'. But just as their wealth protected them, so it also formed the basis of their social standing and they were being counted among the top-most ranks of the gentry of Northamptonshire.

But their ambitions were no longer exclusively confined within their county; having intermarried with so many grander families, the Spencers were almost ready for the most important move of all – upwards into the aristocracy .

In normal circumstances a farming family, however prosperous, but lacking noble ancestry or court connections, would have found this difficult, particularly with the barriers of class and breeding and an ageing Queen Elizabeth increasingly reluctant to dilute her aristocracy with fresh creations. But the Spencers always had what Napoleon demanded of his marshals – luck. And few were luckier than the current heir, Robert Spencer.

After the founding father, Sir John Spencer I, Robert Spencer is the most important figure to emerge so far within the upwardly mobile House of Spencer. He started life with the unusual advantage in this fertile family of being an only child, so that all the resources of the Spencers and the Caitlins funnelled down to him alone. He was to prove remarkably adroit at making the most of them.

While holding to the Spencer virtues – shrewdness over money, discreet ambition and the calm composure of the countryman – Robert appears to have inherited the sharpness and the ready tongue which made the Caitlins such successful lawyers. He had sufficient culture to befriend the playwright Ben Jonson, and saw the necessity in a vulgar age of spending conspicuously to enhance one's standing.

As only son and heir to a rich inheritance, Robert could count on a settlement to tempt the wealthiest heiress, and when his marriage was arranged with seventeen year-old Margaret, daughter of the notoriously rich Nottinghamshire entrepreneur and landowner, Sir Francis Willoughby, great hopes were set upon the union. Margaret dutifully produced three daughters and three sons in swift succession. Then in 1597 she died in childbirth.

Robert records her passing rather like the cool businessman he was: 'Margaret, my most loving wife, having borne me all those children. She was one of the daughters and co-heirs of Sir Francis Willoughby, of honourable parentage, but her virtue surpassed all.'

Although only twenty-seven at the time, Robert never remarried. He was probably too busy, and Margaret, after all, had left him with sufficient children. Had he felt the urge to remarry there was a warning close at hand in the fate of his own rich father-in-law. Sir Francis had taken a second wife, and brought disaster on his family. Heavily in debt, and infatuated with his young bride, he had made all his remaining property over to her, then died intestate not long before Margaret herself, leaving her, and hence the Spencers, next to nothing.

It was a rare example of marriage with an heiress back-firing; but, far from repining, Robert was soon making greater efforts to repair the damage, and adding to the fortunes of the Spencers in the process. He received his full inheritance on the death of his father, Sir John Spencer III, in 1599, and almost immediately started to expand the house at Althorp, increasing it in size and splendour. He also turned his attention to the family business, becoming in the process the nearest thing in Tudor England to a modern marketing tycoon.

He remained very much a farmer, and under his direction the two great Spencer farms at Althorp and Wormleighton were developed to their full potential. But his true achievement was to make these farms part of a carefully worked-out large-scale marketing operation. The Spencer sheep had always been renowned for 'the sweetness and richness of their flesh', and he now concentrated on the regular production of animals for the London market. Thanks to the scale of his business he could cut out middle-men and, with Althorp relatively close to London, could deal directly with the Smithfield butchers to satisfy the growing city's apparently insatiable demand for meat. He was a regular supplier to merchants like Messrs Zackery and Cutts, 'butchers dweling in Est Chepe', and also to the rich wool stapler Henry Moore of Bishopsgate, who purchased what was called 'the single clip', an entire season's shearing from the Spencer flock.

At the end of the sixteenth century it must have taken an organising genius to cope with more than 12,000 breeding ewes and lambs each season, and oversee the portage of several thousand sheep the seventy-odd miles from Althorp to Eastcheap in a state to produce edible mutton on their arrival. Sir Robert would have used expert drovers, but once the Spencer flocks were on the move the logistics must have been formidable, calling for precise arrangements for their pasturing *en route* to London.

With much of his business conducted in the capital, Sir Robert, now a rich young widower, had closer contacts there than previous Spencers, and lived part of every year in London. He was in London early in 1603 when Queen Elizabeth was dying, and must have known the time had come to get his title.

He was so keen to make a good impression on Elizabeth's successor, that he was among the crowd of rich Londoners who rode out specially to welcome James I from Scotland at the gates of London. He followed this a few weeks later with a masque, speedily written by Ben Jonson, which he staged at Althorp in honour of the royal consort, Anne of Denmark, as she journeyed down to London. Thus Anne became the first of many royal guests to stay at Althorp.

Among the many differences between King James and Queen Elizabeth was their attitude to honours, which James regarded rather as Robert Spencer regarded sheep – as an eminently saleable commodity. Anyone with an income of £200 or more was obliged by this hungry king to buy a knighthood. Serious honours cost considerably more and shortly after entertaining Anne of Denmark as his guest, Robert Spencer, like the honest businessman he was, paid James I £3,000, cash down, for a barony.

Now that he had his peerage and was on speaking terms with royalty, it might have seemed as if the new Lord Spencer was about to make another break with family tradition and become a courtier. Since he was rich and handsome, some may have feared the worst when the King, who was notoriously susceptible to young good-looking males, appointed him to head an embassy to the German court of Wurttemberg, to invest its reigning Duke with the Order of the Garter.

This meant crossing France, and as the first of his family venturing abroad the new Lord Spencer was soon exhibiting the true-born Englishman's suspicion of the French. 'The nobility of France are poor; the gentry of France are crafty; the vulgar are rude and unconscionable,' he wrote.

Nor did the splendours of the court of Wurttemberg, which included 'walking on red cloth spread for the purpose' at the investiture, particularly impress him. Despite the Duke's gift of a splendid piece of plate, the only moment when Lord Spencer's spirits rose was when the Duke announced that he would pay for his expenses.

Having failed to enjoy the court of Wurttemberg, it is hardly surprising that Robert also failed to appreciate the court of King James, which was acquiring a dubious reputation. The King was personally repellent, some of his courtiers were worse, and although the court could be a source of personal enrichment, Robert knew better ways of growing rich. Far from being keen 'to serve his king and country', he became one Spencer who henceforth would keep as far away from court and king as possible.

He stuck by this decision for the rest of his life, refusing any further honours. Even the earldom which the King offered him some years later for a mere £10,000, failed to tempt him. Another rising dynasty, the Cavendishes, who were also busily enriching themselves from sheep, did purchase one. But Robert seemed happy with his humble barony, and genuinely preferred the rich green fields of Northamptonshire to the suspect pleasures of Whitehall. He enlarged the original Spencer house at Wormleighton, but seems to have preferred Althorp, where he planted trees and built a gabled 'stand' for his favourite pastime – hawking. It was at Althorp that an eighteenth-century historian described the shepherd baron, like some uncorrupted senator from republican Rome, 'making the countrie a virtuous court where his flocks and fields brought him more calm and happie contentment than the various and mutable dispensations of the court'.

But Robert Spencer was no country bumpkin. By avoiding the court, investing shrewdly, and concentrating on the wholesale meat trade, he amassed a truly fearsome fortune and was widely reputed 'to have by him the most mony of any person in the kingdom'. Actually there were families with ancestral lands and property who were richer, but Robert Spencer was unusual in that much of his wealth was in ready money and could be called on at a moment's notice. This was another Spencer characteristic he had inherited together with his calling. Graziers and cattle dealers traditionally carried large amounts of money – to buy and sell and deal in livestock and in land. And like the grazier that he remained, Robert used his cash in hand to improve still further the quality of his livestock and the standing of his family.

Although he had no problems in purchasing his peerage from King James I, the new Lord Spencer seems to have encountered snobbery from certain members of more ancient families. With his quick wit and self-assurance, this was something he could cope with if the famous story of his House of Lords encounter with the ill-mannered Lord Arundel is any indication.

During a speech, Robert was harking back to earlier times, when Lord Arundel rudely interrupted him. 'When these things were doing, the noble Lord's ancestors were keeping sheep,' he shouted.

'When my ancestors were keeping sheep, the noble Lord's ancestors were plotting treason,' Robert answered.

Uproar ensued, and Arundel was briefly committed to the Tower for contempt of Parliament, before apologising.

But although quick-witted Robert got the better of the graceless Arundel, whose father and grandfather had both met their fate on Tower Hill, the shaft seems to have gone home. Robert's father, Sir John Spencer III, had in fact already done his best to offset any stigma attached to the parvenu status of the Spencers by hiring an official from the College of Heralds to trace their genealogy.

He must have paid him well for, after lengthy study, the herald produced an elaborate family tree linking the Spencers with a far older family whose name was conveniently similar to theirs – the Despensers of Gloucestershire. Although by then extinct, the Despensers had come to England with the Conqueror, and had been extremely powerful in the Middle Ages.

With this descent established, the College of Heralds permitted the Spencers to bear the Despenser arms – which they duly did, and despite the sneers of people like the Arundels, would soon take their place among the ranks of the most ancient families in the land for virtually the next three centuries. Not until 1901 would the famous genealogist, Professor J.H. Round, examine the Spencer pedigree in detail and expose it as an almost total fabrication; apart from the similarity of name there was clearly no real connection between the Althorp Spencers and the ancient race of the Despensers.

But the Professor's revelations came too late to worry the Spencers in the least. By then the aristocracy was being swamped with the new creations of Victorian England – plutocratic dukes, banking earls, industrial barons – making the Spencers seem positively feudal in comparison. In their own right they had grown genealogically old, and if they had missed the Norman Conquest no one noticed.

But in Stuart England lineage mattered, and once the Spencers had established their right to bear the Despenser arms there was little to prevent them rising to the topmost reaches of the aristocracy. In 1614 Robert linked the Spencers with another, considerably grander, family by marrying his son and heir, William Spencer, to Penelope Wriothesley, daughter of the rich and famous Henry Wriothesley, third Earl of Southampton.

As a young man, handsome Henry Wriothesley was Shakespeare's patron, friend, and possibly his lover if, as has been suggested, he really was the mysterious young man of the Sonnets. After a highly chequered career, by the 1620s Wriothesley had emerged among the chief opponents in the House of Lords of an increasingly authoritarian King James. Robert joined him in the Lords as an outspoken critic of the king's policy, and played his part in the dismissal of the corrupt and unpopular Lord Chancellor, Francis Bacon. During the last two years of his life, following King James's death in 1625, Robert continued to oppose the even more absolutist claims of the new king, Charles I.

Economically as well as politically, Robert's world was changing, so that by the time he died in 1627 the great European wool hunger, which had enriched the Spencers for so long, was drawing to a close. Once the profits from large-scale sheep production began to fade, it was clear that the days of old Sir John Spencer's great family business up at Althorp were numbered, and the family started to rely on the more gentlemanly practice of renting out their lands to tenant farmers.

Despite his splendid marriage, William Spencer, second baron, had lived too long in the shadow of his forceful father to be much more than a nonentity. He was extremely rich, but steered clear of court and politics, spending his time on his estates and rarely appearing in the House of Lords.

His son, Henry, seemed more fortunate than his father. With brown eyes, dark skin and curly hair, he was considerably better looking, and in 1636 he had just come down from Oxford when his father's unexpected death at the age of forty-five made him third Lord Spencer, heir to a great fortune and master of almost everything that he surveyed. His friend Edward Hyde (the future historian and politician, Lord Clarendon) described the sixteen-year-old Henry now as 'A lord of great fortune, tender years and an early judgement.'

Since he was not personally involved in the commercial interests that had preoccupied his grandfather, and since his father was no longer breathing down his neck, Henry had something else his predecessors had lacked – freedom to enjoy a gentlemanly life of leisure. He could frequent society, talk, study and travel as he willed. At Oxford he had got to know the Christian humanist, Lucius Cary, Lord Falkland, whose house at Great Tew, outside Oxford, formed a centre for a number of the brightest intellects of London and the University. It is not known whether Henry took part in any of the famous Great Tew debates on religion and politics, but he came to share most of Falkland's views on these subjects – especially on the need for reconciliation between Crown and Parliament and a broadly puritan approach to Christianity.

As his own master, the young Lord Spencer also enjoyed a further freedom granted to few other members of his family – the right to choose himself a wife.

Even today Dorothy Sidney has a certain immortality in English literature as the muse of the Carolean poet Edmund Waller, who met her near Penshurst Place in Kent, the home of her father, Robert Sidney, second Earl of Leicester. She was an intelligent, pretty girl with blond hair and extremely bright blue eyes. Waller called her 'Sacarissa', the sweet one, making her the subject of his best known love poem, 'Go Lovely rose', which urged her to enjoy the bliss of carnal love before, like the rose, she faded.

'Small is the worth of beauty from the light retired.
Bid her come forth. Suffer herself to be admired,
And blush not so to be desired.'

Did Dorothy Sidney blush to be desired? Not by the author of these graceful words, who was eleven years her senior, and who, as a widower and descendant of Buckinghamshire gentry, had little chance of doing as his verse suggested. That was left to Henry Spencer who, following in the poet's wake, met Dorothy soon after, but, unlike poor Waller, happened to possess what she demanded – a great fortune, a gentlemanly presence and a title. When they married at Penshurst Place in 1639 Henry Spencer was nineteen and Dorothy Sidney twenty-three.

Brought up at Penshurst Place in Kent, most romantic of ancestral houses, compared with which Althorp was still a draughty, over-grown Tudor manor house, the new Lady Spencer would become the first of a line of formidable women who were to play important roles in the history of the Spencers. She also brought a fresh addition to the gene pool of the family, which probably introduced some start-ling changes in to the Spencer character in the next few generations.

Dorothy's father, Robert Sidney, second earl of Leicester, came of a famous line of Tudor soldiers and administrators including his uncle, the legendary poet-hero Sir Philip Sidney, author of *Arcadia*, who died so gallantly at the battle of Zutphen in what were then the Spanish Netherlands. His death at the age of thirty-two, caught the imagination of Elizabethan England on something like the scale of the reaction to the death of his distant kinswoman, Princess Diana, four centuries later. Although Queen Elizabeth disliked Sidney, he was mourned across Europe. One nobleman of the day thought it sufficient to put on his tomb – 'Friend of Sir Philip Sidney'. On hearing of his death, Philip II of Spain wrote in his diary: 'He was my godson', and the citizens of London are said to have 'packed the windows and even the roofs of Fleet Street to watch his coffin trundle by'.

After marrying Sidney's great niece, Henry Spencer took his bride to Paris. Lord Leicester was there as ambassador, and they spent the next two years with him, returning to Althorp at the end of 1641 with three young children, Robert, Henry and Dorothy. They were just in time for the outbreak of the Civil War a few months later.

Henry's puritan sympathies and anti-court family traditions inclined him, like his friend Falkland and others among the aristocracy, to side with Parliament. He was wary of both Court and King, and as late as June 1642 Parliament appointed him Lord Lieutenant for Northamptonshire, charged with raising the militia on its behalf against the King. Accepting this duty, Henry put the Roundhead Militia Ordinance into effect with considerable vigour, ensuring that almost all the shire was held by Parliament when hostilities began in earnest.

Then suddenly he changed allegiance. According to Clarendon, 'he was recovered to a right understanding, of which he was very capable, by his uncle, [the Earl of] Southampton'.

Lord Southampton, like Lord Falkland who had also reluctantly joined the King, remained one of the strongest supporters of a compromise peace throughout the Civil War. And Henry, in spite of his conversion to the Royal cause, was actually a most reluctant cavalier, as was his father-in-law, Lord Leicester, who unwillingly settled for the King. It was an indication of how split the country had become that two of Lord Leicester's own sons – Philip, Lord Lisle, and his younger brother, Algernon Sidney – stayed firmly on the side of Parliament.

Early in September Henry rode away from Althorp to join King Charles at Shrewsbury, having sent his wife and children to Lady Leicester's protection at Penshurst. He had done his work so well in organising Northamptonshire for Parliament that he was unable to raise a local regiment for the King. Refusing a commission, he decided to serve in the King's bodyguard instead.

Someone said of Spencer that he shared Lord Falkland's 'belief in the crown, modified by distrust of its wearer'. This distrust increased the more he saw of Charles. But as an aristocrat he faced a problem which had not concerned the Spencers when they were raising sheep and making money – the idea of honour. And as he soon discovered, honour was expensive.

Honour made him lend the King £10,000 and join him when he

raised his standard at Nottingham in September 1642. And at the battle of Edgehill, the first pitched battle of the Civil War, honour led him to the forefront of the cavalry charge against the Parliamentary forces.

After Edgehill, Henry spent the winter with his family, presumably at Oxford, but with spring the fighting and the threat to the city resumed, and they left him reluctantly for the safety of Penshurst. In June, guessing that he would never see the money he had lent the King again, he decided to accept the earldom that James had tried to sell his grandfather in its place. Later, when the King left Oxford to lay siege to Gloucester, it was no longer young Lord Spencer riding with him in the royal bodyguard, but the newly created Earl of Sunderland.

But Lord Sunderland hated soldiering as much as ever. In a letter to his wife from the siege of Gloucester he wrote about 'the noise and tintamarre of guns and drums, the horid spectacles and the hideous cries of dead and hurt men'. He went on to assure her, 'How infinitely more happy I should esteem myself quietly to enjoy your company at Althorp, than to be troubled with the noises and engaged in the factions of the Court, which I shall ever endeavour to avoid.'

But once again he was having to contend with honour. 'Unless a man were resolved to fight on the parliament side, which for my part I had rather be hanged, it will be said without doubt that a man is afraid to fight. If there could be an expert to be found to solve the punctilio of honour, I would not continue here an hour.'

So honour kept him reluctantly in the flooded trenches round the city, but with few illusions now about the royal cause. As a keen Protestant, the more he saw of Charles I and his courtiers, the less he wished to be involved with them. As C.V. Wedgwood writes, 'the growing influence of the Papists on the king deeply disturbed him. The King, he thought, would be in London before the year was out; and this would bring the triumph of extreme and violent men, and there would be no alternative for those, like himself, of moderate and Protestant views, but to go into voluntary exile.'

He continued seeing Falkland, one of the few to whom he could now talk freely. During the siege they often dined together in Lord Falkland's cottage, together with the Protestant theologian John Chillingworth (currently enlisted in the royal forces as an engineer). The three sat long into the night, talking not of honour, nor of tactics, but of the more serious business of theology.

The battle camp, however, was no place for moderate-minded intellectuals. When Lord Essex, the Parliamentary leader, took the risk of leading his army out of London to relieve the siege of Gloucester, the King saw his chance to lift the siege, march swiftly back to London and retake the undefended capital. But before this happened, Charles, egged on by his courtiers spoiling for a fight, decided to engage the Parliamentary army outside Newbury.

Henry Spencer had as little faith in the royal strategy as in the royal person or his followers. But yet again honour made him set aside his doubts and placed him in the forefront of the royal army as the autumn sun was rising and the cavalry prepared to charge the enemy below them.

Clarendon describes what happened next. 'Having no Command in the Army [Sunderland] attended upon the King's Person, under the obligation of Honour; and putting himself that day in the King's troop as a Volunteer before they came to Charge, was taken away by a cannon bullet.'

Henry Spencer, first Earl of Sunderland, was twenty-three when the cannon bullet took him off. His friend Lord Falkland died in the ensuing battle, but before they buried Henry in a common grave, someone cut his heart out and carried it back to Althorp. Here his widow, Countess of Sunderland for just four months, had it placed in the vault in Great Brington church beside those 'costly and self-confident' tombs of her husband's ancestors.

They had had a happy marriage. 'I know you lived happily, and so as nobody but yourself could measure the contentment of it,' her father wrote. 'I rejoiced at it and did thank God for making me one of the means to procure it for you.' She was five months pregnant with a second daughter at the time; her eldest son, two-year-old Robert Spencer, was now the second Earl of Sunderland.

CHAPTER 2

Shameless Sunderland

Robert, second Earl of Sunderland (1641–1702)

Henry Spencer died honourably, but he had done his family no favours by getting himself killed in battle for a cause he barely believed in and leaving behind a pregnant wife with three small children to be taken care of. So it was predictable that his son Robert would not be too preoccupied with honour when he became a man. Honour would prove a luxury that he could ill afford, but through dishonour Robert, second Earl of Sunderland, did more to advance the Spencers than any other member of the family, apart from its founder, Sir John Spencer, who was probably not terribly concerned with honour either.

Sunderland's contemporaries loathed him, almost to a man. 'Shameless Sunderland', they called him, and 'the great apostate of Althorp'. But this was generally said behind his back, for people also feared him. At the height of his power, the future Queen Anne called him 'the most subtil working villain on the face of the earth' as he had led her father to ruin; long after his death Macaulay's damning verdict was: 'Nature had given him a keen understanding, a restless and mischievous temper, a cold heart and an abject spirit.'

Much of this was true. Even today Robert Sunderland appears splendidly despicable – a turncoat and a cynic, a false friend and great betrayer. Unlike the later Spencers, who became so loaded down with wealth and honours that they had little alternative to being honourable and virtuous, Sunderland is slippery as a snake, darting whichever way he feels his fortunes might direct him, changing religion when it suits him, wildly extravagant, an accomplished liar, mercenary and utterly corrupt. If he had a conscience, no one has found evidence of its existence.

All of which makes him absolutely fascinating, and has earned him a unique position in the human chain that links the Spencers with the present day. Balzac remarked that behind every great fortune lies a great crime. Behind the Spencer family lies Shameless Sunderland.

Unlike those of certain of the later Spencers, Robert's face is unforgettable. Someone called him 'the thin great man in Whitehall', and one gets a hint of this in his later portraits – the absurdly haughty mien, the hooded, faintly slanting eyes, the unquestionably aristocratic nose.

As far as the Spencers were concerned, he increased the splendour and importance of the family immeasurably. Thanks to him Althorp was transformed from a Jacobean mansion into a palace worthy of a Prince. Thanks again to him, the family taboo against the court was finally forgotten, which helped promote the Spencers from titled plutocrats into serious members of the aristocracy. He himself became a statesman of the first rank, playing a crucial role in politics and the development of the constitution and the monarchy. And finally, besides all this, he placed his descendants in his everlasting debt by putting them in line for one of the very great inheritances of the eighteenth century. Such were the fruits of Sunderland's dishonour.

One can but speculate on how a family as sensible and solid as the Spencers suddenly produced this quite outlandish character. Perhaps it was those turbulent Sidney genes which became laced with the rustic nature of the Spencers when Lord Leicester's daughter married Henry Spencer.

Four months after Henry's death, Dorothy Sunderland gave birth to a daughter, Penelope, but as the fighting was already spreading through Northamptonshire she was forced to stay on at Penshurst with her parents and the children.

As the Civil War progressed, both sides inflicted damage on the Spencer properties. First the Roundheads sacked Althorp, then the Royalists razed the original Spencer house at Wormleighton to the ground (apart from a gatehouse which survives, a tantalising relic, to the present day). Finally, to crown the disaster, the Spencer estates were sequestered as royalist property after Cromwell's final victory.

Because of this, Dorothy Sunderland and the children had to go on living at Penshurst for seven years as guests of Lord and Lady Leicester, and the infant Earl of Sunderland grew up with the Leicester's youngest son, Henry Sidney. Although he was his uncle, Henry was almost his exact contemporary and became his closest – and at times his only – friend.

It was not in Dorothy's nature to accept the disaster that war had inflicted on the Spencers, and she placed the family firmly in her debt by the way she helped restore their fortunes. First she took advantage of the fact that Sidneys had fought on both sides in the Civil War, and somehow persuaded both her Roundhead brothers, Lord de Lisle and Algernon Sidney, to use their influence to get the Spencer lands released from sequestration. Then, once Althorp was recovered, she set about repairing the extensive damage and making the old house habitable. It was thanks entirely to her that the ten-year-old Robert, Earl of Sunderland, was finally able to return to his ancestral home in 1651.

In the absence of records, how she managed this with the Republic still in power remains a mystery, particularly as her activities did not stop there. Considerable sums of money must have been forthcoming, for during the 1650s the courtyard was roofed over and a few years later work began on the great staircase that is one of the glories of the house. Just as remarkable in its way, Dorothy was able to ensure that, at seventeen, her eldest son embarked on what she felt to be the proper education of a nobleman – a lengthy period travelling through France and Italy

Bear-led by an Oxford don, pious Dr Pierce of Magdalen, Robert Sunderland and Henry Sidney departed for the Continent together, with introductions from Lord Leicester to some of the most noble houses in France and Spain. They travelled indefatigably and, thanks to the reputation of the Sidneys, seem to have been welcome guests wherever they alighted.

After the England of the Commonwealth it must have been a revelation for these two young noblemen to find themselves in Europe with the *entrée* to some of the grandest and most elegant society in France. How Dr Pierce coped with them is not recorded. It seems that in Paris he could not prevent them running into debt; but what they spent their money on is matter for conjecture. For Robert Sunderland was already starting a lifelong love-affair with France, and in particular with the glittering society he witnessed at its court, dancing attendance on the most impressive king in Christendom.

It was in France that his passion for painting and architecture started, and having a considerable flair for language, he was also able to perfect his Spanish in addition to his French, when he and his youthful uncle left Paris for Madrid and visited the Spanish court together. Then, on the eve of the restoration of King Charles II, Sunderland returned to England as what he would remain for the rest of his life – more of a European than an Englishman.

He came back to find his mother remarried – to a handsome, ineffectual Kentishman called Smythe – but she was still calling herself the Countess of Sunderland, and making it clear that Mr Smythe had no authority whatever over his noble stepson. Sunderland would have undoubtedly agreed, since he already possessed the arrogance of a Restoration rake and was hardly likely to take criticism lightly – particularly from somebody called Smythe. At Oxford he survived a term at Christ Church, then left in a hurry for what appears a most unlikely reason – supporting another Christ Church man, William Penn, the Quaker and future founder of Pennsylvania, in a demonstration against the reintroduction of the Anglican liturgy in the college chapel. Not that it mattered very much what Robert Sunderland got up to now. For with his majority approaching, he would soon take his seat in the House of Lords, and with it full control of Althorp and his enviable inheritance.

He was fortunate to come of age in the freer atmosphere following the Restoration, and more fortunate still when King Charles decided to repay the £10,000 which Henry Spencer had lent his father. On the strength of this Sunderland promptly ordered the seventeenth-century equivalent of a Lamborghini – a brand new coach from Paris – and sat for his portrait to Sir Peter Lely. The painting, which is still at Althorp, shows exactly what one would expect – the epicene features and haughty glance of a terribly spoiled young man of fashion.

As such he could not wait to leave England again, spending two more years in his beloved France before returning in 1663 to get married – to seventeen-year-old Anne Digby, the heiress daughter of the Earl of Bristol. But, he being Sunderland, even this could not go smoothly. One the eve of the wedding he bolted, warning his friends 'not to enquire into the reason' . . . but saying that he was 'resolved never to have her'. With this the Europhile Lord Sunderland was off once more across the Channel, this time to Italy, accompanied by Henry Sidney and his brother-in-law, Sir George Savile (later to become the politician Lord Halifax), who was married to Robert's sister Dorothy.

Sunderland's treatment of the buxom Anne is generally seen as typical of his deeply selfish nature, but for once there may just have been a reason for his bad behaviour. At the time of his proposal his prospective father-in-law, the intemperate Lord Bristol, had aroused King Charles's wrath by attacking his First Minister, Clarendon, in the House of Lords; and Sunderland, with a weather eye upon some future court appointment, may well have felt it inadvisable to become linked through marriage with an enemy of the monarch. Equally, he may simply have felt the urge to see Italy before he married.

Long before the 'Grand Tour' became so fashionable in the eighteenth century there was already a conviction that the true home of literature, art and architecture lay in Italy. The Elizabethan paragon, Sir Philip Sidney, spent more than a year studying in Rome and Venice in the 1560s. Now his great-great-nephew was treading in his famous footsteps.

Inevitably the three young noblemen saw Rome and Venice, but what seems to have produced the most lasting impression on Sunderland was a lengthy visit to the youthful ruler of Tuscany, Grand Duke Cosimo III. Although wretchedly married to Louis XIV's cousin, Marguerite Louise d'Orleans, Cosimo's existence was made bearable by his court's apparently unending progress between one or another of the fifteen sumptuous renaissance villas which the Medici still owned in the hills round Florence. These included several great houses like Poggio a Caiano, Buontalenti's Villa Artemisa, and Lorenzo Medici's favourite villa at Careggi, in which the Tuscan court continued to pursue its strangely restless life of pleasure. For Sunderland, Paris had been an overwhelming show of the power of the king of France, but these Tuscan villas of the Medici must have seemed attainable examples of a sort of paradise on earth.

Before leaving Italy for good, one task remained for him – to have his portrait painted. Sir Philip Sidney had been painted in Venice by Veronese. (The portrait has long since disappeared.) Sunderland chose the young and still virtually unknown Roman painter, Carlo Maratta. Unlike subsequent Grand Tourists, who had themselves depicted in the height of fashion in their English finery, Sunderland wore sandals and a Roman toga, and appears against the stormy background of a classical landscape. With his high cheekbones and intense, faintly slanting eyes it is a disturbing portrait. Since Lely painted him he has put on weight, and the languid look has gone entirely, so that the portrait of himself that Sunderland brought back to Althorp was not of an English noble-man at all, but of a young and dangerous-looking Roman senator.

By now Lord Bristol had returned to royal favour, and while still in Italy Sunderland had asked his mother to apologise on his behalf to Lady Anne and tactfully renew his marriage offer. As ever with her son, the Countess did as she was told, and Anne Digby, surprisingly, accepted. But even now Sunderland took his time and stayed on in Venice during carnevale, only getting back to England in time for his marriage at St Giles in the Fields in the early summer of 1665.

It is inevitable that the reputation of Anne, Countess of Sunderland, has suffered from association with her husband. Queen Anne, who never had a good word for the Spencers, called her 'the greatest jade that ever lived', and the anonymous historian in *The Dictionary of National Biography*, repeats as gospel the innuendoes of Barillon, Louis XIV's ambassador at St James's, who of all people had the gall to call her 'a born intriguante', and recounted the gossip of the day about a long affair she may have had with Henry Sidney. As with much in Anne's life, the evidence of this 'affaire' is highly circumstantial.

But if Henry Sidney did become her lover, few could blame her. Sidney was an attractive man and Sunderland at times a quite appalling husband. Henry Sidney did the Sunderlands many favours, and if Anne fell in love with him Sunderland was in no position to complain. More to the point, if Anne was unfaithful to her husband she was more than faithful to the House of Spencer.

Once married, the Sunderlands returned in style to Althorp and set about producing children. They finally had seven, four of whom, Robert, Charles, Elizabeth and Anne, survived into adulthood. But from the start one gets the feeling that Sunderland was more concerned about the Van Dycks and Titians on his walls than about the children in his nursery.

At first he seemed content to play the nobleman of taste and leisure. Thanks to Anne's marriage settlement there were funds to lavish on the house, and just as he had worn a foreign garb when painted by Maratta, so he now decided to clothe homely Althorp in the guise of the princely palaces he had seen in Tuscany.

Again he was well ahead of fashion. Fifty years on and rich Whig aristocrats would be vying with each other to build country houses like Italian palaces, but Sunderland was already transforming

Althorp into his own idea of a country house 'disposed after the Italian manner'. There is some mystery over how the work was done. Workmen's accounts have long since disappeared, and even the architect remains unknown. He is sometimes said to have been an anonymous Italian, but J.C. Kenyon, Sunderland's biographer, believes the earl was his own architect. Given his taste and dominating character, this seems more than likely.

Sunderland retained parts of the old house, including the famous staircase, which was now complete, and the Long Gallery, which made a perfect background for his paintings. But externally he changed the house completely, giving it a classical façade, with Tuscan pillars and a balustrade along the roof. Internally, according to the diarist John Evelyn, who was a friend of Sunderland's wife, he also added 'rooms of state, galleries, offices and furniture such as may become a great prince'.

By creating the setting for a small Italian court in the middle of Northamptonshire, Sunderland was following the example of the independent princes and 'overmighty subjects' he had met in France and Italy. John Evelyn was not the only visitor struck by Althorp's semi-regal status. The indefatigable Celia Fiennes, who visited in 1702 remembered it as being 'like a Prince's Court'.

Sunderland spared no expense in adding to its splendour. Louis XIV's favourite architect, Le Notre, was probably brought over from Versailles to advise on the formal gardens round the house. French deer were specially imported for the park and an ornamental canal created, on which a Venetian gondola floated.

This was all very different from the days when Althorp was the centre of the Spencers' highly profitable farming operation. Now the house existed to reflect the splendour of its owner, and he was soon playing host at Althorp to some of the most influential figures of the day, including the King's current mistress, Lady Castlemaine, his bastard son the Duke of Monmouth, and the heir to the throne, the King's brother, James, Duke of York. Given his situation, it was wise of Sunderland to cultivate such people, but his proudest moment must have come in 1669, when his one-time host from

Italy, Grand Duke Cosimo III of Tuscany, visited Althorp on a tour of England. Cosimo was highly complimentary, calling Althorp 'the best planned and best arranged country seat in the kingdom'.

For Sunderland there was one slight problem. Through his personal extravagance and wild spending on his house, he was running deeply into debt. Unlike his Spencer forebears, he could never manage money. Where they had built their careful fortunes from the land, he showed no interest in farming or in business, and he was doing what the Spencers lying in Great Brington Church would never have forgiven – selling off land to pay his debts. He had become something else money-conscious Spencers would have disapproved of – an obsessional gambler and a most unlucky one, who had reputedly lost £5,000 on one night's play. By 1670 he had been forced to mortgage Althorp for the then enormous sum of £17,000.

Debt could still destroy the greatest families and suddenly the Spencers themselves seemed threatened. It was in a serious attempt to rescue Althorp, that Sunderland embarked on his political career, driven by an overwhelming need for money. At first he relied for support on one of the King's most influential ministers, Henry Bennet, Earl of Arlington, a key member of the governing faction known as the Cabal. Arlington recognised Sunderland's ability and appointed him to several diplomatic posts abroad, including a spell as ambassador in Paris. Further foreign missions followed, but although he was gaining diplomatic expertise Sunderland was still desperately pursued by debt. Nobody knows exactly how he managed. At one point he was borrowing £200 from his chaplain, and his wife had a larger loan from John Evelyn. As a last resort Sunderland tried marrying his fourteen-year-old son and heir, Robert, to the heiress daughter of the city magnate, Sir Stephen Fox, but Robert was so spoiled and uncontrollable that not even Sunderland's famous powers of persuasion could make Sir Stephen force him onto his reluctant daughter.

But help was at hand. Among the fashionable society he and his wife had cultivated so assiduously was Louise de Keroualle, the young French courtesan brought to England by the Duke of Buckingham who had recently become King Charles's favourite mistress. In 1673 Charles made her Duchess of Portsmouth, and two years later he personally requested Sunderland to conduct the delicate negotiations to confer the title of Duke of Richmond on their child.

For Sunderland this was the start of the most important friendship of his life. Unlike the perilous liaison which his younger friend John Churchill was conducting with another royal mistress, the Duchess of Cleveland, this was emphatically non-sexual. Sunderland was not a womaniser, but unquestionably had a way with women, especially women of influence and power like the Duchess of Portsmouth. Speaking fluent French, and acquainted with the French king and his leading courtiers, the Francophile Sunderland could gain her trust and do her further services. It was thanks to him that the infant Duke of Richmond was legitimised in France by Louis XIV, and so enabled to inherit from his mother's family. According to Louise de Keroualle's descendant, Charles James Fox, Sunderland was even suspected of 'offering to obtain the succession of the crown for her son the Duke of Richmond'.

Whether he did or not, the fact is that Sunderland now had an ally at court of immense importance. Charles genuinely loved his 'dearest Fubbs', as he called her, and there was little that he could refuse her. In 1678, when his leading minister, Lord Danby, was bitterly attacked in the panic following the so-called 'Popish Plot', it was the Duchess's influence that helped persuade the King to appoint the relatively unknown Earl of Sunderland to the ministerial post of Secretary of State. From now on Sunderland would not look back.

Within a year, Danby had resigned and Sunderland joined the 'Triumvirate' – the other members being Lord Essex and his brother-in-law, Halifax – who were governing the country. It is hard to know how much Sunderland gained financially from his position, but his appointment undoubtedly redeemed the Spencers from their desperate situation. It was accepted that court appointments were a legitimate source of personal enrichment, and

Professor Habakuk once calculated that Secretary Finch gained £50,000 legitimately from his five year period in office some years earlier. It is hard to imagine Sunderland faring worse. But even now his gambler's instinct all but destroyed him when a movement started with the aim of excluding Charles II's Roman Catholic younger brother, James, Duke of York, from the succession on the grounds of his religion.

Within the tangled web of Caroline politics, the so-called 'Exclusion Crisis' marks the beginning of a genuine divide in English history. Many of the so-called 'Exclusionists' backed the claims of Charles's bastard, the Duke of Monmouth, as well as of the Dutch Prince William of Orange, who besides being Protestant was also grandson to King Charles I and married to another claimant to the throne, the Duke of York's Protestant daughter, Princess Mary. What made this crisis so important for the future was the fact that the Exclusionists were putting forward fundamental claims which the Civil War had left unsettled – such as the right to depose an unjust or unlawful king, Parliament's control of money and taxation and the supremacy of the Protestant religion. For Charles II, claims like these were close to treason, and while at times he compromised with Parliament, he himself would die a Catholic, still believing in the doctrine of the Divine Right of Kings that had helped to destroy his father. It was during the Parliamentary battles of the early 1680s that the 'Exclusionists' first became known as 'Whigs' and supporters of the King and the royal prerogative as 'Tories'.

To start with, Sunderland naturally sided with the King and his friend the Duke of York. But as the Exclusion movement gathered pace, he wavered. Guided as ever by self-interest, he suddenly switched sides and plumped for the claims of Dutch Prince William. During this period he led the Prince's supporters, and it was now that William first appreciated Sunderland's abilities.

But, not for the first or last time in his life, Sunderland had seriously miscalculated. His brother-in-law, Halifax, spoke out against Exclusion in the House of Lords, and when the King told Parliament that he would tolerate no change in the succession, the

Exclusionists collapsed. So did Sunderland. King Charles called him 'Judas' to his face, and dismissed him from the court with ignominy.

Again it was 'dearest Fubbs' who saved Sunderland by finally persuading Charles to forgive him, and in 1683 he was reappointed Secretary of State. Wishing to hear no more about Exclusion, Charles had dispensed with Parliament and needed all the political talent he could find – particularly Sunderland's expertise in foreign policy. It was Sunderland who helped negotiate the secret financial subsidies from King Louis which enabled Charles to dispense with Parliament. In the process, through Ambassador Barillon, Sunderland also secured a French subsidy of his own. Having demanded £10,000, he finally settled for a pension of £7,000 a year from Louis.

This must have helped with his financial worries and saved his much loved Althorp in the process, but it would be wrong to imagine that success and solvency had made Sunderland any nicer. Seventeenth-century Europe was a cruel place. It was Sunderland who appointed Judge Jeffreys, whose Bloody Assize pursued the West Countrymen after Monmouth's rebellion with such terrible ferocity, and it was always said that the only person Jeffreys feared was Sunderland. On a lesser level, Sunderland drove the young Whig philosopher John Locke out of his fellowship at Oxford. And when the old republican, Algernon Sidney, became implicated on flimsy evidence in the Rye House plot to assassinate the King, Sunderland did nothing to save his uncle from the axe – despite the fact that Sidney had helped him to recover Althorp during the Protectorate and that grief at her brother's execution would hasten the death of his mother two months later.

In 1685, when Charles died and James peaceably succeeded him, it seemed inconceivable that Sunderland could remain in office. King James, unlike his pliant brother, had not forgiven his betrayal in the Exclusion crisis. But among the skills of the professional politician, Sunderland had learned the art of managing elections and was able to ensure that James was greeted by a relatively docile

Parliament. Seeing his worth, the King forgot the past and offered him the additional post of Lord President of the Council. Sunderland accepted. The Garter followed, and the most dangerous episode in Sunderland's perilous career had started.

As a devout Roman Catholic, King James had one consuming ambition – the return of England to the faith of Rome. It was an impossible ambition without another civil war, but James had the faith of a believer, and started by using the royal prerogative to place Catholic nominees in positions of influence in the armed forces, the government and the universities, all of which were legally confined to members of the Church of England. He also tried using his prerogative to undermine the rights of the boroughs in the Catholic interest.

This produced alarm among the Protestant majority, many of whom were worried by the news from France, where Louis XIV had just revoked the freedom French Protestants had enjoyed under the Edict of Nantes and followed this with widespread persecution. Disquiet was also growing in other sections of society, particularly the aristocracy and the urban middle classes, at the way their rights and independence seemed threatened by James's assertion of the old doctrine of the Divine Right of Kings.

It will always be a mystery how a politician as experienced and shrewd as Sunderland could have thought that James's reign would end in anything but absolute disaster. But once he had started, any sign of moderation on his part – or 'cowardice', as James and his more extreme advisers would have called it – would have led to his dismissal and he could simply *not* afford to be dismissed. His debts drove him on to advise disastrous policies, but he wasted the huge sums he obtained on gambling and luxuries.

But there was more to it than that. Something in King James's curiously despotic nature seems to have matched his own, as he urged the King to ever more extremist measures. It was as if, having turned Althorp into a palace for an Italianate prince, he was acting like a post-renaissance European prince himself, trying to create an unassailable position as principal minister of an absolutist royal master. Machiavelli, whose book *The Prince* he must have read, presupposes politicians such as Sunderland – subtle bureaucrats, pragmatists who operate behind the scenes, ruthless advisers using all the arts of politics in the faithful services of an autocratic ruler.

By the early months of 1688 it was clear that England would rather change its king than its religion. But the signs which might have prompted Sunderland to cut his losses made him up the stakes and cling to power – even if this meant proving his loyalty to James by publicly converting to Catholicism. Apart from the King, few believed in his change of faith, and the cynical nature of his 'conversion' turned almost everyone against him – his wife included. It was now that he was first called 'Shameless Sunderland' and 'the Apostate of Althorp'. Urchins in the streets yelled insults at his passing.

It was shortly after this that his wife's old friend (and one-time creditor) John Evelyn visited Althorp. Sunderland was still away at court, struggling to contain a situation that was getting out of all control. Since early June, when James's wife, Queen Mary of Modena, had apparently guaranteed the Catholic succession by giving birth to a son, rumours had started that Dutch William, at the urgent invitation of seven influential Whig leaders, was about to sail for England. Since Henry Sidney was among this 'immortal seven' who signed the famous invitation, Sunderland must certainly have known of the situation and he was suddenly making unsuccessful efforts to persuade the King to moderate his policy.

All these problems must have seemed a continent away as John Evelyn and the Countess strolled through Althorp's summer-scented gardens, pausing to admire Le Notre's elegant parterres, so 'exquisitely planted and kept', and the park beyond, 'set with rows or walks of trees, canals and fishponds and stored with game'.

But despite the appearance of tranquillity Anne was deeply troubled by her husband's actions. Like Evelyn she was a devout Anglican, and news of Sunderland's conversion had caused her 'as much affliction as a lady of great soul and much prudence is capable of'.

Evelyn was concerned for her. 'I wish from my soul,' he wrote, 'that the Lord her husband (whose parts and abilities are otherwise conspicuous) was as worthy of her, as by a fatal apostasy and court ambition, he has made himself unworthy.'

But Sunderland was trapped. By October came the news that William had sailed for England. Barring accidents, King James's days were numbered and, once he fell, few would give much for his chief minister's chances of survival.

At court a sharp pair of eyes was watching what was happening. They belonged to Monsignor D'Adda, the papal nuncio, who reported back to Rome that 'my Lord Sunderland shows the utmost fear at the perilous position he is in'. He added that 'his best friends could scarcely excuse the startling transformation in three weeks – from boldness to timidity, from blind courage to wide-eyed terror'.

Sunderland might have kept his nerve – and his dignity – had he realised that this would be a most unusual revolution. Come November, when Dutch William and his troops landed at Torbay, and great men like Cavendish and Marlborough decided to support him, James would decline to fight. And having come to the conclusion that it was in their deepest interests to dismiss the King, the Whigs would conduct the change of monarch with the smoothness of a modern boardroom takeover.

Already James was blaming his misfortunes on Sunderland, and before he left he wanted the pleasure of dismissing him in person. Fearing one final act of regal vengeance, Sunderland humbly begged his pardon.

'My Lord, you have your pardon,' the King answered. 'Much good may it do you; I hope you will be more faithful to your next master than you have been to me.'

Sunderland took his leave and hurried from the court. As he wrote later, 'I thought I escaped well, expecting nothing less than the loss of my head . . . and I believe none about the court thought otherwise.'

This was a crucial moment for the Spencers, with the fate of the family hanging in the balance. Had Sunderland indeed lost his head – as his enemies wanted and expected – and had Althorp and its lands been forfeit, the Spencers would have faced a very doubtful future. It was a future in which it is hard to imagine members of the family making their mark in society or as patrons of the arts, or pursuing any great political endeavour. Given such circumstances, it is most unlikely that three centuries later Diana Spencer would have married Charles Windsor.

And so, if only for the sake of the distant future, it was important for Robert Sunderland to preserve his skin and continue his career. That he could do so now was due as much to luck as judgement, his chief asset being the most unappealing thing about him – the speed with which his arrogance had turned to abject terror in the face of danger. Had he tried to justify himself or save his honour, he would almost certainly have perished. Instead fear drove him back to Althorp, to seek the help of the only person who could save him now, his wife.

She was still angered and ashamed at what she saw as his apostasy in changing his religion, but felt pity at the pathetic state that he was in. 'My Lord, whatever his faults, poor man, they have all been to himself and not to others,' she reflected; and being a religious woman, she was genuinely concerned for his soul. 'Forget not my Lord in your prayers', she ended a letter to John Evelyn, adding that, provided she could be assured of her husband's reconversion, 'I would with comfort live in any part of the world on very little.' At the same time she sent packing the Catholic chaplain Sunderland had brought from London – and possibly saved Althorp from the threat of burning at the hands of the anti-papist local peasantry.

If current gossip was correct, and she really was in love with Henry Sidney, that may have also played its part in Sunderland's salvation. His uncle and his wife were certainly extremely close, and since Sidney was one of the very few Englishmen the aloof King William trusted, his discreet support became invaluable once Sunderland decided he must flee the country.

When Louis XIV refused to grant him asylum Anne wrote to Sidney asking him to use his influence to get them into Holland. No one knows his answer, but someone must certainly have helped them to reach the Hook of Holland, nor could they have subsequently remained in Amsterdam without at least the tacit approval of King William. Later, when Sunderland was inadvertently imprisoned, it was Sidney's intervention that secured his release. Funds arrived – almost certainly by courtesy of influential Uncle Henry – and the Sunderlands were soon enjoying 'a very pretty and convenient house' at Utrecht. Every Sunday morning Lord Sunderland and his wife were seen proceeding to the French Reformed Church in Utrecht following a footman carrying his lordship's Bible.

Shortly before leaving England the Sunderlands had had a further stroke of heavily disguised good fortune in the shape of the death in Paris of their drunken and delinquent son, Lord Robert Spencer. His behaviour had grown steadily more outrageous since Sir Stephen Fox had rejected him as his son-in-law, and when his father sent him on a mission to Genoa, Lord Robert got no further than Turin before debauchery and drink delayed him. From there he returned to Paris and died of his excesses.

His mother mourned him as 'the prettiest boy imaginable' and his death must have been particularly hard on his parents, in addition to their other troubles. But had he survived it is difficult to see how Sunderland could possibly have prevented an heir like Robert Spencer from bringing total disaster upon the family. Luckily, his younger brother, Charles, was a very different proposition. A bookish, precociously clever boy, the new heir was no trouble to his parents, and they specially took up residence in Utrecht so that he could study at the university.

Slowly the crisis in the house of Spencer lifted. Later in 1689 Lady Sunderland returned to Althorp to ensure that everything was still in order – which it was. While back at Utrecht her husband forgot that he had ever been a Catholic and reverted to whatever religion he believed in. It would soon be time for him to end his exile and resume his rudely interrupted political career in England.

One of the Sunderland's descendants, Winston Churchill, speaking of his own return to the Conservatives after deserting to the Liberals some years earlier, remarked that 'rattling isn't difficult ... What takes real skill is to re-rat' – and it was now that Sunderland 're-ratted' with all the virtuosity of his wonderfully devious nature.

With Dutch William and his wife Mary now established as joint sovereigns on the throne of England, they published an Act of Indemnity forgiving almost everyone who had been against them in the recent revolution. Sunderland was not included. Nor was he included when ex-King James, in exile outside Paris, extended his pardon to almost anyone who would now support him.

The name of Sunderland was still anathema. So when King William wanted his advice, the royal yacht had to be surreptitiously despatched to Holland to collect him. It was some time before anyone realised that he was back in England. Rumours started. He had been sighted in Whitehall. He had attended the House of Lords. He had kissed hands with the King at St James's. For most of the time he was in fact safely back at Althorp with his gardens and his pictures, only gradually emerging into a sort of twilit royal favour. Not until 1692 was he finally accepted as one of King William's principal advisers, but even then he called himself 'the minister behind the curtain' – which more or less summed up his situation.

Historians have argued over how he made this final come-back. Professor Plumb, who was fascinated by him, ascribed it to charm, and Professor Foxcroft, who hated him, to sorcery. Neither explanation is convincing. Sunderland would seem to have possessed the charm of a rattlesnake, and King William was not susceptible to magic.

Curiously, for a man so congenitally disloyal, the answer lay partly in his undoubted loyalty to King William – if only because, as the Earl of Portland drily pointed out, 'he must serve the King faithfully since his whole future depends on his success'. Also as Kenyon writes, 'in their cold appraisal of men and things, their willingness to forsake principle for expediency, and their impatience with fools, William and Sunderland were not unalike. Sunderland's brazen rudeness also impressed a man who had never had much time for flatterers'.

But the true key to Sunderland's return was simple. The King needed him. William was unacquainted with England, which he regarded chiefly as a useful ally in his war in the Netherlands against the French, and Sunderland was the most effective and experienced politician in the country, an unprejudiced adviser with a matchless skill at managing – and bribing politicians.

In 1692 he publicly re-entered society by taking up his seat in the House of Lords. Given his notoriety, even for him this must have been a considerable ordeal. In spite of this, 'his mask of sarcastic indifference saw him through, but at the cost of what little reputation he had left'. In fact he was probably past worrying what people said about him, and a year later came the crowning coup of his extraordinary career.

In August 1693 an anonymous correspondent was writing to Lord Halifax: 'The great news is about the meeting of the Great Men at Althorp, viz the Lords Shrewsbury, Godolphin and Marlborough and Messrs Russell, Wharton, etc. Every politician is making his own reflections about it.' As well they might, for this so-called 'Althorp Conference' marks an important moment in English political history, which has also given Sunderland his place in the history of the English constitution.

Like all his predecessors, King William was suspicious of political cliques, and tried to assert his right to use any politician he pleased in a coalition government. But, smart as ever, Sunderland had made another private transformation by siding with the Whig majority, and finally convinced King William that the Tories were so tainted by Jacobite dealings with 'the Kings across the Water' that only Whig politicians could be trusted. By such arguments Sunderland persuaded William to accept the notion of definite party ministries, which foreshadowed the ultimate adoption of full-scale party government.

But as far as Sunderland was concerned, his purpose in arranging the Althorp Conference was a personal show of strength to convince this impressive gathering of mainly Whig grandees that it was in their interests to support the King in Parliament. Not for nothing was Sunderland still the most persuasive man in politics, and after several days in which the great Whig lords savoured the Italianate charms of Althorp they reached an all-important understanding. In return for Whig support in the country and in Parliament, the King would respect the immortal principles of what was already being called the sacred 'Whig Revolution' of 1688.

If it was odd to have the man who had been the hated chief minister of tyrannical King James now arguing the case for Whiggish solidarity, no one said so. For Sunderland had not invited these great men to his house empty-handed. In return for their support he was able to promise, on behalf of William, dukedoms for the great Whig families of Bedford, Devonshire, Clare, and Shrewsbury.

If anyone deserved a dukedom it was Sunderland, but he was far too disreputable for honours, and had probably grown too worldly-wise to want them. But after the success of the Althorp Conference his true power steadily increased. In 1695 King William, on a pre-election tour, spent three whole days at Althorp, enjoying the conversation and the hunting. Later in the year John Evelyn found himself dining at the fine house in St James's Square which was now the London residence of Lord Sunderland. Despite the rise of the latter's fortunes it was still hard for Evelyn to find a good word to say for the man he called 'the great royal favourite and underhand politician', who was still 'obnoxious to the people for having twice changed his religion'.

Evelyn had put his finger on the problem which, despite Sunderland's power, would finally defeat him. In 1697 King William thought the time had come for his chief minister to be 'underhand' no longer but to take his place in public at the centre of his government; so he appointed Sunderland Lord Chamberlain and one of the Lord Justices who governed England in his absence. Times might have changed since the Revolution, but there were still limits to what members of Parliament would accept. Appointing the Althorp Apostate to these two great offices of state overstepped them, and the uproar against Sunderland was more sustained and scurrilous than ever.

In the old days he would probably have shrugged this off and angrily continued in his great position. But no longer. He was not quite sixty, but the stress of life had prematurely aged him, particularly the added recent strain of trying to prevent the murderous in-fighting among the Whigs in Parliament. When the Whig leaders, some of whose necks he had saved a year earlier, failed to defend him against the attacks of the opposition, Sunderland panicked, returned the Lord Chamberlain's silver key to the King and, for the last time, took the road to Althorp.

William tried hard to make him change his mind, and for several months refused his resignation; but Sunderland was adamant, and although continuing to advise the King 'behind the curtain' at times of crisis, his career in active politics was over.

The truth was that, give or take the odd betrayal, Sunderland had served his country rather well – and Althorp and the Spencers even better. Had he been a man of honour he could never have achieved this. For he had lived through stormy times and, like the true gambler he was, had taken the most exaggerated risks, not only with his life and his career, but also with his house and the future of his family. Amazingly some of his gambles had paid off, and he had been a great survivor, having helped to govern England under three separate, very different monarchs. He had been wildly profligate, but with every twist and turn in his career he had advanced the Spencers' interests and their expectations. Now as his life was ending he was placing everything in order.

Sunderland, the one-time Catholic and protagonist of absolutist government, was backing the Protestant Whig aristocracy to run the country through constitutionalist, parliamentary means. It was a shrewd decision, for with his assistance the Whig grandees were entering into their inheritance. Distrustful of the crown, assured of their position following their revolution, and enthusiastic in encouraging trade and industry (unlike their continental counterparts) these great landowners were set to run the country for the greater part of the coming century and enormously enrich themselves and those around them in the process. Sunderland's extravagance with his ill-gotten gains had prevented the Spencers from joining them in his lifetime; and his widow would have to sell still more of the depleted family estates to pay the most pressing debts. But like the great gambler he was, he had still to make one final wager which, by succeeding against the longest odds, would raise the Spencers far beyond their wildest dreams after he was dead.

At Althorp the one task still requiring his attention was the marriage of his son and heir, Lord Charles Spencer. Two years earlier, acting for once according to family tradition, Sunderland had married Charles to Arabella Cavendish, heir to the wildly rich Earl of Newcastle. Being Sunderland, he didn't lose out on the marriage, discreetly pocketing £20,000 of Arabella's £50,000 dowry to pay off debts and improve Althorp. Charles raised no objections. For unlike his father he was the most uxorious of men, and was deeply happy in his marriage. When Arabella died, barely a year later, he was broken-hearted.

But it was not in Sunderland's nature to let sadness come between him and family advancement. Over the years he had developed an uneasy friendship with the handsome courtier and soldier he had first met at the court of Charles II – John Churchill, who was now the Earl of Marlborough. Simultaneously Anne Sunderland had befriended Marlborough's fair-haired countess, Sarah, and the Sunderlands had recently decided that the Marlboroughs' second daughter, fifteen-year-old Anne Churchill, would make the perfect wife for widowed Charles Spencer.

It was an unexpected decision, for as a marriage this was not in the same financial league as Charles's union with Arabella Cavendish. Anne was not an obvious heiress, having both an elder sister and a brother, young Lord Blandford, who would presumably inherit Marlborough's money and possessions. Nor were the Churchills in a particularly strong position at the time. Marlborough was still emerging from prolonged royal disfavour, and not even Sunderland could have possibly foreseen the series of astounding victories which the great 'Captain General' was to win against the French a few years later – victories which would make him and Sarah the most famous – and possibly the richest – couple in the country.

As it happened, the marriage was not easy to arrange. Charles, still grieving for one wife, was not anxious for another, and Marlborough had no wish to force his favourite daughter onto this mournful intellectual. So while Sunderland needed to convince Marlborough that his son would make an ideal son-in-law, who 'would always do his lordship's bidding', Anne was busily persuading Sarah that he would make her daughter happy. Anne's turned out to be the easier task, for Charles was susceptible, and on meeting Churchill's daughter he fell as deeply in love with her as he ever had been with Arabella. His enthusiasm was contagious, and plans for the union of the Spencers and the Churchills now proceeded.

In fact the marriage was to prove the richest gift that Sunderland bestowed upon his family – making it ironic that, after all the risks and near-disasters of his extraordinary career, the 'Great Gamester' would not live to see its outcome. But already Althorp was itself immeasurably enriched from his stewardship, and he was leaving everything in readiness for a calmer future.

In the Long Gallery the Lelys were gleaming from the gilded frames he had had made for them many years before by craftsmen in Madrid. Le Notre's gardens had reached maturity. The woods were full of game, and the deer were belling in the park. In the first month of the first year of a new and hopeful century, the wedding on which so much of the future of the Spencers would depend took place at Marlborough House: and to ensure that nothing could go wrong it was held in secret.

CHAPTER 3

The Great Inheritance

Charles Spencer, third Earl of Sunderland (1675–1722)

Lord Marlborough's fears for the happiness of his daughter Anne were quite unfounded. True, her husband, Charles Spencer, in contrast with his unlamented elder brother Robert, was not particularly attractive. His mother-in-law described him as 'tall and of a large make', with 'no more genteelness than a porter'. His face was badly scarred from smallpox contracted as a child and, according to one contemporary, 'his manners also were repelling and his disposition harsh'. But not, apparently, with Anne. Within the privacy of his family Charles Spencer was the most uxorious of men, and loved his young wife dearly. Pretty Anne was happy with her large ungainly husband, and within a year they had a son. They called him Robert, but whether in honour of Charles Spencer's father or in memory of his brother is uncertain.

Charles himself was essentially a private man and something of a scholar. Evelyn who knew him in his late teens had called him then 'a youth of extraordinary hopes, very learned for his age, and ingenious', and after his time at Utrecht, 'studying the laws and religion of the Dutch', he started to build himself a library on a considerable scale, buying early volumes of the classics and the whole of Sir Charles Scarborough's famous mathematical collection.

As a book-loving intellectual he could permit himself the luxury of being an extreme radical in his political beliefs. Utrecht had long been a stronghold of Dutch republicanism and Jonathan Swift, who got to know him soon after his return, claims that he was a convinced republican who, despite his lineage, hated lords as well as kings. This hostility to the peerage, though topical today, was unusual at the time, even his Republican great-uncle, Algernon Sidney, having valued the aristocracy, provided it was independent of the court. But he apparently believed that 'the worst republic was better than the noblest of kingdoms', and Swift describes how, among his friends, Spencer refused to use the title 'lord'. He 'swore he would never be called otherwise than Charles Spencer, and hoped to see the day when there would not be a peer in England'.

Even in Parliament, which he entered in 1695 as member for Tiverton, 'Mr Spencer' made no secret of his extreme beliefs. This clearly was a man of passionate conviction, and one senses something of his personal frustration when interrupted in the course of a debate by someone who invoked the authority of the House of Lords. 'Sir, I would p-ss upon your House of Lords,' he shouted. This irritated that most cynical of men, his father, who heard about it later; even his mother said that at times Charles did 'show too much heat and over-earnestness in politics'.

The one person who unfailingly agreed with him was his young wife, Anne. Loving him, she shared eagerly in his political beliefs and was herself known as 'the Little Whig'.

In fact, her husband was the last person anyone would have picked on to become a successful politician. He was far too passionate, too tactless, too disinclined to suffer fools gladly, and there was more than a touch of silliness about this heir to a rich eighteenth-century earldom who dreamed of abolishing the peerage and the royal family.

In an ideal world he should have been allowed to study in his library, enjoy his family, and make the most of the earthly paradise his father had created up at Althorp.

But thanks to the Marlborough connection none of this would happen. Like it or not, the Marlboroughs would involve him in the practical pursuit of power. Because of their support, combined with his considerable intelligence, he would become surprisingly successful, but in the process even he would inevitably be corrupted. Just as inevitably, he and his children would become entangled with the vast inheritance of the Marlboroughs, and the Spencers would finally emerge enormously enriched, but with the dynasty split, and its members fighting one another. As for Charles Spencer himself, the Marlborough connection, which empowered and enriched him, would finally destroy him.

As it happened, Charles and his wife were lucky to enjoy two peaceful years of marriage before the great upheaval in their lives engulfed them. This occurred in the spring of 1702, when King William, thrown from his horse in Windsor Park, caught pneumonia and died three weeks later. He was succeeded on the throne by his sister-in-law, James II's younger daughter, Princess Anne, who helped to make her dearest friends, the Marlboroughs, one of the richest and most influential couples in the kingdom.

Both had waited long for this joyous moment to arrive. Indeed, until now, Churchill himself had led a curiously frustrating life for a military genius. Born in 1650, son of the eccentric royalist historian Sir Winston Churchill, he had served his military apprenticeship with the English garrison in Tangiers, then joined the court of Charles II in the entourage of his brother, James, Duke of York.

With his faultless manners and appearance, John Churchill always seemed as much a courtier as a soldier. According to his wife, as a young man he was 'handsome as an angel'. Early portraits show a dark, long, handsome face, with soulful, slightly feminine brown eyes, making all-too predictable his dangerous love affair in his early twenties with Charles II's voracious mistress, the Duchess of Cleveland. This ended only when that easy-going monarch caught the lovers *in flagrante*. It was probably the famous Churchill charm that saved him.

'You are a rascal but I forgive you, for you do it for your bread,' the King remarked, a reference to the rumour that the Duchess had paid him £5,000 for his services. For even then John Churchill was notoriously keen on money.

Then at the age of twenty-five he fell in love with Sarah Jenyns, a fifteen-year-old maid-of-honour in the service of King James's new wife, Mary of Modena – and more than met his match.

A wilful girl with pale skin, bright blue eyes and 'golden hair that people said she washed in honey', almost everyone remarked on Sarah's boundless energy and determination. Unlike the High Tory Churchills, the Jenynses were a Roundhead family who in the Civil War supported parliament. Churchill himself described his wife as 'a true-born Whig', and from childhood she seems to have imbibed an innate distrust of kings and courts and anyone who tried to stop her doing as she wanted. At fifteen she made it plain that she intended to control her private life completely.

Brushing aside the young Colonel's valiant efforts to seduce her, she told him that marriage was his only option. This was the one occasion when John Churchill knowingly surrendered; and having done so, the great hero of his age remained domestically under Sarah's thumb for the rest of his life. As he put it, 'A man must bear with a good deal to be quiet at home.' On this basis one of the richest husband-and-wife partnerships in English history began.

While not in the Shameless Sunderland league, Churchill was a very cool careerist who relied on charm and looks to advance his fortunes as a military commander. When the Duke of York became King James II, he gave him a peerage, and it was as Lord Churchill that he effectively commanded the royal forces that destroyed the Monmouth Rebellion. Then, in 1688, seeing how the wind was blowing, he rapidly switched kings and helped Dutch William to suppress King James's followers in Ireland – for which he was made Earl of Marlborough.

By now he and Sarah had five children – four daughters, Henrietta, Anne, Mary and Elizabeth, and the all-important male heir, John Churchill who, on his father's elevation, was called by the courtesy title of Lord Blandford. But throughout these early years of marriage Sarah never let her husband or her children come between her and the strange relationship on which the hopes of the family now depended – her passionate friendship with King James's daughter, Princess Anne.

As younger daughter of King James II, by his first wife, Anne Hyde, Princess Anne was in direct succession to the throne, but in spite of this she lived a fairly miserable existence. A solid, unappealing child, she was left motherless at the age of six and, being brought up an Anglican, was largely ignored by her Catholic father. Neglected and unloved, the sad princess appeared 'a pathetic little soul in that false and glittering court' of Charles II.

Later she was in the unenviable position of royalty-in-waiting; one day she might be Queen of England, but until this happened she would always be potentially a source of trouble and annoyance to the reigning monarch. Even her marriage in 1683 to the amiably stupid Prince George of Denmark, though affectionate, gave Anne little in the way of consolation, since every year it brought her yet another failed pregnancy. Between 1683 and 1700, she had twelve miscarriages and a still-born child. All of her five children who did survive birth died in infancy of encephalitis.

Pity must have played its part when Sarah Churchill first befriended Princess Anne, but Sarah was also thinking of the future. As her recent biographer, Frances Harris, puts it, what Sarah Churchill really wanted out of Anne was not so much 'the personal intimacy of this rather dull girl, five years her junior, but the tangible benefits of royal favour for herself, her husband and her children'.

Vivacious Sarah cannot have found it difficult to captivate this vulnerable princess, whose body was becoming bloated with so many pregnancies and whose unsophisticated nature yearned for the sympathy her husband could not give her. What Anne needed was a lover, but without the physical demands of sex. And with Sarah this was precisely what she got. Where Sarah was strong-willed and masterful, Anne was devoted and profoundly grateful. When Anne was lonely and defeated, Sarah was passionate and full of life. To all intents and purposes the result was a long and utterly absorbing love affair.

It had one curious feature. As a 'true-born Whig', Sarah had a deep distrust of royalty, which she overcame within their friendship by acting as if Anne were not a future queen at all, but a simple homely body she addressed as 'Mrs Morley'. Sarah in return was known as 'Mrs Freeman', and by dispensing with her royal status Princess Anne could actually enjoy the rare illusion of equality and everyday humanity. Within this strangely serious game of royal make-believe, gentle Mrs Morley was usually the supplicant, while strong Mrs Freeman, as dominant and carefree as her name, was very much the male partner.

At the beginning of the joint reign of Anne's cousin, William and his wife, her elder sister, now Queen Mary, the Churchills acted as protectors and advisers to Princess Anne, who was on bad terms with the royal couple. Like many public figures of the day, Churchill had taken out political 'insurance' by making contact with the exiled former James II at his court in France, just in case he or his son returned to power. His activities discovered, Churchill was briefly imprisoned in the Tower on suspicion of Jacobitism, and although he was rapidly released, it was largely thanks to Sunderland's support that the Churchills regained a measure of the royal favour. But as soon as Mrs Morley became Queen of England she could show the depth of her affection for the Freemans with all the patronage and honours at a queen's command.

Once on the throne, the new Queen's eagerness to shower honours and appointments on the Churchills was extremely touching, but there is something deeply unappealing in the Churchills' even greater eagerness to seize everything on offer. As Evelyn put it, they were soon 'ingrossing all that stirred and was profitable at Court', rather as if, after all those years of hard work fussing over poor dear boring Mrs Morley, they were intent on getting every penny out of their investment.

Sarah was actually appointed, not to one, but to three of the most lucrative and influential posts at court – Mistress of the Robes, Keeper of the Privy Purse, and Groom of the Stole (originally Groom of the Stool, who performed the lowliest of functions at the court. Over the years the resultant intimacy with the royal person had made the Groom one of the most influential members of the court, as his original employment was forgotten.) The income from these three posts alone was in excess of £6,000 a year.

Mr Freeman did still better, his rewards including the Order of the Garter and the immensely profitable positions of Captain General in command of the Army and Master General of the Ordnance, with payments of around £60,000 a year and the opportunity of making even more from military contracts. With all this in addition to the sale of honours and positions from the court, the Marlboroughs were soon enjoying 'huge joint salaries' from the Crown of more than £100,000 a year.

This must have made John Churchill happy, but for him the most important royal gift of all was his appointment by Queen Anne to command her army. This had come only just in time. During his period out of favour with King William, Churchill had had to watch himself beginning to grow old for a military commander. Now he was anxious to embark for Holland, where Louis XIV of France, in the first year of the War of the Spanish Succession, was trying to annex the Netherlands. As Captain General of the allied Anglo-Dutch forces opposing him, Marlborough found his last and greatest chance of glory.

As Marlborough sailed for the Netherlands to fight the French, his son-in-law, Charles Spencer, would soon be facing an equally determined enemy at home – his mother-in-law, Sarah Churchill.

When Shameless Sunderland died that autumn, there was no sign of undue grief from his son Charles who, as third Earl of Sunderland, had to take his seat in the hated House of Lords. As a man of principle, he would use the occasion to assert his republican beliefs – but he chose a somewhat tactless moment to proclaim them.

Sarah herself was currently engaged in something close to her ambitious heart – marrying her daughter Elizabeth to Lord Egerton, heir to the vastly rich Earl of Bridgewater – and was counting on Queen Anne for a generous contribution to the marriage settlement. So this was not the moment for the new Earl of Sunderland to lumber to his feet before their lordships, state his precious principles and attack the monarchy. Still less was it the moment to denounce the pension of £100,000 out of public funds being granted to the royal consort, George of Denmark.

Sarah was beside herself with fury on hearing of his speech, for in truth she was in a vulnerable position. As a sort of Whig herself she theoretically disapproved of court corruption, but as the queen's closest friend she wanted her due share of its benefits. Sarah's favourite daughter, Anne Sunderland, cannot have helped the situation when she primly told her mother that 'Lord Sunderland would never do anything against his conscience for any obligation in the world'.

Luckily, warm-hearted Mrs Morley was so deeply attached to her great friend Mrs Freeman that in spite of Sunderland's behaviour she still produced £10,000 for Elizabeth Churchill's marriage settlement. But while the Queen was willing to overlook the incident as far as the Churchills were concerned, she did not feel the same about the 'most uncivil' Earl of Sunderland, whom she saw as the incarnation of his shameless father, untrustworthy, probably treasonable, and the living embodiment of everything she most disliked about the Whigs.

But Sarah soon had something worse than Sunderland to contend with. No sooner was Elizabeth safely married to Lord Egerton than her son Lord Blandford, who had been studying at Cambridge, contracted smallpox. Sarah had always had a morbid fear of illness, and with the pitted face of her son-in-law as a reminder she was terrified to think of what this fell disease might do to her handsome son. But whereas smallpox had merely robbed Lord Sunderland of his looks, Lord Blandford was soon in danger of his life. Frantic with worry Sarah summoned her husband back from Holland, and in early February he was with Sarah at their son's bedside when he died.

For the Marlboroughs it was the cruellest of blows, and for all their wealth and honours they were suddenly reduced to a middle-aged couple overcome by grief. They did their best to comfort one another in the privacy of Holywell, their house outside St Albans, and told their friends that they were renouncing all the pomp and pleasures of the world. Marlborough would resign as Captain General and Sarah retire from the court.

On hearing this the Queen's reaction was a cry of horror: 'Never desert me,' she implored them, 'for what is a crown when the support is gone? . . . We four [by which she meant herself, Prince George, Sarah and Marlborough] must never part till death mows us down with an impartial hand.'

Not entirely surprisingly, the Freemans changed their minds about retiring. But nothing could bring them back their son, and death indeed had shown the hollowness of the great dynastic dream which Marlborough had been planning for the future. Sarah would go on hoping for another son, and a few months later was actually convinced that she was pregnant. But she was forty-three, and when that hope vanished, Marlborough's dream for his great dynasty seemed to vanish with it.

But even now devoted Mrs Morley offered a solution. Not only did she grant poor Mr Freeman the final honour in her gift, a dukedom; but in order that the dukedom should continue it was arranged by Act of Parliament for the title to pass through the female line to his eldest daughter, Henrietta, making her Duke of Marlborough in her own right on his death.

As Henrietta was married to Lord Godolphin's son, Francis, their only son, William, known as 'Willigo', now stepped into line to inherit the dukedom after his mother. But as Sunderland well knew, after Willigo stood his own first-born son, Robert Spencer. Blandford's death, and the creation of the dukedom, had happened just as the warlike duke himself was about to add immeasurably to the Marlborough inheritance.

Marlborough was fifty-four. At his age Napoleon would be dead and Wellington would have fought his final battle with the French. But Marlborough seemed untouched by age. In Holland he had been hard at work creating an allied army of 56,000 Dutch and British troops and German mercenaries with which he planned to attack the armies of King Louis, who, in alliance with the Bavarians, was threatening England's other allies, the Austrians. To do this meant marching his army across Europe 'from the North Sea to the Danube', almost to the walls of Vienna. It was there, in mid-August, that he encountered the combined armies of France and Bavaria near the village of Blindheim. At the conclusion of the fearful battle that ensued Marlborough rested briefly in his saddle and, using the back of an inn bill, scribbled his wife one of the great messages of military history:

> I have no time to say more but to beg you will give my duty to the Queen and let her know her army has had a glorious victory. Monsieur Tallard and two other Generals are in my coach.

For once in his life Marlborough was being modest. The battle of Blindheim, or Blenheim as his soldiers called it, was the greatest European victory won by an English commander since Agincourt. By humbling the pride of Louis XIV he had not only saved Vienna but stopped the French king dominating Europe.

He was an instant hero, and among the kings and princes anxious to reward him was the Austrian emperor, who showed his gratitude by showering him with riches – jewelled swords, priceless paintings, gold plate, and what the Duke appreciated most of all, the title of Prince of the Holy Roman Empire and his own small German principality, called Mindelheim, to go with it.

At home, more modestly, Parliament voted his family a £5,000 pension in perpetuity, and endorsed Queen Anne's grant of the royal manor of Woodstock. She committed the government to pay for erecting there a triumphal palace to be called Blenheim, without placing any limits on its cost – a dangerous omission.

Blenheim was no ordinary English stately home. Designed by the restoration playwright and great baroque architect, Sir John Vanbrugh, it was to be a grandiose memorial to the greatest conqueror Europe would see until the arrival of Napoleon. And there was a foretaste of Napoleon in the way this warrior prince was picturing his everlasting fame within the dynasty created round his dukedom. Had the Dutch agreed to the Emperor's suggestion that they make him Governor-General of the Netherlands, Marlborough and his descendants would have joined the ranks of minor European royalty. He was deeply disappointed when the Dutch refused, but in spite of this he still hoped to establish something like a regal dynasty to reflect his glory.

In Germany and Central Europe he had been impressed by the great semi-independent principalities owned by grand-ducal families like the Esterharzys. Nor would he have failed to notice how the Princes of Orange had used the small county of Orange in the South of France as a springboard for their family's advancement. With Queen Anne's support he was hoping that one of the great court positions, like the Groomship of the Stole, together with its valuable emoluments, could be made hereditary within his family. Endowed with the riches and the massive fortune he was now accruing, and with further victories to come, Marlborough could make his family a European style grand-dukedom, largely independent of the crown, and with its privileges, court position and pensions passing from one descendant to the next.

As if to prove Blenheim no accident, barely two years later Marlborough defeated yet another great French army under Marshal Villeroy at Ramillies, near the border city of Namur. This was an overwhelming conflict, with 25,000 cavalry locked in combat on a narrow front. (Winston Churchill called it 'the largest cavalry battle of which there is a trustworthy account'.) By this second crushing victory, Marlborough destroyed for ever King Louis's dreams of conquering the Netherlands and brought the victorious Allies ever closer to the frontiers of France.

That winter, with Ramillies fresh on everbody's mind, the Whig majority in Parliament, which in contrast with the Tories had tended to support Marlborough, felt the time had come for their reward. As a dedicated Whig, Sarah agreed, and convinced her husband that, since in her eyes the Tories were little more than pro-French Jacobites, the only guarantee of political support for continuing the war against the French was for a leading Whig to be included in the Queen's government. Her favoured candidate was Sunderland.

Having patched up their differences, she and Sunderland were currently enjoying a rare spell of amity, and Sarah now proposed him on the grounds that, as Marlborough's son in law, Lord Sunderland 'had especial claims upon the Queen's favour'.

Nothing in fact was further from the truth, for the Tory Queen detested Sunderland as much as ever, and had come to see him 'as the incarnation of everything she hated in pure Whiggery'.

Now in his early thirties, Sunderland the one-time idealist was calming down and would certainly not allow his principles to stop him sharing in the rising fortunes of the Marlboroughs. He might still be a republican at heart, but he also needed money. He had inherited more than a touch of his father's extravagance along with his love of gambling, but his greatest expenditure of all was still on books. His library was his passion and its fame was growing. He used it as security for the loan of £10,000 he had recently borrowed from his father-in-law. To help him repay this, Marlborough had found him some profitable appointments – as special envoy to the Austrian emperor at Vienna, and then as one of the commissioners for the planned union of England and Scotland. Sunderland performed successfully, and it was more as a tribute to his rising prospects than to his learning that Oxford University awarded him a doctorate.

None of this impressed the Queen in the least, and the winter after Ramillies was followed by another hard-fought conflict – this time between the Freemans and the Morleys, over admitting Sunderland to Queen Anne's government.

For the first time in their long and passionate relationship it appeared that Mrs Freeman might not get her way. As usual she was most insistent, but the years in power had made Queen Anne surer of herself and more confirmed in her beliefs as an innate Tory. Soon the two devoted friends were locked in bitter conflict.

True to her nature, Sarah railed at the Queen as no other subject would have dared. As always she was counting on their friendship, but she also knew that, however much the Queen hated Sunderland, even she could not oppose the wishes of her greatest general, who had made her name resound across the battlefields of Europe – and who, if a shade cautiously, was endorsing the appointment of his son-in-law.

Discussion raged for several weeks before the Queen sullenly gave way, as she knew she must with Marlborough against her. So, in the end, it was thanks entirely to the Marlboroughs that Queen Anne accepted the thirty-one-year-old Earl of Sunderland as one of her principal secretaries of state. This was an important moment in the development of English politics, setting a precedent for the Monarch's strongest private wishes being overridden by Parliamentary considerations. It was also, naturally, a great advance for Sunderland, who, however much he still privately disapproved of kings (and queens) and titles, now found himself principal minister in what gradually became a Whig administration.

But for the Marlboroughs, this decision to support their son-in-law against the Queen proved a terrible mistake. By humiliating Mrs Morley, Sarah had forced the royal worm to turn at last.

What followed was essentially the long dragged-out, bitter ending of a dying love affair. There was, of course, another woman, Sarah's now hated cousin, Abigail Masham, who had originally entered the court with Sarah's backing. There were denials from the Queen, and bouts of jealous rage from Sarah, with accusations pouring back and forth as Sarah found herself supplanted. All that distinguished what was happening from the break-up of some humdrum relationship between two ageing matrons was the one thing Sarah chose to overlook – the fact that her faithless lover was no longer poor dependent Mrs Morley, but that she happened to be Queen of England. Since her husband's appointment as head of the allied forces depended on Her Majesty, their quarrel was bound to have dramatic repercussions.

Sarah being Sarah, repercussions were the last thing she considered. Single-minded woman that she was, all she could see was that her place in Anne's affections had been usurped by the common, shameless, fellow-travelling Tory, Mrs Masham. Overcome with jealousy, she went so far as to accuse the Queen of England of 'an unnatural passion for her chambermaid', but even this was not entirely the end of the relationship.

On the battlefield the Duke was still invincible, winning two more overwhelming victories against the French – Oudenarde in 1708 and the bloodbath of Malplaquet a year later – and with so much depending on the Queen's support, anyone but Sarah would have seen the need for caution. But caution was foreign to her nature, and she was now so jealous that she seemed past caring. At the thanksgiving service for Oudenarde at St Paul's Cathedral, Sarah was sitting near the Queen and, hearing her talking loudly, told her to keep quiet.

In former days Sarah might just have got away with it, but she was no longer dealing with the woman who had once adored her. Dependent Mrs Morley was no more; Queen Anne had very firmly taken over, so that when she broke with Sarah she produced what A.L. Rowse described as 'a noise that reverberated all over Europe and down the corridors of time'.

When Sarah came to her senses and realised the full extent of her appalling rudeness, there were of course apologies and embarrassed meetings between Marlborough and the Queen, at one of which the Duke was on his knees before her, begging for his wife to be forgiven. The Queen was gracious, but she had taken her decision. All Sarah's royal appointments ended and her connection with the court was effectively over. So was the bond between the Freemans and the Morleys, which had always been the true foundation of Marlborough's fortunes.

England, like Europe, was tiring of the war and there was little real support for Marlborough's great ambition 'to carry his sword to the very gates of Paris'. The Whigs in government were losing popularity, and the public outcry following their decision to impeach for sedition the popular High Church Tory preacher, Dr Sacheverell, showed that their days, like Marlborough's victories, were numbered. The government would have to go, and no one was terribly surprised that the first minister the Queen dismissed was Sunderland.

He had been an unpopular if effective minister, playing an important role in the Act of Union bringing England and Scotland together in 1707. Typically, he had spent the considerable (and legitimate) profits he had made from office not on restoring Althorp or the family's distinctly shaky fortunes, but on building the new Sunderland House in Piccadilly on the site occupied today by the Albany. As he badly needed the pension of £3,000 a year which the Queen offered him in compensation for the loss of office, his words of refusal show him trying to remain a man of principle. 'Your Majesty,' he said self-righteously, 'since I can no longer serve my country, I will not rob it.'

Hard times had come upon the Marlboroughs and the house of Spencer. Thanks to Sarah, Marlborough was now without the friendship and support of the Queen in London. This proved crucial, for it left him vulnerable, and when accusations of corruption followed from the new Tory government, his dismissal as commander-in-chief of the army was inevitable.

Blenheim Palace stood unfinished, amid bitter squabbles over money, so it was fortunate that the Marlboroughs still had the use of the splendid country house at Windsor which went with Sarah's original appointment by the Queen to the Rangership of Windsor Park. Anne generously let them keep it, but from now on Sarah had really turned her heart against both court and monarchy for ever. Marlborough was threatened with prosecution and disgrace, and left the country.

But despite his fall from favour and the defeat of his ultimate ambitions for his family, he and Sarah had created one of the great fortunes of the age. And since in money terms alone Marlborough was worth close on a million pounds – an enormous sum in present-day currency – within the family itself concern for the great inheritance began in earnest.

The ever fertile Spencers had advanced their chances by increasing the reserves of Spencer males. Whereas Henrietta, Marlborough's eldest daughter and heir to the dukedom, would only manage to produce two further daughters – and one of them by the playwright William Congreve – the stalwart 'little Whig', Anne Sunderland, had given birth to two more healthy males, Charles Spencer, born in 1706 and John, born two years later, these in addition to her daughter, Anne, born in 1702, and Diana in 1710. So the Sunderlands were by far the most thriving branch of the family, and the presence of three robust Spencer grandsons made it most unlikely that the 'dear Duke's' precious English dynasty would ever fail for lack of heirs.

With Marlborough now in exile and disgrace, it was clear to Sunderland too that, politically, there was nothing left for him in England while Queen Anne remained alive. But Anne's health was doubtful, and in Germany, at the court of Hanover, lived Sunderland's best and brightest hope for the future – another of the Queen's personal enemies, who under the Act of Succession was heir to the throne of England, the Elector, George of Hanover.

Embittered by exile and the shipwreck of his great ambitions, Marlborough, now very much in league with Sunderland, approached Elector George and the other European allied leaders with an extraordinary request – to provide him with a continental army with which he could invade England, and by dismissing Queen Anne's Tory government, stop them making peace with France.

Although the Elector was opposed to the policy of peace at any price with France, he could not possibly support this hare-brained scheme, and it seems to have convinced him that Sunderland, like Marlborough, could be dangerous. As a result, in 1714 when Queen Anne died and Elector George became King of England, Sunderland failed to receive the great political reward he had been counting on. Instead he was made Viceroy of Ireland which meant exile to Dublin, and little in the way of income. Deeply disappointed, and using his wife's refusal to leave the new Sunderland House as an excuse, he continued to postpone crossing the Irish Channel until his fortunes suddenly revived, thanks to events in Scotland.

Until defeat at the battle of Sheriffmuir, the 1715 Jacobite uprising seemed a serious threat to the new Hanoverian dynasty of King George, from the Old Pretender, James Edward Stuart. With panic in the air, Marlborough was restored to his post as Captain General, and was soon directing operations from London with remarkable incompetence, whilst secretly sending £5,000 to the Stuarts just in cast they won. Sunderland, with his knowledge of Scotland dating back to his negotiations for the Act of Union, made himself indispensable in Whitehall.

Branded as crypto-Jacobites, the Tories were totally discredited, and the Whigs would be in power for almost a generation to come. At a time when senior Whig politicians were dying or retiring, Sunderland came to a conclusion: Republican or not, his best hope for the two things in life he needed – power and money – lay in close contact with the person of the King and as if to prove him right, the King rewarded him with the position of Lord Privy Seal.

But as so often happened with Sunderland, no sooner did it seem as if his luck had changed, than he was hit by a fresh disaster. Thirty-six year-old Anne Sunderland fell ill with pleurisy. She had not inherited her mother's robust constitution and, after a careless blood-letting, she contracted septicaemia and died. (In fact, it seems more than likely that she was actually suffering from the tuberculosis which would afflict the Spencers for the next two generations.)

Since the day they married she and Sunderland had been devoted to each other, writing to each other every day when they were parted. Now that she was gone, this passionate, abrasive man was suddenly beside himself with grief, as were the children and Sarah and the Duke. In their sorrow the whole family was overwhelmed by one of those great outbursts of emotion that break through the stiffness and restraint of this outwardly formal age.

'Pray get my mother the Duchess of Marlborough to take care of the girls ... a man can't take the care of little children that a woman can ... For the love she has of me, I hope she will do it, and be ever kind to you who was dearer to me than my life.'

This from the last pathetic letter Anne wrote to Sunderland shortly before she died. He sent it on to Sarah, and briefly the ill-assorted couple were united as they shared their loss – but only briefly.

Sarah was more than willing to take her daughter's place with the children, and particularly anxious to take charge of her favourite grandchild, the baby of the family, seven-year-old Diana Spencer, for whom she started to prepare a nursery at Holywell. Then came a fresh disaster. Marlborough, the great war-lord, had always been susceptible to sorrow; now he was so affected by his daughter's death that he had a stroke a few weeks later, tumbled down the stairs at Holywell and lay for three days in a coma.

He recovered – after a fashion. But from now on, the once-great Duke of Marlborough was a weakened, melancholy shadow. Sometimes recovering, but always liable to profound depression and attacks of weeping, he was no longer able – or permitted – to stand up against his Duchess. With the Queen dead, there was nobody to stop her giving her husband and her family her full and terrible attention.

Many years before Sarah had persuaded her husband to agree that her fortune was her own. Now she effectively took charge of the trust controlling Marlborough's money too, and the joint fortunes of the family. As the Duke's grasp weakened, Sarah's strengthened. As Marlborough's dreams of founding his European dynasty dissolved, so the troubled saga of the Marlborough inheritance began in earnest.

Sarah and Sunderland should have remembered Anne's last letter and stayed united, if only in her memory, for her motherless children needed their joint affection and support. But this was clearly impossible, particularly for Sarah, who could not help quarrelling with any member of the family who remotely disagreed with her. It is not entirely surprising that this mother who methodically recorded the misdoings of her children for posterity in a small green notebook should by now have alienated all of her three surviving daughters. Nor is it surprising that before long she would turn upon this son-in-law who had once been 'dearer to her daughter than her life' with particular venom.

Part of Sarah's trouble was that from the age of fifteen, when she married Marlborough, she had grown used to what she called 'that inestimable blessing, a kind husband', who had always let her have her way. Sunderland would not and stood up to her.

As it was, they just managed to agree over the one thing it might have been better had they not – the marriage of Sunderland's elder daughter, Elizabeth.

At fifteen, Elizabeth Spencer was no beauty, but Sarah had set her heart on marrying her to the son of the extremely wealthy Lord Bateman, a former Governor of the Bank of England. When conferring his title on Lord Bateman, George I had remarked, 'I can make him a lord but not a gentleman', and Sunderland seems to have felt the same, both about Lord Bateman and his son. He finally agreed to Elizabeth's marriage, partly to ensure that this motherless daughter was taken care of, and partly to keep the peace with Sarah. Neither can have realised that rich Lord Bateman's son was homosexual, and that in years to come an increasingly embittered Lady Batemen would go on blaming Sarah for her wretchedly unhappy marriage to the day she died.

But while Sunderland was suffering domestically, he prospered politically. With Marlborough now incapacitated, Sunderland had taken over (although with periodic interference from Sarah) Marlborough's old political faction, together with his claim to the Groomship of the Stole. After the Jacobite campaign of 1715 he and his fellow Whig grandees were better placed than ever to convince King George I and his successor George II that only good Whig governments could save them from conspiracies and invasion attempts by the exiled Stuarts. The result was effectively a one party state as government by Whig oligarchy started.

Since George I (like George II after him) made frequent summer visits to Hanover, there was a great political opportunity for those ministers who accompanied the King, particularly if, like Sunderland, they spoke fluent French and German, and were ready to carry out policies benefiting Hanover rather than Britain.

Through his unscrupulous readiness to follow King George's wishes, Sunderland outmanoeuvred his Whig rivals, Lord Townshend and Robert Walpole, becoming First Lord of the Treasury in 1718, and as such was effectively the junior partner in a joint prime ministership with the brilliant diplomat, James, Earl Stanhope, in charge of foreign policy.

Now into portly middle-age, Sunderland had come to resemble his father as a master of political intrigue and also as a skilful courtier and as such now got himself appointed to Sarah's old position as Groom of the Stole, with its invaluable proximity to the person of the King. This was important for Sunderland in his role of power-broker for the Whigs, since it gave him access to the royal patronage that won elections and built political alliances.

Although this must have meant that Sunderland had finally abandoned his Republican beliefs, this did not stop him being, on occasion, as outrageous and politically extreme as ever, as he demonstrated during King George's very public disagreement with his son, the Prince of Wales, in 1717. Such was the King's anger and frustration with his son and heir that the First Lord of the Admiralty seriously suggested kidnapping the Prince and marooning him on a desert island until he begged forgiveness and recovered his sense of duty. Typically, Sunderland went one step further and in one of the most outrageous state papers ever presented to a British monarch, calmy suggested that the King should have the Prince of Wales murdered. As he told him, 'It is true he is your son, but the son of God himself was sacrificed for the good of mankind.'

Since the rift between King George and his son was soon repaired, it was fortunate that His Majesty had the sense to ignore Sunderland's somewhat extreme advice, and placed the unusual memorandum in his private safe, where it was discovered after his death by the intended victim, George II.

To be fair to Sunderland, it was also in the course of this quarrel that he helped to define the status of the royal grandchildren, in a legal judgment which by a strange coincidence today continues to affect his own extremely distant but direct descendants, Prince William and Prince Harry. In order to resolve the argument between the King and the Prince of Wales over who controlled the upbringing and education of the royal grandchildren, it was Sunderland who suggested putting the question to the judges – who by an overwhelming majority stated that according to the constitution the ultimate decision on such matters unquestionably rested with the monarch.

But while prospering politically, Sunderland again fell foul of Sarah when he decided to remarry – this time to the fifteen year old heiress, Judith Tichborne. Lord Hervey had nicknamed Sarah 'Mount Etna' after the great volcano, and when she heard the news she instantly erupted, raining down slander and obloquy on Sunderland like red hot lava. On one day she was telling everyone she knew that he was homosexual, the next that he was visiting the women of the town. He was dishonest and utterly despicable. Then she finally produced an allegation for which there could be no forgiveness – that by his behaviour as a husband, Sunderland had killed her daughter.

'If she had been the wife of any man in the world but my Lord Sunderland, she had been now living, which had been happy for her poor children and for me.'

Sunderland was more than tough enough to cope with this. As J.C. Kenyon puts it, 'his rudeness complemented her intolerableness', and finally the slanders ceased. But so did contact between the two sides of the family, leaving Sunderland to savour married life for the third time round as devotedly as ever.

He had loved all his wives, and within three years of marrying Judith had fathered as many children. Without Sarah's fatal intervention he seems to have been a kind and a devoted father, treating his young wife and children with a bluff sort of older man's *bonhomie*. One gets a touch of this in a short note tucked away among his papers in which he tells his 'dear wife Judith' that he will be late coming home, and in case any of the children miss him, she is to 'kiss the little bastards for me'.

By now it must have seemed that Sunderland had finally escaped from Sarah's influence for ever. He had grown powerful and rich on his own account, and besides Althorp he could enjoy Sunderland House in Piccadilly, now virtually complete. Here he had gardens and an orchard and would soon begin to plan an elaborate library to his heart's content. Away from the Marlboroughs and the storms around them, he should have been a happy man at last. Then there was suddenly another crisis, which yet again brought Sarah back to his attention.

As First Lord of the Treasury he became involved in the scheme to reduce the National Debt by encouraging the public to exchange government bonds for shares in the profitable South Sea Company. Together with several other leading politicians, he was undoubtedly bribed with shares to gain his backing, and as speculation mounted it produced the great financial racket known to history as the South Sea Bubble.

Shrewd as ever over money, Sarah had been investing in the South Sea Company for several years and continued doing so, both on her own account and as a trustee for her husband. Sunderland invested heavily as well. But whereas Sarah, with what Winston Churchill called 'her repellent common sense', saw that the bubble had to burst and pulled out just before it did, Sunderland, like most of the investors, including George I, did not.

For Sunderland it was a disaster. Much of the financial establishment was ruined, in the City bankers were committing suicide, and Sunderland himself had lost heavily. To make it that much worse, he knew that Sarah and Marlborough had made a fortune, estimated at more than £100,000 between them. Then came the final blow – a threat of impeachment in parliament which looked like ending his career in politics. As it was, he was just saved by an inspired speech and some skilful backstage pressure and bribery by the extremely able Norfolk squire Sir Robert Walpole – for which Sarah never forgave him.

As a *quid pro quo* for Walpole's support, Sunderland had to relinquish to him his post of First Lord of the Treasury, but he clung to his position of Groom of the Stole, which meant that the power and income of this once professed Republican now came entirely from the King.

It might have been better had Sunderland now retired from active politics himself and enjoyed the pleasures of his private life – studying in his splendid library at Sunderland House, becoming a better father to his children and returning to the country roots of the Spencers in the peace of Althorp. But once again lack of money stopped him doing this, even had he genuinely wished to. For once again, exactly like his father, he had failed to use any of the gains from office to increase the Spencer fortunes, which were barely adequate to sustain his earldom. Since most of his savings had vanished in the Bubble, he was forced to continue his career in politics, but ambition must have also spurred him on. Not yet fifty, and in the prime of life, he was far too proud and angry to yield to an upstart, however talented, like Robert Walpole.

He did his best to put the little Norfolk squire in his place in the general election of April 1722, but it was an uphill task, with Walpole free at the Treasury to use the Secret Service money for electioneering. And as the first electoral returns began to show that Walpole's followers were winning, Sunderland fell ill with pleurisy.

Sunderland House was already a place of mourning, his eldest son by Judith having died there two days earlier after an unsuccessful smallpox inoculation. Mortally sick himself, Sunderland, the one-time atheist, sought comfort from a Church of England clergyman. Despite his prayers the illness worsened and, as inconsistent in his death as in life, Charles, third Earl of Sunderland died in the bosom of the Church of England at the age of only forty-eight on 19 April 1722.

Sunderland House remained unfinished and, although he theoretically left his wife and children £75,000 in shares, the face value on many of the share certificates proved obsolete. His two other children by Judith both died young, as did their mother. After the

Earl's death the King of Denmark offered his executors the then enormous sum of £30,000 for his library, but since they were counting on the children soon inheriting much larger fortunes from the Marlboroughs, the offer was refused. As for Sarah, Sunderland's welcome death now left her free to treat her Spencer grandchildren exactly as she wanted.

CHAPTER 4

A Liberated Woman

Sarah Marlborough (1660–1744)

Marlborough, like Nelson, should have died in battle. Instead, with Blenheim Palace now complete, he lingered on thanks largely to Sarah's devoted nursing. After seeing him, the politician James Craggs wrote: 'I love him well enough to wish it were over; he is a melancholy memento.' But it was as if Sarah would not let him die, and when finally he did, just two months after Sunderland, she sank into deep depression.

'Whoever has been once so happy as I have been and have nothing left but mony which from my humour, I don't want much of, deserves to be pity'd,' she lamented.

Hardly surprisingly, few did pity her, certainly not the members of her family, who knew that, although one of the richest women in the country, her eagerness for 'mony' was as strong as ever. But just as nobody could doubt her devotion to the 'dear Duke' while he was alive, with his death the actress in her made her play the tragic widow tending the sacred flame of his memory. She was good at feeling sorry for herself, but this could clearly not continue. Now in her early sixties, she was as full of energy as ever, and since she had preserved not only her 'mony' but her looks, people wondered if she would remarry. Finally her friend the proud Duke of Somerset plucked up courage and proposed. Some thought she might accept, but then, dramatically, she turned him down in words that belong to Sarah Marlborough's legend.

'If I were young and handsome as I was, instead of old and faded as I am, and you could lay the empire of the world at my feet, you should never share the heart and hand that once belonged to John Duke of Marlborough.'

Nobly said – but as with so many of the best lines in history, it is doubtful that she spoke them. Almost certainly she wrote them later, partly for posterity and partly to obscure the truth. For the truth was that, had Sarah wed the Duke of Somerset, it would have meant sacrificing not only the hand once sanctified by Marlborough's love but something more important still – her secret role as Mrs Freeman. For Mrs Freeman had not died with the end of the relationship with Mrs Morley, nor with the Queen's own death in 1714. With Marlborough's demise Mrs Freeman really came into her own. And it was as Mrs Freeman that Sarah came to the decision which was to have such amazing consequences for the Spencers.

By the time of Marlborough's death in 1732 there were already two great separate fortunes – over a million pounds left in trust by the Duke himself, of which Sarah was principal trustee, and her personal fortune, which was entirely her own and fast approaching similar proportions. What did she intend to do with it?

The fact that her daughter Henrietta was now Duchess of Marlborough in her own right had done nothing to endear her to Sarah, especially as she always referred to her as 'the Dowager Duchess', a method of address she found offensive. But as Henrietta's son Willigo Godolphin would finally inherit both Blenheim and the title, it was assumed that finally the two fortunes would be united to create the sort of massively endowed grand dukedom that Marlborough himself had hoped for. Certainly, had Sarah been truly anxious to carry out the wishes of her dear departed, this would have been her ultimate intention, and the joint fortunes would have provided the future Dukes of Marlborough with a vast endowment to maintain their honour and position as the first Duke had intended. But Sarah did not rush to do this. Already she had other plans which were more in tune with her highly independent nature.

The overriding theme of Sarah Marlborough's life was her

determination to control her destiny. As an old woman, she was still boasting to the Duke of Bridgewater that 'nobody upon earth ever governed me nor ever shall'; just as when little more than a child of fifteen, she had shown the same instinct to control her life when she made John Churchill marry her.

Once married, she had acted in the only way she could, bearing his children, backing his career and sublimating her considerable ambition in his success. This was not difficult for her, since she was devoted to her handsome, brave, resourceful husband. But as the relationship with Princess Anne developed Sarah had found a separate role for herself as Mrs Freeman. And Mrs Freeman's priorities were different from those of happily married Sarah Churchill. As Mrs Freeman, she was increasingly asserting the rights of a 'free man' in the presence of the Queen of England and she learned to make the most of them, for by dominating Mrs Morley, Sarah was able to extort all those honours and riches from the court for Mr Freeman and herself. Once she had adopted these two very different roles in life, Sarah started to become two different women.

As Sarah, Duchess of Marlborough, she was still the proudest and most supportive wife of the greatest hero of his age. But as Mrs Freeman she was increasingly aware that without her years of dedicated labour with the Queen, there would have been no fortune, no power and precious little in the way of honour for her or for her husband. At times she used to grumble that she had 'laboured like a pack-horse' for her husband's glory, for without the work of Mrs Freeman, Churchill would not have been a Duke, let alone have reached the battlefield of Blenheim.

After his great victories, the gap between Mrs Freeman and the Duchess of Marlborough widened. As she gloried in his vast success, the Duchess was genuinely proud to have been his pack-horse, but for Mrs Freeman the Duke's achievements served as a reminder of the handicaps she suffered as a woman, for the contrast between her situation and her husband's could not have been more glaring. Simply because he was a man, Marlborough had been free to live a life of extraordinary richness, devoted to politics, diplomacy and the pursuit of glory. But for Sarah none of this had been remotely possible, and at times she grew bitter on the subject. She knew her worth and genuinely wished she had been born a man.

The political disadvantages of her gender particularly frustrated her. 'I am confydent I should have been the greatest Hero that ever was known in the Parliament Hous if I had been so happy as to have been a man,' she said impatiently. She was haunted by the thought. Why was it, she asked, that 'the things that are worth naming will ever be done from the influence of men?'

She knew the answer, and now that the Duke was dead Mrs Freeman decided to assert herself. In the process she made herself one of history's great precursors of the modern liberated woman.

With all her failings, Sarah was profoundly realistic, and she knew that in a world where privilege and power were exclusively reserved for men, no woman, even one of her considerable determination, could enter such strict male preserves as politics, warfare, or the law, which produced 'the things that are worth naming'.

But there was just one area she could enter, and where her extraordinary flair had already revealed itself. This area was money. For money was one of the few things in seventeenth and eighteenth century England that was gender free, and thanks to Marlborough's willingness to let her treat her fortune as her own, she could compete with men on terms of relative equality.

As Frances Harris writes, 'As much a Whig in private as in public affairs, she had come to consider this financial independence to be not merely an indulgence on Marlborough's part, but an essential human right and liberty; without it she'd have been reduced to the level of the dispossessed country peasantry, "who neither plow nor sew, because they can't call it their own".'

Marlborough understood this and, being astute enough to realise that Sarah was a match for him financially, had increasingly left her to manage their joint fortunes during his frequent absences abroad. With her 'repellent common sense', she had a sort of genius for investment and it was largely thanks to her that Marlborough's own fortune reached such great proportions.

Another area in which she acted with the freedom of a man was property and building. She loved to be involved in building, and had all the instincts of a modern property developer. It was she who finally took charge of the disastrous muddle over Blenheim Palace, and it was largely thanks to her that it was finished. She also took total charge of acquiring a piece of royal land opposite St James's Palace in London, and then building on it the Duke's proud London residence of Marlborough House.

But financially Sarah's greatest coup had come with the collapse of the notorious South Sea Company. Again her 'common sense' prevailed against what she knew to be the sheer stupidity of all those sheep-like male investors – the King and her own son-in-law included – who had let their greed impair their powers of judgement. She made a fortune by selling before the crash and one can understand how much this fortune, won in the face of overwhelming male competition, must have meant to her.

But the £100,000 she had earned for herself and Marlborough meant even more to her than this. In England, where land and property had always been regarded as the best and safest form of investment, there was normally no eagerness to sell and landed estates rarely came on the market. But the South Sea crash occurred on such a scale that the countryside was littered with failed investors desperate to avoid bankruptcy and the debtor's prison. This placed her in the wonderful position of not only having made a fortune at the expense of the male race and several of her enemies, but of having a whole range of virtually unheard-of bargains to invest it in.

Being Sarah, she took her time and chose extremely shrewdly, at first buying estates in Surrey and Northamptonshire. She was particularly pleased to get the estate at Chippenham, conveniently situated near her house in Windsor Park, which had been confiscated from Robert Knight, the South Sea Company cashier, and which she liked to boast was 'the finest farm in England'.

But there was one purchase which gave her particular satisfaction. One of the most spectacular losers in the crash had been the City mogul Sir Theodore Janssen, whose prized estate, Wimbledon Park in Surrey, had also been forfeit because of his role as a director of the Company. Sarah bought it for £25,000, cash down, and obtained one of the great property bargains of the eighteenth century. It included over a thousand acres of well-stocked woodland and farmland, a forty-acre pond, manorial rights over Wimbledon Common, the villages of Putney and Roehampton, the half-demolished ruin of a Tudor mansion and the site of the present All-England Tennis Club, all within five miles of Hyde Park Corner.

Not that she needed the estate or particularly wished to live there. Although she had Holywell, Marlborough House and the use of Blenheim, her favourite residence was still the enchanting Ranger's Lodge in Windsor Park. But once she had purchased Wimbledon her building mania overtook her and she was soon busily engaged in getting the remains of the Tudor mansion torn down and commissioning the architect Roger Morris, a pupil of the great Lord Burlington, to design her a Palladian villa in its place. Since she was already suffering from the arthritis which would finally cripple her, she made Morris place the *piano nobile*, normally on the first floor, at ground level, so that she would not have to climb the stairs. She never cared for the result which, as she said, made the house 'appear to curtsey', and rarely stayed at Wimbledon herself. She explained that she was building for the future.

Now that she had her great fortune and was busily acquiring what amounted to a private kingdom, Sarah started planning what should be done with it following her death. It meant so much to her that she had no intention of simply leaving this to chance, and just as her fortune had become her greatest source of power, so, with old age approaching, she felt that it could also be her surest hope of immortality.

Had her son Blandford lived, there would have been no problem. All would have gone to him. But the more she saw of Henrietta and her son Willigo (who was now Lord Blandford), the less could she endure the thought of wasting all her hard-won fortune on them. Besides, as Mrs Freeman, she had already realised that were she clever, there remained one further very special male prerogative she could indulge in – that of establishing a dynasty.

It is hard to know how much she originally envisaged this as Mrs Freeman's answer to the Marlborough dukedom, but certainly her personal dislike of Blenheim Palace influenced her decision. As Duchess Sarah she had played her crucial part in creating that great monument to her husband's glory, but from the start she had seen the palace as 'his greatest pride and his greatest weakness'. Then, with all the troubles that ensued, her dislike of Blenheim grew apace, until she saw it as that 'cruel, unmerciful house', imbued with the very qualities which she as a true-born Whig detested. Built like a royal palace, Blenheim was steeped in majesty and ostentation, everlastingly proclaiming one man's overwhelming power and domination. The fact that that man had been her husband made it even less acceptable. She had done her duty by 'the dear duke' in ensuring that his house was finished, and when her own time came she would be buried in the chapel there beside him. But none of this would ever make her like it.

The house she really loved was Althorp, which she remembered from its heyday after Shameless Sunderland had made it such a place of beauty, and she and her husband had visited as guests of hospitable Anne Sunderland. She had cherished the memory of it ever since and had come to regard it as a sort of idealised Whig country house. As she put it, 'there was room in it to entertain a king, if one could have the bad taste to like them, or the company that surrounds them. And yet it was so contriv'd that one might live there mighty comfortably with a few friends.'

It was also the family home of her Spencer grandchildren. Having completely alienated all her living children, these grandchildren offered her a promise for the future, and she knew that, whatever happened, no future duke of Marlborough would ever get his hands on Althorp, or undermine the independence of the House of Spencer.

At the centre of all Sarah's plans was twenty-year-old Robert Spencer, who, on the death of his father, had become the fourth Earl of Sunderland and taken up residence in Althorp. His brothers, fifteen-year-old Charles and thirteen-year-old John, were still at Eton and their sister Anne was on her marital bed of nails as Lady Bateman, leaving Sarah free to bring up her favourite grandchild, eleven-year-old Diana Spencer. 'Lady Dye', as Sarah called her, was a pretty child who reminded Sarah of her daughter, Anne, and Sarah seemed entranced with her, telling everyone that she 'already has more sense than any body that I know of my sex'.

But Sarah's real interest was in Robert Spencer, for she was already planning to make this fortunate young man principal heir to all her fortune and her property. Just as Blenheim and the duke-dom were her husband's monument, so she was hoping that with her own inheritance added to the Spencer lands at Althorp she could turn the Spencers into a supremely rich and powerful Whig dynasty, who would stand as her memorial.

Central to her thinking was her hatred of what she saw as the corruption of government produced by the alliance of Sunderland's successor as prime minister, Sir Robert Walpole, with King George II, through whom he controlled the wealth and patronage of the court. Now that her own courtier days were over, she had come to resent the court and the monarchy with a jealousy and bitterness of which only she was capable, and she seems to have hoped to turn her grandson into a great and incorruptible Whig statesman who might yet defeat her enemies. Backed by her wealth, and fired by her inspiration, he and his descendants would one day vindicate the Whig ideals that she believed in.

Soon she was taking steps to prevent 'her jewel' from succumbing to the blandishments of Robert Walpole and the court, who might yet bribe him with a pension and a court appointment. No sooner had Robert come of age and taken his seat in the House of Lords than she offered him a pension of her own of £1,000 a year and told him he would be her heir as long as he never sided with the court, the government or Robert Walpole.

Young Lord Sunderland was perfectly prepared to indulge his interfering but immensely wealthy grandmother. She was in her seventies by now and seemed unlikely to survive much longer. So he did what any sensible and self-indulgent young nobleman would do in such circumstances. He was most charming when he saw her, always agreed with her, flattered her outrageously, then went on living exactly as he wanted. He was a sociable young man and his life consisted chiefly of hunting, gambling, travelling abroad and borrowing heavily against his expectations as he waited to inherit his grandmother's money.

While he waited, so did Sarah, who was becoming impatient for her charming grandson to marry and produce the all important heirs to her fortune and her property. But even the promise of Wimbledon as a wedding present failed to make him settle down. Six years after his father died Lord Sunderland was still unmarried, and Sarah, one of whose favourite occupations was match-making, was becoming seriously perturbed. Needing a scapegoat, she accused his sister, Lady Bateman, of providing Robert with a mistress especially to flout her wishes.

Wisely, Lord Sunderland refused to argue, and it may well have been to escape from all this talk of marriage that he slipped quietly away to France in the summer of 1729. Out of sight of Sarah's spies, he was free to indulge in what he most enjoyed – the whirl of Paris and the gambling at Versailles. But early that September came the news that Sarah always dreaded. Robert was back in Paris and had fallen ill with fever.

Practical as ever, she instantly despatched a parcel of medicines, and was about to leave for France herself when she heard it was too late. So many celebrated doctors had been bleeding Robert Sunderland with leeches that, as his fever subsided, so had he. Enfeebled though he was, he was still worrying about his debts, as he makes clear in his final letter to his brother Charles:

'Dear Brother, I am now a-dying, and therefore desire when I am dead that you will do according to the directions in this letter.'

Listing his debts, he begged Charles to repay them for him – 220 guineas to Sir Michael Newton, £1,128 to Matthew Lamb the moneylender (and future scourge of the Spencers), and 'Mr Herbert who has a mortgage of £6,300 upon my estate'.

His conscience cleared, Robert Spencer, fourth Earl of Sunderland, closed his eyes and went to meet his maker. Since his dying wish was to be taken back to Althorp and buried with his ancestors in Great Brington church, 'they sent the corpse in the Calais coach with his former valet, M.D'Olignon, and a footman to attend it'.

Sarah was not present at the funeral, but was soon blaming the French doctors for murdering her grandson, and her grandson for dying. When her anger had receded, she felt deeply sorry for herself. It was, she told Lady Mary Wortley Montagu, 'the cruellest of blows to have one droop so untimely from the only branch that I can ever hope to receive any comfort from in my own family'.

For Sarah the worst consequence of the untimely death of Robert Sunderland was that it upset her deep-laid plans for the inheritance and forced her to begin again with the new incumbent at Althorp, twenty-three-year-old Charles Spencer, who had overnight become the fifth Earl of Sunderland. Like both his brothers, Charles had been wildly spoiled by the prospect of inheriting from Sarah's ever-growing fortune. But in contrast with his tactful, if evasive, brother, Charles had not a hope of winning Sarah's tempestuous affection.

He seems to have irritated her from the start, probably because he looked exactly like his father. In character, too, he was his father to the core – the same abrasiveness and lack of charm, the same 'large make', but without the cleverness. The best that Sarah could say for him was 'they say hee has sence, but hee has nothing at least before me that is entertaining'. Try as she might, she said, she could never bring herself to love him.

Although he had conscientiously settled Robert's debts, she refused to help him pay them. Once he was settled into Althorp trouble inevitably started – and inevitably over money.

In fact, he seems to have inherited something of the family's artistic taste, which, combined with his passionate love of horses, now gave Althorp two of its greatest treasures – John Wootton's near life-size paintings of his favourite horses which still dominate the entrance hall, and the great Palladian stable block for over a hundred horses. This equine palace is something of a masterpiece of Georgian architecture which Professor Nikolaus Pevsner rated higher than the later restoration of Althorp House itself.

But Sarah was outraged when she heard about the stables, partly because of the expense and partly because, contrary to her advice, Charles had employed as architect 'that infamous fellow' Roger Morris, the architect responsible for her house at Wimbledon. Inevitably she and Morris had had an angry falling out once the house was built and, intolerant as ever, she could not bear to think of any member of her family disagreeing with her wishes.

All this apart, Sarah was right to be disturbed about her grandson's expenditure. For, as his brother had before him, Charles was banking everything on Sarah's fairly imminent demise. Having been brought up, like his brothers, with the prospect of finally inheriting all the money he could ever need, there seemed no reason to worry overmuch about expenditure, and soon he was proving even more extravagant than Robert. Only the strongest willed of heirs could have resisted borrowing against such expectations, and strength of will was not his forte. Charles could hunt and womanise and gamble, but he could only pay for these expensive pleasures by mortgaging his future with moneylenders such as Matthew Lamb, at quite extortionate rates of interest.

It was now that Sarah's great plans for the future started going wrong, due largely to her own behaviour. For clearly there was a fearsome downside to the courageous, freedom-loving woman riding like a fury through the storms of eighteenth century politics. She could also be vindictive, manipulative, obsessively suspicious and totally insensitive to other peoples' feelings. And since she would ultimately depend upon her family to achieve what had become her life's ambition, it was through feuding with its members that she put at risk everything she wanted.

The first sign of trouble came when, irritated by her grandson Charles, she began to show unusual interest in his cousin, the Duke

of Marlborough's previously neglected heir, Willigo, Lord Blandford. Having become a Jacobite, a Catholic convert and an alcoholic, Blandford was not exactly ducal timber and since his sexual
tastes inclined him to stable-boys, few expected him to marry. But
in 1729, during one of the lengthy European tours that he indulged
in, marry he did – to the daughter of a rich Dutch burgomaster
called de Jong. The former Miss de Jong was not the type that
Sarah would normally have embraced as a potential Duchess of
Marlborough, but when, in 1730, Willigo brought her back to
England, Sarah, to everyone's surprise, welcomed the couple effus-
ively, expressing fond affection for Lord Blandford and saying how
much she hoped the couple would soon start a family. Sarah knew
quite well that news of this would get back to Charles Sunderland
at Althorp, and presumably felt that it would do no harm to remind
him of potential competition in his hopes for the great inheritance.

So far, Sarah's behaviour was relatively harmless. More serious
was the vendetta which was growing up between her and her eldest
granddaughter, Lady Bateman. Another enemy within the family
was the last thing Sarah needed, but she could not resist the temptation to upset poor Anne Bateman when they were together, and
since Anne had inherited every ounce of Sarah's own vindictiveness,
trouble loomed between them.

Where Sarah now appears at her meddling worst is over her
marriage plans for the one member of the family she really loved –
her youngest Spencer granddaughter, 'Lady Dye'. Sarah had already
paid an expensive London doctor to cure Diana of scrofula, and
was determined to find her a rich husband when, according to
Robert Walpole's son, the diarist Horace Walpole, Sarah hit upon
a plan of breathtaking presumption. The Hanoverians had a habit
of feuding with their offspring, and at the centre of the opposition
to King George and Queen Caroline stood their own disaffected
son and heir, Frederick, Prince of Wales. The Queen herself
described her son as 'the greatest ass and the greatest *canaille* and
the greatest beast in the whole world, and I heartily wish he was
out if it'.

Frederick felt much the same about his parents and, according to Horace Walpole, Sarah found irresistible the idea of scoring the ultimate victory over the court and the Royal Family itself by capturing the Prince of Wales as a husband for Diana. Knowing that he was always short of money, she supposedly offered him a dowry of £100,000 and he accepted.

If this was true – and in fairness to Sarah it must be said that the only account of this comes from Horace Walpole – it seems unforgivable that, in order to score off Queen Caroline and George II, Sarah was perfectly prepared to sacrifice the happiness of her own beloved Diana Spencer, by marrying her to that 'cad and cur', the Prince of Wales.

Fortunately for Diana, little escaped the notice of wily Robert Walpole, and, hearing rumours of what was happening, he promptly put an end to Sarah's plans for the secret marriage. Diana was well out of it and showed no sign of sadness or regret when, soon afterwards, she married Lord John Russell, the plump brother of the Duke of Bedford.

No sooner had Sarah married off Diana than death stepped in to rearrange the succession of the Spencers. Poor Willigo Godolphin had not managed to stay sober long enough to father an heir, and in August 1731, during an all-night feast at Balliol College Oxford, he drank so much that he suffered an attack of delirium tremens from which he never surfaced. Sarah was deeply shaken by his sudden death, and for once picked on the right person to blame for what had happened when she muttered that she 'hoped the devil is picking the bones of the man who taught him to drink'.

Willigo's estranged mother, Henrietta, was still Duchess of Marlborough in her own right, but Charles Sunderland was now inescapably her heir. He would succeed to the dukedom on her death, and not even Sarah Marlborough could prevent it. Nor could she affect the succession to Althorp, which was governed by the terms of her husband's will, in which it was clearly stated that if a Spencer became the heir to the Duke of Marlborough, Althorp and the family possessions would pass unencumbered to the next in line among the Spencers.

Now that the Spencer family between them had become the exclusive heirs of the fortunes and honours of the Marlboroughs, this if ever was the moment for Sarah to have made her peace with all the grandchildren, Charles included, and even with embittered Lady Bateman. But reconciliation was not in Sarah's nature, any more than it was in Charles's, and with his prospects suddenly enhanced to the tune of £8,000 a year from the Marlborough trust, which had previously gone to cousin Blandford, all his old resentments rose against her. Soon he was heard boasting in his cups that the money would free him from dependence on 'that unloving, capricious, extravagant old fury of a grandmother'. A few more drinks and he was promising 'to kick the old fury's A– . . . and make her kiss his own', words which inevitably got back to Sarah, who, surprisingly, kept her counsel and did nothing.

But not for long. Soon there was further news from Charles that set Mount Etna into full eruption: the ungrateful wretch who had just become heir to her own dear Duke of Marlborough had decided to get married, and without consulting her. Worse still, the shameless hussy who would one day bear the title of Duchess of Marlborough was none other than Elizabeth Trevor, daughter of the unmentionable Lord Trevor, one of twelve servile Tory peers who had been created to ensure the passage through the House of Lords of the infamous Peace of Utrecht, which had brought such suffering and shame on her late husband.

Then, as if all this were not enough, every one of her Spencer grandchildren, apart from ever faithful 'Lady Dye', had used the occasion to defy her by attending Charles's wedding, to which, of course, she was not invited. Sarah was convinced that the ringleader had to be the woman who was now her greatest enemy, her own granddaughter, evil Lady Bateman.

She was probably right, but again she only had herself to blame. For ever since forcing Anne Spencer into her miserable marriage, Sarah had taken every opportunity to provoke her, either inquiring why poor Lady Bateman had no children, or comparing Lord Bateman's lack of affection with the way her own dear duke had always treated her. Childless, ugly and embittered, Lady Bateman had come to loathe her grandmother.

Sarah might have learned by now that rows in families, like civil wars, are the bitterest of all, but nothing could quell her hatred for Lady Bateman. 'The vilest woman I ever knew in my life; and deserves to be burnt', was one of her milder descriptions of her own granddaughter – and so that no one would misunderstand her feelings she blacked out the face on Lady Bateman's portrait in the dining room at Marlborough House, telling her startled guests that, 'Now her outside is as black as her insides.'

Convinced that her whole family had turned against her, Sarah then informed them all that she would burn her will, and got as far as making an overlarge bequest for the creation of almshouses at St Albans to show that she meant business.

As for her grandson Charles, who was now happily married to Elizabeth Trevor, words could not express Sarah's indignation at his base behaviour, so she did what she had long been threatening and disinherited him of his promised share of her fortune. His reply can hardly have improved her temper:

As for your cutting me out of yr. Will, it is some time since I neither expected nor desired to be in it. I have nothing more to add, except to assure your Grace that this is the last time I shall ever trouble you by Letter or by Conversation.
    I am yr. Grace's grandson,
        Sunderland

Not a letter to be left unanswered, certainly not by Sarah, who had always insisted on having the last word in everything:

You end yr. letter that you are my grandson; Which is indeed a melancholy Truth; but very lucky for you. For all the world except yourself is sensible that had you not been my Grandson, you would be in as bad a condition as you deserve to be.

Game, set and match, it seemed, to Sarah, but of course it was not. For after the death of Willigo, Lord Blandford, not even Sarah Marlborough could prevent her grandson Charles from entering into at least part of his inheritance as third Duke of Marlborough on the death of her daughter Harriet – which happened sooner than expected two years later.

But even now that Charles Spencer had become the undoubted third Duke of Marlborough, Sarah could not resist keeping the hatred in the family alive by making his life as difficult as possible, first by banning him from Blenheim, which was hers for life, and then by refusing to help financially with the large expenses he incurred by moving out of Althorp.

The new Duke was a domesticated man at heart; he bought himself a charming red-brick house at Langley in Buckinghamshire, started a family, stayed unexpectedly faithful to his wife, and continued borrowing heavily against his expectations. Like everybody in the family, he was waiting for Sarah to die, and it seemed as if her grand dynastic plans were over. She was growing old and bitter, and eighteen months after Harriet's death came news that she had dreaded.

For some time she had been concerned about Diana, whose husband, Lord John Russell, had become Duke of Bedford on his brother's death in 1730. Diana was convinced that she was pregnant, but Sarah thought her far too thin. She was in fact in the final stages of tuberculosis and died a few months later. Sarah was overcome with grief which, true to form, she expressed at the funeral by accusing the inoffensive husband of having killed poor Dye 'stone dead' by his behaviour. Unused to such treatment, the roly-poly Duke of Bedford fainted.

Sarah genuinely mourned her 'dearest Dye'. But, as she often said, 'the heart is a long time a-breaking', and she remained a long time a-dying. Now in her mid-seventies, her energies were undiminished and her will-power seemed as strong as ever. Nothing could deflect her, and despite her bitterness she continued with the three things she excelled at – making money, buying property, and making the lives of everyone around her as intolerable as possible.

But Diana's death affected her more than anyone suspected, and just as it seemed as if her great dynastic plans had been forgotten, she turned for affection to the last remaining heir to Althorp, Diana's brother and the youngest of the Spencer grandsons, the Honourable John 'Jack' Spencer.

Had Jack Spencer not been in line for one of the great inheritances of England, he would probably have led a long and relatively harmless life. People liked him, for he was a charming, lively character, and his portrait at Althorp shows a manly figure with strong legs, a commanding presence and something of the Churchill features. But the portrait is deceptive. Jack had always been notoriously idle, and what energies he possessed had been directed into three absorbing interests – gambling, drink and women. A younger Sarah would not have tolerated him for long, but since she was old and lonely and Jack her one remaining heir, she did her best to like him. 'I am sure I love him more than anybody that is in the world,' she said and soon informed him that provided he obeyed her wishes she would make him virtually sole heir to her entire estate.

For Jack this proved a most deceptive blessing, for as Sarah's heir he rapidly became a walking demonstration of the various afflictions which the promise of great riches can inflict upon one amiable but weak willed human being. Sarah both spoiled him and tyrannised over him, and while at times he seemed to resent his grandmother's incessant domination, he lacked the strength of will to do anything about it. So he went on flattering her, playing up to her and counting on his looks and cheerful manner to placate her when she felt neglected. But he seems to have revealed his real feeling for her at her seventieth birthday party when she remarked how good it was to see all the branches of the family flourishing around her, and John was heard to mutter that 'branches flourish better when their roots are buried'.

Remembering the fuss following his brother's marriage, Jack wisely took no chances with his own. The story goes that when Sarah showed him a list of marriageable young women in alphabetical order he picked the first, Lady Georgiana Carteret, the daughter of John Carteret, second Earl Granville, simply because her name began with C. Probably more to the point was the fact that Granville was one of Walpole's most serious political opponents and Sarah wanted his support.

There was a slight delay while Jack was cured of gonorrhoea, but once recovered, he dutifully walked Georgiana up the aisle of fashionable St George's, Hanover Square, where the Spencer family had briefly and uncomfortably assembled on Sarah's orders. Afterwards Jack took his bride to St James's Palace, but when he presented her to King George II, His Majesty turned his back on them and it was left to Queen Caroline to remark, 'Mr Spencer, I believe I have not seen you since you was a child.'

'No madam, I believe not,' Jack replied, and the audience was over.

But Sarah soon made up for the king's rudeness by treating her grandson as a prince, and offering him and his wife Marlborough House, together with the use of Roger Morris's 'curtseying' villa at Wimbledon, once intended for his long-dead brother Robert. Her own verdict on Wimbledon by now was that it was 'an ill sod, very damp, and I believe an unhealthy place, which I shall seldom live in'.

However, Jack's marriage seems to have confirmed her interest in the future of her all-important dynasty. Procreation was one area in which Jack was willing to oblige, and Sarah was delighted when his wife produced in swift succession two extremely pretty children, John and Diana. But despite the children, Jack was not a family man, and he increasingly resorted to the house at Wimbledon, staying there for weeks on end with groups of friends, enjoying the drinking and wenching and, presumably when sober, the shooting.

If Sarah knew what was going on, she did not seem to care. What really concerned her was the next generation, and she doted on the two children, who often stayed with her at Windsor. Despite the arthritis which was plaguing her, she used to sing to them to make them laugh, and played what she called 'romping games' with them before they went to bed. But, like everyone in the family, even the children were becoming wise about her money. When they played a game of draughts she asked them what they wanted as a prize – money or a kiss?

'Money,' the tots replied in unison.

And still Sarah would not die. Somehow she struggled on into her eighties, and despite the singing and the romping games, arthritis now confined her to her bed in winter and to a crab-like existence in the summer. But even as she clattered round her house on crutches nothing, it seemed, could stop her making money.

She was now unquestionably the richest woman in the land – and still trying to use her wealth to dominate the lives of others. She was still convinced that land was the best and safest form of investment, and from time to time took pleasure in embarrassing the government by disposing of a tranche of government stock when it would cause the greatest trouble to the Treasury, then using the money to invest in yet further purchases of real estate. Thus her kingdom went on growing, and would soon consist of estates in twelve counties, and reserves of something over £250,000 in capital.

She had made herself what Mrs Freeman had always longed to be – free, all-powerful, and famous. It was now that she suddenly conceived the idea of getting her chosen heir the title of Lord Churchill in his own right. 'By this I thought I should make one of the dear Duke of Marlborough's grandsons represent him in this world by His Name, supported by my own estate' – which would presumably have meant that the Spencers would have borne the Churchill title to the present day. But without resorting to the court, or asking a favour of hated Robert Walpole – both of which she emphatically refused to do – this was not possible. So the Spencers remained Spencers and her grandson had to face the world without a title.

By now her hatred of George II and Queen Caroline and their apparently indestructible prime minister was so obsessive that it became the cause of one final and far-reaching encumbrance with which she would lumber the next two generations of the Spencer family.

It all began in 1738, when what has been described as 'a bombshell' burst within her family. By now Sarah had mellowed sufficiently to be back on speaking terms with her grandson Charles, who was increasingly enjoying his role as third Duke of Marlborough. Since she still insisted on retaining Blenheim, he had got himself yet further into debt by extensive alterations to the house and gardens at Langley, but in compensation for depriving him of Blenheim, Sarah had permitted him and his family to use the Little Lodge at Windsor, and was dropping promises about remembering him in her will in order to ensure his loyalty against the government in the House of Lords.

But she firmly refused to advance him money to pay off the most pressing of his debts, and finally he became so desperate that he did the one thing Sarah would not forgive – accepted a sinecure from Robert Walpole in the form of a well paid colonelcy in a West Indian regiment, in return for his promise to support the government. A still more valuable court appointment as Gentleman of the Bedchamber was to follow, and Sarah became particularly enraged on hearing Walpole's smug reaction to the news in the House of Commons: 'You see, I know the way to get every body I have a mind to.'

The outcome was inevitable – a final breaking off of all relations between Sarah and Marlborough and an instant cancelling of the various bequests which she had been going to leave him and which, as she icily informed him, 'had been more than anybody could have expected'. On becoming Duke of Marlborough, Charles had already carried off not only the major part of the Sunderland library but also the two Spencer peerages, Earl of Sunderland and Baron Wormleighton. There was nothing Sarah could do about this, but she did demand the return of numerous possessions and mementoes of her husband, all of which were now to go to Althorp. As a final insult she insisted that the Duke return his grandfather's jewelled sword, 'lest he pick out the diamonds to pawn them'. He and his family were summarily ejected from the Little Lodge at Windsor.

It was an occasion Jack made the most of in Sarah's presence, by 'bursting into tears . . . and saying he was so much ashamed he could not stand it'. But, ancient though she was, Sarah was not stupid, and however convinced she may have been that Jack loved her while she was alive she had no illusions over how he would behave after she was dead.

So, summoning her lawyers, the old woman penned one further clause to that puissant document, her will. By it she debarred both John Spencer and his son from inheriting a penny of all she was leaving them, should they ever accept any post or pension from the government. 'She was determined, even from beyond the grave, to ensure that no minister would ever be able to buy the allegiance of her heirs, although the cost would be to exclude them from any role in public life except a parliamentary one.'

She was pleased with herself for devising such a smart manoeuvre. Seeing it as a final scoring off against the monarch and the court, she even insisted that 'It would have been of great use to the Nation , if People of great Estates had taken the same Method.' For she believed that this would keep the Spencers free from the contagion and corruption of the court until the arrival on the scene of a later generation who might use her wealth as she intended. She hoped that one day a Spencer might become the sort of staunch champion of liberty which, had she but been a man, she might have been herself.

But she was very old, and she had done the best she could. Now it was up to future generations to carry out her wishes, while those around her let her die in peace.

It was not until 1744, at the age of eighty-four, that she did so. The novelist Tobias Smollett's epitaph was brief and to the point. 'Her death in the 85th year of her life was very little regretted, either by her own family or the world in general.'

For twenty-two years her husband's body had been lying in

Westminster Abbey waiting for this moment. Now in accordance with his will it was taken to the grave she had prepared for them both in the chapel at Blenheim Palace, and she was placed beside him. Thus was she finally reunited with her 'dear Duke' in the palace she had helped create and which she hated.

After his death she had effectively flouted the great man's wishes, corrupted and undermined his heirs, split the Spencer dynasty, created a vast inheritance and started two quite separate lines of Spencers for the future. For an uneducated woman in the predominantly male world of the eighteenth century it was no mean achievement.

CHAPTER 5

The Divide

The Hon. John Spencer (1708–1746)

For the Spencers, Sarah Marlborough's death was like the moment when a river suddenly divides, continuing as two separate branches to the sea. There were deep reasons for the split among the Spencers, but the immediate cause lies almost entirely with Sarah. Through her gross favouritism of her youngest grandson Jack, at the expense of her other grandson Charles, Sarah made these two brothers bitter enemies, who had no further contact with each other after her funeral. From then on the two families, although all Spencers, were quite different, and they have stayed so to the present day.

Since one branch of the Spencers bore the great Duke's title and inherited his palace, it is not entirely surprising that the Marlborough Spencers have been dominated by his memory. In 1817 they would even change their name to Spencer Churchill in his honour, and just as the family has remained firmly to the right in politics, so it has always been strongly influenced by John Duke's warlike shadow. As a dynasty these nineteenth-century Spencer Churchills would produce two worthy successors to their great progenitor, the volatile precursor of modern conservatism, Lord Randolph Churchill, and his greater son Sir Winston, much of whose life both as soldier and statesman was inspired by his ancestor, John, Duke of Marlborough.

The Althorp Spencers were another matter. Sarah's inheritance made them far richer than their Marlborough cousins, and at Althorp, freed from the overwhelming presence of the Duke, they stayed loyal to their Whig traditions, as Sarah wanted. Thanks to the terms of her will these Spencers would remain immensely rich throughout the eighteenth century, aloof from both court and government for the next two generations, leaving them free to enjoy their great inheritance. In the process they became celebrated figures in society, patrons of the arts, great travellers and keen collectors.

At first one feels sorriest for irascible Charles Spencer who, as third Duke of Marlborough, was so badly treated by his grandmother. Not only did she disinherit him, and was deeply offensive to his inoffensive wife, but at his expense she also outrageously favoured his brother John. Until his death in 1758, Charles and the dukedom would be plagued with debt, but he managed to survive and in his way he prospered. He was neither a great man like his grandfather, nor a particularly clever one like his father, and he made a rather unassuming duke, being essentially a family man, with a love of gardening and expensive tastes in building.

But however traumatic at the time, his break with Sarah, far from being an absolute disaster, seems to have brought him certain long-term advantages. Primarily it allowed him to enjoy a political career, enriched with the spoils of government. Once his foot was on the ladder of political preferment, the Duke climbed slowly upwards to an honourable position in the political establishment, eventually becoming Lord President of the Council in the Duke of Newcastle's government and honoured with the Order of the Garter. Although officially a Whig like everyone in government, Charles was by inclination and ambition considerably to the right in politics – a position which the subsequent Dukes of Marlborough have adhered to to the present day.

On finding himself Duke of Marlborough the influence of his warlike grandfather seems to have affected him in other ways, and he was soon exchanging his lucrative colonelcy in his West Indian regiment for a colonelcy in the Dragoon Guards, before moving onto the even smarter second Regiment of Horse Guards. His military career began in earnest when war again broke out with France in 1740 and the Duke, by now a lieutenant general, took his regiment to Germany, with George II. He was with him at the inglorious Battle of Dettingen, the last occasion when a king of England fought in battle.

There can be no greater contrast to the Duke's financial situation than that of Sarah's favoured heir, his brother Jack. Where Charles was effectively disinherited by Sarah, Jack was that rich old woman's unchallenged legatee. When the full extent of all she owned had been computed, it was revealed that Jack had inherited not so much a fortune as an empire – with no less than thirty-nine separate manors in a dozen counties. Some, like Crowhurst in Surrey and Hailweston in Northamptonshire, were relatively small. But other houses and estates were of considerable size and wealth. There was Sarah's old home at St Albans, which effectively returned its own member of parliament. There was the shootingbox and fenland estate of North Creake in Norfolk. There were large tracts of land in Bedfordshire and Northamptonshire. Above all there was Wimbledon Manor with its potential urban goldmine at Putney and Mortlake. There was also half a million pounds in money and investments. When added to the 12,000 ancestral Spencer acres in Northamptonshire and Althorp this meant that, in terms of sheer resources, Sarah had made the Althorp Spencers into one of the wealthiest families in England. Since Charles Spencer remained fifth Earl of Sunderland on becoming Duke of Marlborough, Jack was still without a title, but with money this could soon be rectified, and the Althorp Spencers were vastly richer than the nearly bankrupt Dukes of Marlborough.

For Jack Spencer it must suddenly have seemed that all those years of dancing attendance on Sarah had finally paid off, and he should have been the happiest of men as at last he entered into his great inheritance. But it was not that simple. With Sarah, things rarely were. Before she died she had made absolutely sure that there were several awkward catches to the enjoyment of his fortune.

In the first place there was that all-important clause in his grandmother's will which prohibited both him and his heir from taking any pension or position with the court. This meant that at the age of thirty-two Jack was politically castrated and totally excluded from political preferment, a career at court, or government largesse. More serious still was the discovery that his 'old fury of a grand-mother' had effectively tied up all the lands that she had left in trust, and that the trustees themselves were utterly intent upon preserving every item of the great inheritance in the future interests of the family. This caused Jack serious problems. Sarah had lived so much longer than anyone expected that both he and Charles had been borrowing for years against their expectations, and now Jack's debts were even larger than his brother's. Whereas Charles was said to have been owing half a million pounds at Sarah's death, one estimate put Jack's indebtedness closer to a million.

Jack, not unnaturally, had been assuming that he could use at least part of his inheritance to repay his debts, but this was shown to have been a most unwise assumption. He discovered that with all his property in trust he was banned from selling it to realise his assets. Nor could he even touch the income from the property and investments which, according to Horace Walpole, amounted to at least £30,000 a year. But Sarah's death was the signal for creditors like Matthew Lamb and Sir Theodore Janssen's son (who seems to have been lending Jack large amounts of money in the hope of recovering Wimbledon) to fall upon Jack, clamouring for payment. It must have been particularly disappointing for the easy-going he-donist to find himself having to convince these tough financiers that in spite of his inheritance he could genuinely not repay them, since his trustees were using all the income from his vast estate to pay off other debts and legacies.

There is a certain amount of sympathy for him, but it is also hard not to feel impatient at his weakness and stupidity. Surely even he could have done something to make money out of this enormous legacy? He could have found himself sensible advisers. He could still have lived economically and happily at Althorp – which his brother had considerably enhanced in his years of tenure – or at Hollywell, or Wimbledon. And although forbidden to take any profit from the government or the court, there was nothing to stop him trading his electoral influence for money or a title. His situation, while difficult, was far from hopeless, and no property owner like him needed to despair. But despair he did. For, having just won the greatest inheritance of his age, Jack now seemed paralysed. His doctor summed the situation up as follows: 'He didn't have experience in the world sufficient to conduct himself and his affairs, was very negligent, and averse to business. Nor was he prudent in his dealings.'

Sarah Marlborough had been making all the real decisions in Jack's life for so long that she seemed to have destroyed his will. So it was that, instead of benefiting from her fortune, the greatest inheritor in England became its victim. Jack lacked the character and skill to cope with it, to the extent that it actually brought him far more misery than pleasure. In a sense he only had himself to blame, but Sarah should also bear some of the responsibility for Jack's disaster. By spoiling and bullying him for so many years, she had effectively destroyed Jack Spencer before she died.

A.L. Rowse believed that Jack's decline was due to undiagnosed tuberculosis which he caught as a child from his mother Anne. Although there is no direct evidence that Anne Sunderland died of the disease, Jack's sisters, Anne and Diana certainly did, and both his children were probably consumptive. For Jack himself the evidence is inconclusive. Certainly, shortly after Sarah's death his doctor was assuring him that he found him 'of strong and healthy constitution, and likely to live many years in good health'. But it is also clear that he was drinking more than was good for him. The ebullient Jack Spencer, who had once made Sarah laugh by re-entering her drawing room by the window when she had shown him the door, had turned into the notorious 'Sack' Spencer, best known for his addiction to the bottle.

Drinking heavily, he grew morose. There was no sign of affection to or from his wife and family – nor did women or gambling seem to interest him any longer. Instead he withdrew from life, and the more he drank the more his health deteriorated. But even now when he consulted an apothecary in Chelsea, Jack was assured that 'provided he could refrain from chewing tobacco and drinking of drams, he might still live a great while'. But did he want to?

'From time to time', as his doctor suggested, Jack would take a cure at Bath, hoping that the waters would 'remove the disorders of his stomach'. For a while, it seems, they did, for soon his doctor was prescribing Jack what he called 'a strict regime' which he insisted could still save him. But Jack was too weak willed to follow it. And in 1745, barely twenty months after inheriting one of the greatest fortunes in the country, Jack Spencer died. In recording his death, Horace Walpole wrote his epitaph: 'With an income of £30,000 a year, Jack Spencer had died, because he would not be abridg'd of those invaluable blessings of an English subject, brandy, small beer and tobacco.'

Even now Sarah's influence continued to affect the Spencers, and Walpole it was who also described the strange postscript to Jack's death.

'The great business of the town,' he wrote, 'is Jack Spencer's will, who has left Althorp and the Sunderland estates in reversion to Pitt, after more obligations and more pretended friendships for his brother than is conceivable.'

It seems that this alarming clause in Jack Spencer's will was due to Sarah's influence, and it left a most worrying situation for the family. Not long before Sarah died she had been delighted by Pitt the Elder's angry attacks on the Hanoverian influence on George II and the foreign policy of Walpole. She had made Jack agree to the reversion of all the Spencer property being left to Pitt – anything to stop it going back to Charles and the Marlborough side of the family. This meant that everything depended on the heir Jack Spencer left behind him. Small wonder that his brother Charles was so unhappy when he heard the news. For far from strengthening the house of Spencer, as she had once intended, Sarah had left its future hanging by a slender thread of a single life – Jack's only son, John Spencer. At the tender age of twelve, John found himself the 'richest schoolboy in England'.

CHAPTER 6

The First Earl

John, first Earl Spencer (1734–1783)

Young John Spencer was not only the richest schoolboy in England, but also the most precious as far as the Spencers were concerned, since he was all that now prevented Althorp and Sarah Marlborough's fortune passing to William Pitt the Elder. This must have made his adolescence a time of some anxiety, and as a consequence his mother seems to have lavished more care and attention on him than was good for his character. Even as a grown man he would never quite get over all the spoiling he received in childhood.

His mother's behaviour was understandable, however, for as well as being so important he was also beautiful, having inherited his father's looks, with the same fine eyes and clear complexion. But he was always delicate, and after his sister, Diana, died in late childhood, his mother became doubly anxious for him.

Sarah Marlborough's death, followed so rapidly by Jack Spencer's, had provided a breathing space for the family trustees to address the problems of the estate, settle Jack's debts, invest in yet more land, including Wandsworth and Battersea, and amass a surplus of £25,000 in cash for John Spencer to receive on his majority. And although his mother had married for the second time kindly Lord Cowper, she continued to dedicate her life to looking after her delicate son, and thereby saving Sarah Marlborough's vast inheritance for the Spencers.

After his sister's death, John's health improved sufficiently for his mother to send him off to be educated at Harrow, where she made sure he was looked after by a private tutor. However, towards the end of his schooldays John's health was causing fresh anxiety, and instead of being sent to university or on the Grand Tour, he returned to Althorp and his doting mother, having grown from a pretty child into an unusually handsome young man. Although there is no evidence of the exact nature of his illness it was almost certainly tuberculosis, which affected him intermittently for the rest of his life and would ultimately kill him.

Whether or not Lady Cowper knew what was wrong with her son, she was obviously extremely worried, but at the same time she must have realised that this was not the moment to be over-sentimental. If her son's life was threatened, when so much depended on it, the sooner he was married and producing little Spencers the better. Just as she took care of most things in his life, Lady Cowper seems to have taken care of this as well.

In December 1755 she gave a party at Althorp on the eve of her son's twenty first birthday, in the course of which it had been arranged that he should slip upstairs to his mother's dressing room with seventeen-year-old Georgiana Poyntz. Lady Cowper and Georgiana's mother were waiting for them with a local vicar, who proceeded to marry the young couple there and then in the simplest of ceremonies. Shortly afterwards, when they returned to the party as man and wife, none of their guests was any the wiser.

It was most mysterious, and when the marriage was made public, Horace Walpole expressed surprise that somebody as rich and grand as Spencer should be marrying 'a mere Miss Poyntz', when he seemed to be ideally placed for another of those splendid marriages so beloved by his family.

Miss Poyntz was neither rich nor famous. Her father, Stephen Poyntz, the son of a London upholsterer, was a self-made business-man who had risen to become a courtier, a diplomat and tutor to the Duke of Cumberland. He was also a trusted friend of the Duke of Devonshire, and his social connections explain how his lively daughter came to meet the young John Spencer, and fall in love with him, and he with her. But a romance between them would have gone no further without positive encouragement from both their families. While the Poyntzes must have seen marriage with rich John Spencer, however ill he was, as a splendid opportunity for their daughter, Lady Cowper must also have detected in Georgiana Poyntz the sort of wife her son so badly needed.

Not only could this serious and affectionate young girl bear her sickly son's all-important children; she could also look after him and give him all the love he needed. His health was so uncertain at this time that someone later said, 'It was a question of which came first, the marriage or the funeral', which almost certainly explains why the wedding was performed so hurriedly and with such discretion. The ailing groom was thought unlikely to have coped with a grander ceremony, and he was really marrying his nurse. But they loved each other, and Georgiana would devotedly look after him in sickness and in health for the rest of his life.

It was thanks to her that the marriage swiftly proved a much greater success than anyone – apart presumably from Pitt the Elder – can have hoped for. (Pitt, in fact, had more serious matters on his mind, having just effectively taken charge of the war against the French, and he made no mention of the matter.)

But no sooner was John Spencer married than his health dramatically improved. He and his wife seemed more in love than ever and, before long, everyone concerned about the future of the Spencers and their great inheritance could breathe again. Young Mrs Spencer was pregnant and, provided all went well, the family would have an heir for Althorp and for Sarah Marlborough's inheritance. The relief was enormous and, to celebrate, John Spencer decided to use part of his great legacy to build one of the most beautiful houses in London.

Although he owned more grand houses than he knew what to do with, the one place where he lacked a residence was London. His Sunderland grandfather's house in Piccadilly had been sold, following his death, and Marlborough House in Pall Mall had gone to his uncle, Charles Duke of Marlborough, leaving the newly married Spencers with nothing more than what Horace Walpole would probably have called 'a mere abode' in Grosvenor Street. It was in fact extremely comfortable, but it was not in keeping with the Spencers' wealth and their suddenly expanding social aspirations. But like most things in John Spencer's now enviable existence, this was something else that money could provide.

As luck would have it, shortly before the Spencers married, Henry Bromley, first Baron Montfort, an overweight and none too scrupulous City businessman, was involved in a financial scandal that ruined him. After dining at Whites, he called on his lawyer to countersign his will and, while the man was in another room, put a pistol to his head and pulled the trigger. His suicide placed the most desirable building site in London on the market. He had recently bought some land between St James's Palace and Green Park, and had already dug the foundations for what was intended to be Monfort House. John Spencer purchased the site from the dead businessman's estate and proceeded to build Spencer House instead.

Thanks to Sarah Marlborough, with so much money at the couple's disposal the result was no ordinary house. They could have exactly what they wanted, and they were fortunate to be building at a time when it seemed impossible to create anything ugly – whether a book, a tombstone, a carriage or a house – particularly a house overlooking Green Park, with the pick of London's architects to call on.

They chose John Vardy, a follower of the architect William Kent, a choice revealing something of the way their minds were working. For Kent's accepted masterpiece was the rebuilt Devonshire House, the grandest of all the great Whig palaces and home of the Cavendish Dukes of Devonshire, which faced them just across Green Park from Piccadilly. And although the mansion Vardy planned was very much in Kent's Palladian manner, it was based on the smaller and more elegant Palazzo Chiericato in Verona.

There was great joy when, in January 1757, Mrs Spencer gave birth to a healthy baby girl. To express his gratitude to his wife, John Spencer insisted on naming her Georgiana, and the following year the arrival of a son and heir, George John, guaranteed the future of the Spencer dynasty. Their third and last child, Henrietta (always known as Harriet), arrived two years later.

The Spencers were a particularly devoted family, due partly to John Spencer's still delicate state of health and also to his wife's profoundly earnest dedication to their children's needs. Coming from a close-knit middle-class family herself, she would always be involved in her children's lives, taking an unusual interest in their education and religion.

After four years, Spencer House was still not finished, and Spencer and his wife had become disenchanted with their architect. Kent and Vardy were going out of fashion. Stylistically, ancient Greece was superseding ancient Rome, and there was now a new genius for everyone to turn to, James 'Athenian' Stuart, who was freshly back from Athens where he had been studying the art and architecture of Ancient Greece. He was considered the architectural *arbiter elegantiarum* of his day, and the Spencers appointed him to take over from Vardy and impart additional refinements to the house, assisted by many of the most gifted craftsmen from England, France and Italy.

The result was the most beautiful neo-classical house in London, which alone of the great Whig London mansions miraculously survives today. It has been as miraculously restored thanks to Lord (Jacob) Rothschild, who fell in love with it and whose investment company bought a 124-year lease on the house in 1987. Walking through its rooms today one glimpses something of the style and splendour in which John and Georgiana Spencer lived their married life in London.

Now that John Spencer had a son it was time to think about a title. At twenty-one he had been offered – and had rather languidly accepted – a seat in parliament, but he does not seem to have enjoyed it. His distant cousin, Lady Mary Coke, heard him speak in a debate and commented, 'as much as could be heard was very pretty, but he was extremely frightened and spoke very low'. If he was so uncomfortable in parliament, the clause in Sarah

Marlborough's will banning him from any ministerial appointment, cannot have seriously worried him, particularly not with so much else in a life as rich as his to relish and enjoy.

He certainly had no intention of becoming like Thomas Pelham-Holles, Duke of Newcastle, who finally became prime minister in 1754 and ended up £300,000 the poorer after spending forty years, and almost all his fortune, on the unrewarding game of politics. Not only did Sarah's ban save Spencer from such a fate, he was even able to turn the ban to his own advantage. At twenty-six he wrote to Newcastle pointing out that he had always supported the government and that since he was unable to accept office, he was unable to receive any favour from the King except a title.

'Only a title? My dear fellow, we must see to that!' said Newcastle, or words to that effect. Since Newcastle's government was in desperate need of fresh supporters in the House of Lords, John duly found himself created first Viscount Spencer in 1761, and was effortlessly earled some four years later. Henceforth as first Earl Spencer, he was free to follow the blessings of a very grand and very private life at the apex of polite eighteenth-century aristocratic society.

And what a life it was, with all those houses crammed with art and books and hordes of servants. There was Althorp, somewhat neglected but enjoying the fine new stables generously built by Uncle Charles, fifth Earl of Sunderland before he left for Blenheim to become the Duke of Marlborough. There was Holywell, Sarah Marlborough's family house at St Albans, which she had had largely rebuilt by the architect William Talman before he turned to greater things at Chatsworth. They leased Pytchley for the hunting, and owned North Creake in Norfolk for the shooting. And last, but emphatically not least, there was Sarah's proudest purchase, Wimbledon Park, which now included the picturesque villages of Mortlake and Roehampton, a forty-acre lake, abundant woodlands, several farms, unrivalled views across to the Surrey hills, and a costly new menagerie of exotic birds and beasts, together with

Sarah's very grand Palladian mansion – all within five miles of Hyde Park Corner.

The Spencers seemed a happy and devoted pair, if somewhat self-indulgent, and wildly extravagant. Even the cynical old Lord Queensberry grudgingly conceded that they offered the best argument for the married state he had ever seen. Nothing appeared to mar their happiness until suddenly the Earl's health once again betrayed him.

It must have been tuberculosis, for in 1763, at the age of twenty-eight, he was suffering from what was described as 'a weakness of the lungs', which necessitated wintering abroad. Even this was undertaken on the grandest scale. Two separate packet boats were needed to transport the Spencers from Gravesend to Harwich – one for the Earl, family and personal servants, the other for the baggage, lesser servants and his Lordship's furniture and carriages.

Even so, it took this caravanserai more than a month to rattle down to Rome, much of it spent bumping over unmade roads. When the Spencers reached the Eternal City, they were welcomed by the Pope, the palazzi of the city swung open their great doors in their honour and, between outings into the campagna, Georgiana sat for her portrait to the most fashionable Roman painter of the English nobility, Pompeo Battoni. The Earl, meanwhile, bought paintings by Andrea Sacchi and Salvator Rosa for the empty walls of Spencer House in far-off London.

In warmer climes the Earl's health had steadily improved, making him happy to return to England in early summer. Once back, the Spencers' lives seemed governed by perpetual motion as they moved from one great mansion to the next. At Althorp the Earl was obsessed with hunting, and as master of the Pytchley Hunt would go out regardless of the weather and his state of health. Back in London, he and Lady Spencer were privileged spectators of the great Augustan age in art and literature, enjoying the company of such men as Samuel Johnson, David Garrick and their close friend, the great painter Sir Joshua Reynolds. Lawrence Sterne, a particular protegé, dedicated part of *Tristram Shandy* to them.

If one could choose a time in which to be alive and young and very rich, it must have been around the time when the first Earl Spencer was living in newly-built Spencer House with his wife Georgiana. And yet the Earl grew increasingly irritable, and was sometimes overcome by black bad temper. It was now that Lord Hervey wrote about how deeply involved Georgiana was with the poor of Althorp. She was a dedicated Christian and was the first member of the family to show any real concern for them and set up Sunday schools for the children. With her love of the country and her commitment to the local poor, 'nothing', Lord Hervey wrote, 'could tempt Lady Spencer to London but the restlessness of her poor husband'.

How, one asks, could one so blest be 'restless' – and why was one so rich described as 'poor'?

There were several reasons. The first was that all the spoiling in his childhood seems to have left the Earl permanently discontented. Apart from travelling and spending vast amounts of money, there was not a great deal for his restless nature to accomplish after Spencer House was built. Although he happened to buy pictures, and his friendships with Reynolds and Gainsborough produced some magnificent portraits, particularly of his wife and daughters, he was in no sense a patron and connoisseur like his great grandfather, the second Earl of Sunderland. And, although he rather casually purchased 5,000 Elizabethan volumes from Dr George, the Master of Eton, to fill some of the empty shelves at Althorp after his uncle Charles took so much of the famous Sunderland Library to Blenheim, he was in no sense a bibliophile and scholar like his formidable grandfather, the third Earl of Sunderland.

There was another reason for Spencer's discontent. Remarkably for one so rich, he was often worried about money – or the lack of it. Throughout his adult life, his income stood at around £40,000 a year, which – at a time when a servant was rich on £50 a year, and Sarah had bought the Wimbledon estate for £25,000 – should have seemed like boundless riches. But even in the 1760s a determined man could get through £40,000 a year – and the Earl was such a man. Admittedly, he seldom received his full theoretical income, particularly during periods of agricultural depression, and his stewards and rent collectors were not well supervised by the ageing agents inherited from Sarah or the Trustees. But nothing was likely to check John Spencer from overspending in an age when even the greatest nobles were usually in debt. He might reasonably feel that, in establishing the new dynasty socially and politically, he had done his duty by his successors even if he had failed to realise the moment when indebtedness passed from being a normal burden on a great estate to a threat to its survival.

Servants might be cheap, but when you staffed as many establishments as he did, wages – and the cost of clothing and feeding an army of retainers – mounted up. So did the maintenance on so many houses, particularly the roofs. Roofs were the bane of the eighteenth-century aristocracy.

There were also the Earl's random extravagances. Hunting was always a great expense, particularly with the hounds and horses he was expected to maintain as Master of the Pytchley. He was also spending lavishly on the gardens at Althorp, and currently employing the aristocracy's favourite landscape gardener, Lancelot 'Capability' Brown, to sweep away what was left of the ancient formal gardens, replacing them with the now fashionable 'natural' landscape. Brown was also employed widely at Wimbledon. But all of this still left the Earl two areas where he could spread himself financially – politics and building.

Although Spencer's St Alban's estate enabled him to control one of the town's two MPs, at neighbouring Northampton, electoral influence was split between the Comptons, Earls of Northampton, and the Montagus, Earls of Halifax. Soon after he came of age, John Spencer became determined to break this control, but the showdown finally came with what became known as 'the contest of the three earls' at the 1768 general election.

From the start he fought with the determination of his great-grandfather, Marlborough, beating back the French. It was a battle of attrition – more Malplaquet than Blenheim – and proved disastrously expensive, with all three families upping the bribes offered to the thousand or so highly-favoured local electors.

It was the most corrupt election of the century. Sarah would have turned in her grave, and the story goes that as potential voters were welcomed into Althorp House, each was offered a sandwich by a footman at the door, only to discover that the sandwich filling was a golden guinea. They were then coralled in the park by Spencer agents to prevent their opponents' agents carrying them off before they voted. Even so, the opposing families' candidates were elected, but thanks to fact that the Comptons had committed even more illegalities than the Spencers, the Spencer candidate was finally elected on petition.

It had been cripplingly expensive for all concerned. Lord Halifax was ruined and sold his estates, the Northamptons had to live abroad for a generation, and Spencer was henceforth never free from financial problems. One estimate put the cost to him at a staggering £120,000.

In terms of sheer extravagance, however, not even the Northamptonshire election could match the final cost of Spencer House, which severely dented even the Spencers' ironclad resources. For Spencer House, as an exercise in luxury, style and high fashion, proved inordinately costly. (Some idea of its cost in present-day terms can be gathered from the fact that, after leasing Spencer House from the family, Rothschilds spent something like £16 million restoring it and its decorations to their former glory.)

Intended to impress a world already very rich, Spencer House appears a supreme example of what the economist Thorstein Veblen called 'Conspicuous Consumption', or the showing off of wealth on the grandest scale to impress the neighbours. What the house did – and did superbly – was to place the Spencers firmly in the centre of the smartest Whig society of the time, by making the point that not only was the family very rich, but that it was among the unsurpassed leaders of style and fashion. Certainly in social terms Spencer House would prove a wonderful investment, and owning this gem, so strategically placed between St James's

Palace and Devonshire House, made them pre-eminent as social figures.

This endorsement of their social position went with the shift in the Spencers' situation following the exclusion clause in Sarah Marlborough's will. For now that they were banned from office, they were picking up a different role as leaders, not of politics, but of a London Society which was swiftly overtaking Paris as the most fashionable in Europe. This move from the male world of politics to the female one of fashion and society, meant that the most memorable Spencers were suddenly women, and Spencer House became quite different from the male world of Althorp.

Althorp had always been the centre of the Spencers' political and territorial influence, which together with the hunting, made it very much a world of men. Whereas Spencer House was dominated by two essentially feminine activities from the start. The first was love and child-rearing, and just as it was built by a young, newly-married couple who were very much in love, so the result is still an unmistakably romantic house. Even the gilded plaster mouldings are concupiscent – from the egg and dart motif in the friezes and the cupids with their scattered garlands, to Georgiana Spencer's bedroom with its golden palm trees, symbols of fertility, copied from Inigo Jones's plans for the Queen's bedroom in her house at Greenwich. In such surroundings, one has left the rustic male domain of Althorp for the seductive, eighteenth-century world of the boudoir, the ballroom and the glancing world of female fashion.

There was also the social side of Spencer House, with its whole tenor set by the progress (known as the 'rout') made by the Spencers' guests through an enfilade of rooms towards Athenian Stuart's magnificent Painted Room in green and gold, where the Countess (not the Earl) received her guests, gossiped, dispensed *politesse* and – the acme of sophistication – offered them the latest novelty, ice-cream – an ice-house for its manufacture having been built beside the house in 1762.

While the Countess was growing in importance in this social world, so, as the years passed and ill health took over, the Earl increasingly relied upon her for affection and support. She had changed from the earnest teenage girl of the time of her marriage into a strong-willed, quietly dominating character. She was intelligent, loved travel and had inherited her entrepreneurial father's firm belief in self-improvement. But although something of a bluestocking, Georgiana, like all the Poyntzes, had a very different side to her character, and enjoyed life with a gusto foreign to her increasingly sick, reclusive husband. She was a great dancer and party lover, as well as an accomplished billiards player, but, above all, like most of her family, she was a compulsive gambler.

'I have known the Poyntzes in the nursery,' said Lord Lansdowne, 'the Bible on the table, the cards in the drawer'; and both Althorp and Spencer House became notorious for what were often all-night gambling parties. The guests were rich and often serious gamblers, and the stakes could be enormous. With a tradition of gambling in the family, the Earl needed little encouragement from his wife but he was rarely lucky, and the Spencers increasingly drew upon their income to cover their continual losses.

Lady Spencer was a devoted mother, supervising her children's studies and making sure that George the son and heir received tuition from the Oriental scholar learned Dr Jones. Like a very modern parent, above all she craved her children's friendship – an idea which would have been unthinkable a few years earlier, and which she certainly retained for the rest of her life as far as her son, George, was concerned.

As for the Earl, by his early forties he was appearing increasingly redundant in this overwhelming world of women. At Althorp he still hunted with the consumptive's hectic desperation, but he had clearly started to decline, and he who was once so handsome and decisive was increasingly described as shy and shadowy. His lungs were again affected but in addition he was now afflicted by a series of unrelated illnesses, which eighteenth-century doctors invariably diagnose as gout.

Never was a man more vulnerable to that excruciating malady than poor John Spencer. When gout attacked his feet Georgiana took him off to Bath, from where she wrote about him in his 'wheeling chair', unable to stand because his feet and ankles were so red and swollen. His sad decline had now begun in earnest. So had his anger and frustration, and soon he was coughing blood in what sounds like the final stages of consumption.

But his doctors still insisted it was gout, which they diagnosed in both his head and stomach. Early in 1783, he and Georgiana were staying quietly at Wimbledon, and he seemed slightly better. She had taken charge of him completely, and later in the year took him to Buxton Spa in Derbyshire, hoping the waters would cure him.

'I get up at 6,' she wrote to her son. 'Walk. Breakfast in pump-room on excellent muffins, brown toast and tea. Home to see how father is. Home for father's b'fast. In evening play whist while father retires to read till near 10. Your father and I then sup and converse on our own till 12.'

It is a touching demonstration of the closeness of their marriage but by July they were back at Spencer House, and Georgiana was once more writing to their son. 'Father very ill indeed, with gout in head and stomach. Takes nothing but a little veal broth . . . God grant, my dearest George, you may go thro' life w'out the feeling and anguish which I have suffered these last three days. He is coming out of his room, so I hasten to seal up this letter.'

Ever hopeful, in August Georgiana took her husband off to Margate, trusting this time that the sea air would help him. It seems it did not, for in October they returned to Bath, from where Georgiana had to tell her son that 'father is no better for taking the waters'.

By 23 October she writes: 'He is so oppressed with sleep that he dozes incessantly. Now wanders when he wakes. Not sure where he is. Am more miserable than I have been in my life . . . You must come to me, my dearest George, if he grows worse. I do not believe I could support myself without you.'

Lord Althorp was a good son and went to Bath to join his mother at her vigil. Eight days later he was present when his father died, aged forty-eight, leaving his widow broken-hearted.

For in spite of his chronic ailments and uncertain temper, she had always loved the Earl, and on the day following his death she described herself in her diary 'stunned with affliction and stupefied with laudanum'. She could still not bear to leave him. 'There is something inexpressibly painful to me in the thoughts of abandoning him to servants and of so soon avoiding what I have so long and ardently loved.'

Next day she wrote, 'I can never describe or forget what I felt when they came to fetch me. My reason almost forsook me. I was half frantic, and wanted to get into his room. I had no power to pass by his door, and my brother and George were forced to drag me downstairs and lift me into the coach.'

A week later, when he was buried at St Mary's, Great Brington, she found consolation in the sorrow of the local people. For all his weaknesses, John Spencer had made himself popular with the people of Northamptonshire. As his wife wrote: 'the unsolicited attendance and the uncommon degree of gratitude, affection and respect shown to my Lord's memory has soothed and gratified my aching heart.'

But as his family would discover, the man who was once 'the richest schoolboy in England' had left them something else to remember him by – his debts. For whilst enriching them, Sarah Marlborough's fortune had encouraged the Spencers to be more profligate than ever and, before his death, Lord Spencer's extravagance was coming close to ruining the family.

CHAPTER 7

'A Wild and Scrambling Life'

Georgiana, Duchess of Devonshire (1757–1806)

Although the first Earl Spencer died a sad and disillusioned man, he had lived long enough to see all his three children settled. The future of the family was safe now that his heir, George Spencer, had married Lavinia Bingham, daughter of the Irish peer Lord Lucan and Lavinia had recently given birth to a son called Jack. The Earl's youngest daughter, Harriet, had finally resisted the dishonourable advances of the young Prince Regent and had settled instead for marriage with Frederick Ponsonby, who received the courtesy title Lord Duncannon, and who would later inherit the title of third Earl of Bessborough. As for his favourite child, Georgiana, the Earl had often had to hide his worries, but he could at least die happy in the knowledge that with her he had fathered one of the most extraordinary women of her age.

Georgiana was the prize creation of her two devoted parents – and particularly of her mother and namesake. Throughout Georgiana's childhood, Lady Spencer's passionate belief in education – combined with her social ambition – had consciously prepared her daughter for the great success her family expected.

By sixteen she was already something of a prodigy. She had travelled widely, was well read, spoke fluent French and had all the social graces. Much of the charm of this tall, slim, slightly gawky girl with the grey eyes and the mass of reddish gold hair, lay in her unpretentiousness. It gave her something of the allure of a young unspoilt romantic heroine; and, from an early age, Georgiana

111

clearly had something that no mother could ever teach a favourite daughter – magic.

How else can one explain the extraordinary effect that she had had upon that most impassive aristocrat, the twenty-four-year-old William Cavendish, fifth Duke of Devonshire, when she met him with her parents as they were taking the waters for Lord Spencer's health at the fashionable Ardennes resort of Spa in the autumn of 1773. The Spencers had known William since he was a child, for the Cavendishes were another great Whig family, and even richer than the Spencers.

The two families had similar origins. Both had come to prominence with the Tudors and, just as with the Spencers, the true founder of the Cavendish family, four times married Bess of Hardwick, had made her original fortune out of sheep. Since then the Cavendishes had advanced through a series of spectacular marriages, which had left them with the dukedom and no less than ten of the greatest houses in the country. These included Bess's two original homes in Derbyshire, Chatsworth and Hardwick Hall, and in London they owned Devonshire House (opposite the present Ritz Hotel in Piccadilly, and just across the Park from Spencer House), Burlington House (a few doors away towards today's Piccadilly Circus and now housing the Royal Academy), and that jewel of Palladian architecture in West London, Lord Burlington's Chiswick House. On the death of the fourth Duke of Devonshire in 1764, the dukedom, the houses and their great estates descended to the Duke's motherless sixteen-year-old son, William, who would soon be hailed as 'the Crown Prince of the Whigs'.

But none of this had served to raise the young duke's rather weary spirits. One writer called him 'the perfect image of a wintry day', and according to another, 'constitutional apathy formed his distinguishing characteristic'. However, during the time at Spa something must have happened, for the Duke in his undemonstrative way was sufficiently excited by the young Georgiana to request her hand in marriage.

While not discounting the impact of Georgiana's presence on

the wintry duke, he may have had some less romantic reasons for proposing. The pregnancy of his current mistress – a milliner whose name, by a strange coincidence, was Charlotte Spencer – may have reminded him that the time had come to think of producing legitimate heirs to his vast possessions. A further consideration which must certainly have crossed his mind was connected with that other great inheritance – the wealth and the estates with which Sarah Marlborough had so enriched the Althorp Spencers.

True, Georgiana would not be first in line to inherit from her father, the already infirm Lord Spencer. First would come her brother, George, but as the Duke well knew, over recent years the Spencer males had not been healthy. The present Earl was ailing at the time. His father before him had died in his early thirties and, before that, Marlborough's fortune had descended through the female line. As a betting man the Duke would certainly have known that the odds were not entirely against history repeating itself. His own mother, who had been the daughter of Lord Burlington, had brought the great Burlington inheritance to the Cavendishes on her father's death, and with Georgiana Spencer, something similar might happen.

All this apart, the Duke appeared to be in love – as much as he ever could be – and was positively eager for the wedding. So were Lord and Lady Spencer, knowing that such a chance would not come their way again. As for Georgiana, marriage to her Duke appeared to offer everything in life that she had ever wanted.

There was one point on which everyone agreed – the need for secrecy. The Duke was a favourite subject for the gossip-mongers, and the populace, which could easily get out of hand in the days before the regular police, had to be kept in ignorance of the occasion. So on Saturday 4 June 1774, the Duke made a public show of partnering Georgiana at a ball in honour of the King's birthday. They danced late, after which the Duke returned to Devonshire House and Georgiana to her parents' house at Wimbledon. The following morning she was wakened early, attired in a silver dress with satin shoes and a silver head-dress set with pearls, then driven to the local parish church. The Duke was waiting, together with a few close members of Georgiana's family, and just before matins her disreputable uncle, the Revd Charles Poyntz, performed the ceremony which made Georgiana Spencer, on the eve of her seventeenth birthday, wife of William Cavendish and Duchess of Devonshire.

Georgiana was not conventionally beautiful. She was too tall for current tastes and her face lacked the classical perfection much admired at the time. But she was so obviously in love and full of life that even King George III was visibly impressed when she swept into his unfashionable court to be presented to him following her wedding. As Horace Walpole carefully explained, 'The Duchess of Devonshire effaces all without being a beauty; but her youth, figure, flowing good nature, sense and lively modesty and modest familiarity, make her a phenomenon.'

Garrick put it more succinctly. 'Were I five and twenty, I could go mad about her. As I am past five and fifty, I would only suffer martyrdom for her.' The one man who didn't seem to feel the same about her was her husband.

The Devonshires honeymooned together up at Chatsworth, the Duke's great house in Derbyshire, known as the 'Palace of the Peaks'. They rode and walked through the autumnal countryside and went to a ball at Chesterfield. But soon the Duke began to miss the company at his club, Brooks's, the cold mackerel he enjoyed for breakfast after a long night's gambling, and the company of Miss Charlotte Spencer who, unbeknown to his wife, had just given birth to a daughter. (Using their joint first names, the Duke and his mistress had christened her Charlotte Williams.)

In his deadpan way the Duke still tried to make the honeymoon a success – as, with considerably more enthusiasm, did Georgiana. To surprise him she imported the great violinist, Giardiani, up from London, unaware of the Duke's aversion to surprises and the fact that, being tone deaf like all the Cavendishes, he detested music. She lectured him about religion, and he agreed to having prayers recited every morning in his chapel. She invited her parents over from Althorp, and since, emotionally at least, the Duke was closer to them in age than to their daughter, they got on rather well together.

On one thing Georgiana and her Duke were totally united – the need to make an heir. Even this, however, was not easy, and it was not until the following summer, just before her eighteenth birthday, that Georgiana discovered she was pregnant. But come October her father was writing to her from Paris to console her for having 'fail'd making me a grandfather; however what has been may be again, and you will succeed better another time if you will have a little patience'.

As the Earl must have known, patience was foreign to Georgiana's nature and, back in London, she consoled herself as only someone with her energy and very grand position in the *beau monde* could. With dowdy Queen Charlotte sitting on the throne, the role of social queen of London was there for the taking – and Georgiana took it.

This was a period when Whiggism, so long the political expression of the rich inheritors of the 1688 revolution, was turning into something very different. The so-called New Whigs, with Edmund Burke as their philosopher and Charles James Fox their parliamentary leader, had been agitating in support of the American colonies against the oppression of King George III and his prime minister, Lord North. These New Whigs were radical, libertarian and passionately ranged against the growing power of the King and his supporters. At the same time, Whig society itself was becoming more sophisticated and fashionable than the predominantly masculine, hard-drinking gatherings of the political families who had ruled the country for so long under Robert Walpole. Shorn of much of their political power, Whig families like the Spencers, were switching their interest to the serious pursuit of pleasure.

'As types of distilled civility,' wrote Harold Nicolson, 'the Whig aristocrats of 1770–1830 have never been surpassed or equalled'; and he rejoiced that 'before respectability came to dull the skies of

England, they were there, like fallow deer, to sparkle in the sun'. Few sparkled more entrancingly, or with less regard for drab respectability, than Georgiana.

She was ideally suited for the role of queen of this frivolous yet highly civilized society. While not an intellectual, she had inherited sufficient of the Poyntz intelligence to match the conversation of Sheridan or Charles James Fox, and could lighten up the 'cynical moroseness' of the aged Dr Johnson when he came to Chatsworth. 'He din'd here,' she reported, 'and does not shine quite so much in eating as conversing, for he eat much and nastily.'

She was in fact a loyal friend, with a natural love of human beings; she had wit, a sometimes excessive sense of fun and she adored the social whirl. Above all, she clearly had that suspect but unstoppable quality – outrageous charm, and for a while it must have seemed that she could get away with anything.

Once she was into her social stride, it was as if she had recreated all the power of the Spencers and Devonshires in her female image. By totally taking over Devonshire House, she made it something it had never been since William Kent rebuilt it following the fire of 1733 – the most fashionable great house in London. The Duke felt more at home at Brooks's Club or Almack's where he could gamble, drink and quote his favourite Latin authors in the presence of his ever faithful cronies. But in Devonshire House, with its great white and gilt reception rooms, and its spacious gardens in the midst of London, there 'flowered the female aspect of Whiggism ... Here in the flesh was the exquisite eighteenth-century world of Gainsborough, all flowing elegance and melting glances, and shifting silken colour'.

The house became a unique institution, part Georgiana's private salon, part fashionable show-place for the smart set, known as 'the ton', and also the political headquarters for the Foxite Whigs, who had now adopted the buff and blue of General Washington's army to demonstrate support for 'Liberty' and the American revolution.

By 1784, America had won its independence and Georgiana's friends were now engaged in bitter parliamentary warfare with the

'He had amassed a truly fearsome fortune' – Robert, first Baron Spencer
(1570–1627).

The unwilling cavalier –
Henry Spencer, first
Earl of Sunderland
(1620–1643).

The earthly paradise –
Althorp amid gardens built
by Robert, second Earl of
Sunderland.

'A restless and mischievous temper, a cold heart and an abject spirit' – Robert, second Earl of Sunderland (1641–1702).

Sarah Marlborough's hated son-in-law – Charles, third Earl of Sunderland (1675–1722).

The Matriarch. Sarah, Duchess of Marlborough (1670–1744).

The great inheritors. Sarah Marlborough's heir, the Hon. John Spencer (left), who died in 1746 at thirty-seven, leaving his son, John, the future first Earl Spencer (on horse-back, right) 'the richest schoolboy in England'.

Georgiana, Duchess of Devonshire (1757–1806), sister of the second Earl Spencer.

Nelson's friend and patron: George John, second Earl Spencer (1758–1834).

The new Althorp –
as rebuilt by Henry Holland
for the second Earl Spencer.

Saviour of the family: John
Charles, third Earl Spencer
(1782–1845).

The family's greatest
extravagance –
Spencer House.

A saint in the family? The
Hon. George Spencer
(1799–1864), also known
as Fr. Ignatius of St Paul.

John Poyntz, fifth Earl Spencer (1835–1910) with his wife Charlotte at a rifle shoot on Wimbledon Common.

Charles Robert, sixth Earl Spencer (1857–1922).

newly appointed prime minister, twenty-four-year-old William Pitt, who enjoyed the backing – and the patronage – of their sworn enemy, King George III. This warfare culminated in a spring election, which the opposition Whigs already looked like losing, as did Fox himself, who was standing as a candidate in the 'Peoples' Constituency' of Westminster.

Unlike most constituencies, which were controlled by the Crown or the local landowners, at Westminster householders enjoyed the vote, and during a six-week long election, they had the right to return two candidates to parliament. The victory of the popular Pittite candidate, Lord Howe, was a foregone conclusion, and Fox's challenge for the second seat was going badly when Georgiana effectively took charge of his campaign, using all her influence as fashion leader and unrivalled social celebrity against Pitt and the power of the King.

Sarah Marlborough would have been proud of her great-great-granddaughter's championing of sound Whig principles, and also of the way she was asserting the rights of women for an active role in politics. Whether she would have approved of the way Georgiana did this is another matter.

No one had ever before seen anything remotely like what happened as the Duchess, her sister, Lady Bessborough, and her sister-in-law, the Duchess of Portland, dressed in fox furs and all their finery, unashamedly set out to bring the humblest of voters to the hustings in the cause of Liberty and Charles James Fox. Pitt's supporters expressed outrage at the behaviour of these so-called ladies who were so blatantly offending social decency and feminine decorum in the scramble for votes. And when Fox, thanks entirely to Georgiana and the power of these upper-class ladies, won second place in the election and a seat in parliament the press attacks upon Georgiana grew.

She had to bear the brunt of governmental fury, and the disapproval of a male-dominated society. She was shown no mercy by a scurrilous press, which accused her of the most appalling vices – from prostitution in return for votes, to encouraging revolution and undermining social order and propriety. It was a fearsome onslaught, and Georgiana's reputation and her power in politics never recovered; nor, for many years to come, did the cause of women's rights in politics. As Amanda Foreman writes in her recent biography of the Duchess, Georgiana's 'methods were too modern for eighteenth-century society . . . and it would be another hundred years before women once more ventured boldly into street politics as Georgiana had not been afraid to do in 1784.'

For all her courage, and her loyalty to Charles James Fox, the fact remains that Georgiana had made herself vulnerable to attack because of the disorder of her private life. In the words of the diarist Charles Greville, 'the private history of Devonshire House was very curious and amusing as a scandalous chronicle, an exhibition of vice in its most attractive form, full of grace, dignity, and splendour, but I fancy full of misery and sorrow also.' Most of the 'misery and sorrow' now fell upon Georgiana.

She and the Duke kept up appearances, but they had grown more incompatible than ever. He remained totally unimpressed by her social triumphs and, apart from desultory efforts to produce an heir which had twice resulted in Georgiana miscarrying, they had less and less to do with one another.

By 1782 the marriage was effectively over, apart from the one task Georgiana was still required to perform – the creation of the all-important male heir to the dukedom. For however much the Duke neglected her, she felt that this was something she could not refuse him and his family. Early that April the ill-matched pair arrived in Bath, hoping the waters would alleviate the ducal gout and encourage the twenty-four-year-old Duchess to conceive. Neither happened. However, while at Bath they met the woman who would bring salvation of a sort to the Devonshire marriage.

Acting as always with the very best intentions, the now widowed Lady Spencer had written to Georgiana at Bath asking her to contact the unfortunate Lady Elizabeth Foster, Lord Hervey's daughter, who had recently been deserted by her husband. Georgiana did so, but instead of finding a pathetic victim, Lady Elizabeth proved to be a lively, very pretty creature, of much the same age as herself. Her father was the notorious 'Earl Bishop' who, while still Bishop of Derry, had inherited the rich earldom of Bristol from his brother and had been travelling on the Continent ever since, in such splendour that his name is remembered to this day in the countless 'Hotels Bristol' named after him.

All this travelling had left Lord Hervey little time to bother with his daughter, but Georgiana and the Duke both found that they enjoyed her company. When they left Bath for the nearby town of Plympton, where the Duke was attending summer camp with the Volunteers, they asked Elizabeth – or Bess – to join them, and the trio got on splendidly together; the weary Duke no longer weary and the Duchess finding in Elizabeth the friend she felt she had always needed.

Where the Devonshires were bored, Elizabeth was full of life and she made them laugh by giving them all pet names. The Duke was 'Canis', because of the way he loved his dogs, Georgiana was 'Mrs Rat' and Elizabeth was 'Racky', because of her irritating cough. 'Canis', 'Mrs Rat' and 'Racky' they would be until they died.

Elizabeth was clearly something of a sexual tease. A devotee of slightly risqué novels, she introduced the Duke and Duchess to two of her favourite books – Laclos's primer of refined seduction, *Les Liaisons Dangereuses*, and the gospel of Romanticism, *La Nouvelle Heloise* by Jean-Jacques Rousseau. She read them passages each evening, and by doing so may well have brought a little 'soft romantic feeling' to what for Georgiana and the Duke must have been becoming an extremely basic chore.

Perhaps as a result, Georgiana not only managed to conceive at Plympton, but also avoided miscarrying. By the end of the year her childless state was over and she was able to present the Duke with a pretty daughter, christened Georgiana Dorothy, but called 'Little Gi' within the family.

It was an exciting moment for them all, and although Little Gi was not the longed for heir, she seems to have transformed the marriage. Georgiana felt fulfilled, the Duke believed that next time he would have a boy, and they were happier than they'd ever been together, thanks entirely to 'Sister Racky'. In the euphoria, Sister Racky even persuaded Mrs Rat to accept Canis's daughter, Charlotte Williams, into the family. The Duke was pleased, but worried by the possibility of scandal. Racky suggested a solution. She would take little Charlotte on an extended European holiday to put potential gossip mongers off the scent of her origins.

This clearly suited Elizabeth, who was very much her father's daughter and she spent several months enjoying herself travelling through Europe at the Duke's expense, without letting Charlotte Williams cramp her style. She visited the sights of Italy, saw Florence, Rome and Pompeii, stayed with the Hamiltons in Naples and returned through Switzerland, where she visited Edward Gibbon and apparently had the author of *The Decline and Fall of the Roman Empire* on his knees before her uttering words of tender adoration – or so she told her friends upon her return.

Racky, accompanied by 'her' child, Charlotte, was fondly welcomed back to Chatsworth by Canis and Mrs Rat. Georgiana seems to have genuinely believed that her happiness was due entirely to the fact that 'my dearest, loveliest friend and the man whom I love so much and to whom I owe everything, are united like brother and sister'. After Bess's absence none could endure the thought of parting company again, and the trio returned to Devonshire House together. It was time for a fresh attempt to make an heir, and by Christmas time the Duchess was pregnant. And so was Elizabeth.

The Duke was responsible for both almost simultaneous conceptions.

Georgiana claimed to be delighted, but Elizabeth was more practical. She had no wish to bring scandal on the Duke, so before her pregnancy began to show, she left once more for Italy, where the wilting, soft, romantic Bess showed just how tough she was by thoroughly enjoying life and concealing her condition even from the friends she stayed with. She refused to blame the Duke for her situation. As she wrote in her diary, 'His nature is noble, tender, honourable and affectionate . . . Passion has led us both astray.' And early in August 1785, in the house of a Palermo midwife, she bore the Duke a third daughter, naming her Caroline St Jules. Less than two weeks later, back in Devonshire House, Georgiana followed suit, presenting the Duke with yet another daughter, christened Harriet.

Although he was now the father of four daughters, the Duke remained convinced that his wife would still produce the all-important son, provided they could both rely on the support of 'Dearest Bess'. So when Bess returned to London, having left Caroline St Jules with a nurse in Paris, the Duke's previous concern with appearances was entirely forgotten. After the public battering she had been receiving in the press following the Westminster election, Georgiana was grateful to have those she loved around her, and the Duke seemed positively brazen as he took both his women back to Devonshire House. Both had a call on his attentions, Bess because he was now in love with her and Georgiana because she was his wife and she and she alone could still produce the heir he needed.

The Duke seemed happy with this rational arrangement. So was Elizabeth, and so, in theory, was Georgiana, who had her dearest 'Mrs Bess' back with her at last. The press and the scandal mongers could do their worst, and there seemed no reason now why all the Duke's children, legitimate and illegitimate alike, should not live happily beneath the all-embracing roof of Devonshire House. There was room for all of them and, if gossip started, why should anybody worry? They loved each other.

But however rational a *ménage à trois* may seem, and however much its members speak of mutual love, it can prove difficult to maintain. One member is usually left out in the cold, and with the personalities involved at Devonshire House this was unlikely to be Bess. Seeing Georgiana now, Fanny Burney noted, 'She appeared to me not happy. I thought she looked oppressed within, though there is a native cheerfulness about her which I fancy scarce deserts her.'

This was not surprising given the strain of the life that she was leading. 'She verges fast to a coarseness', wrote her one-time admirer, Horace Walpole, and although Georgiana was not yet thirty she was suffering chronic headaches, using sleeping draughts and her looks were fading.

On the surface, everything at Devonshire House continued as before and Georgiana was as much the queen of society as ever, at the centre of the balls, the dinners and the grand receptions, at a time when Charles James Fox was still unsuccessfully attempting to unseat William Pitt in parliament. But behind the scenes 'sorrow and misery' were starting to afflict her, through her addiction to the same vice which brought such trouble to her parents – obsessional gambling.

Everyone around her gambled, especially her mother who now blamed herself for the bad example she had set. Georgiana answered, 'I do assure you that it is innate, for I remember playing from seven in the morning until eight at night at Lansquenet with old Mrs Newton when I was nine years old and sent to the King's Road for the measles.'

In fact her gambling was destroying both her health and happiness, and the debts were a constant worry; although the Duke usually ended up paying them they inevitably became a source of anger and distrust between them. Lady Spencer was increasingly concerned for her daughter's health.

'For God's sake try to compose yourself. I am terrified lest the perpetual hurrye of our spirits, and the medicines you take to obtain a false tranquillity should injure you ... Why will you not say fairly; – I have led a wild and scrambling life that disagrees with me. I have lost more money than I can afford. I will turn over a new leaf and lead a quiet sober life from this moment, as I am sure that if I do not, I shall hurt myself or my child.'

One may as well ask an alcoholic to give up drink. For Georgiana, gambling was an addiction she could not control. When Little Gi was born, Walpole said Georgiana would probably 'stuff her poor babe into her knotting-bag when she wants to play at Macao, and forget it'. Since then the self-destructive gambling had increased and enormous losses had mounted.

Throughout this time Bess continued to consolidate her role in Devonshire House. No longer the dependent victim who had once relied upon the Duke and Georgiana's pity, she had made herself indispensable. With her abounding health and sense of purpose, she had the strength the others lacked and could offer both the love and the support they needed. Through love she had the now gouty, often fuddled Duke totally beneath her thumb and could persuade him to brazen out the situation as he would never have dared do on his own. Love kept Georgiana dependent on her too, but dependence was not the same as happiness and Georgiana's situation was profoundly wretched underneath the surface gaiety. She was suppressing emotions which, as a wife, she must have felt in such a situation. If for a moment she allowed such feelings to emerge, she was in danger of losing everything – husband, children, 'dearest Bess' and the glittering world around her.

By the beginning of 1789 Georgiana was desperate. She had borrowed from everyone to pay her debts – her maid, Anne Scafe, Louis XVI's former Minister of Finance, Calonne and the London banker, Thomas Coutts. Her acknowledged debts were £60,000 and the Duke refused to meet them.

Georgiana felt she had one hope remaining. The Duke still wanted one thing that she alone could give him – his long overdue heir – and she felt that if she finally succeeded in providing a son the Duke would forgive her, pay her debts and all her problems would be over. Somehow she convinced the Duke that in London, with its endless distractions, she was unlikely to conceive. Instead they would take a lengthy holiday in France, along with Bess and all the family. In June 1789 – a fateful year in European history – the Devonshires embarked *en masse* for France from Dover.

First they stayed in Paris in order to give the Duke and Bess a chance to see their daughter, the now four-year-old Caroline

St Jules, before going on to Versailles for an audience with Queen Marie Antoinette. It is some indication of the social standing of the Spencers that the Queen was an old friend of the family, and was particularly interested in Georgiana as the acknowledged fashion queen of London.

By a curious trick of history this visit of the Devonshires to Versailles offered the Duke, as hereditary standard-bearer of the English Revolution, a chance to witness the beginning of its counter-part in France. For he and Georgiana were in the palace talking to the Queen when the people staged their historic march from Paris and forced themselves into the presence of the King. What is fascin-ating is how little attention Georgiana or the Duke appear to have given to what was happening. When the populace departed, the ceremonial of the court continued as before and Georgiana appar-ently enjoyed her conversation with the Queen. Even back in Paris she was not particularly disturbed by the threatening presence of the revolutionary mob. It was tiresome, but it took more than the threats and catcalls of the common people to distract Georgiana from the joy of being back in Paris.

Besides, as enlightened Whigs, the Devonshires and Spencers were all in favour of popular liberty, and however charming the fat, balding Marie Antoinette might be, the French monarchy could only be improved by some of the constitutional reforms that had already been imposed on the English monarchy in 1688.

'I confess I amuse myself,' Georgiana wrote a trifle smugly from Paris in July, 'and have been well the whole time I have been here.' A few days later came the fall of the Bastille and the French re-volution began in earnest.

Back in England Charles James Fox exulted. 'How much the greatest event that ever happened in the history of the world, and how much the best!' Georgiana, and probably the Duke, agreed, although they sensibly kept their comments to themselves. Only the realistic Bess foresaw trouble for them in Paris when noticing the arms of noblemen being obliterated from their carriages. The Devonshires had more important matters to attend to and, before the mob had finished demolishing the Bastille, they were on their way again to Spa in the Ardennes, with the Cavendish succession now at stake, together with Georgiana's personal salvation.

The Duke and the waters did their work. By the end of August Georgiana was pregnant and, this time, Elizabeth was not. Georgiana was probably unwilling to risk the unborn baby by returning to London and her creditors. Instead, the whole Devonshire ménage, including Bess, installed itself in considerable style in Brussels in readiness for the great event. Georgiana's daughters, Georgiana Dorothy and Harriet, hurried over with their governess, Miss Trimmer. They were followed by her sister and brother-in-law, the Duncannons. Doctors and fresh servants arrived, and finally the deeply disapproving Lady Spencer overcame her bitterness against what she saw as the immoral presence of Lady Elizabeth, and joined the party.

The most crucial moment in Georgiana's life had almost come, and as an addicted gambler she must have realised the high stakes for which she was playing. She was only thirty-two but her looks and health were going and she would not get another chance like this. Another daughter or a still-born child would spell her ruin. Either an heir to the dukedom or disaster.

Even Bess's nerve was shaken. 'I can't express to you how my courage fails me as your time draws near,' she told Georgiana. But Georgiana faced the outcome with the born gambler's equanimity. Even the sudden threat of revolution in the Belgian capital failed to shake her, when the whole family had to hurry back to Paris. They arrived just in time, and were in Passy, on the outskirts of the city, when Georgiana's labour started. Practical as ever, Lady Spencer sent Bess off to the Paris Opera to appear among the audience showing her slim figure, just to prove that it was not she who was giving birth – otherwise, with the *ménage à trois*, later Cavendishes might claim the child was hers. Then on 21 May 1790, in the house of their friend the Marquis Boulainvilliers, Georgiana's gamble paid off and she was able to present the Duke with an heir to his possessions and his title. He was christened William George

Spencer Cavendish, and as heir to the dukedom took the title Viscount Hartington. In August the strange threesome – Bess, Georgiana and the Duke – brought him back to London.

'The family is all arrived safe here,' wrote Anne Scafe from Devonshire House. 'Many hearts are made glad at a young heir being brought home. He is three months old – a fine strong healthy child. The Duchess suckles him and is quite well.'

All should have ended happily, but even now the travails of Georgiana were not over. Lady Spencer went on making trouble over Bess; her sister, Harriet, fell ill; and the Duke was none too eager, even now, to pay her debts. It was somehow typical of impulsive Georgiana to choose this very moment to involve herself in a fresh emotional disaster.

She may have felt that, having finally performed her unromantic duty by the Duke, she was free to fall in love at last. For several years Charles Grey, the clever, uncomfortably good-looking young Whig politician, had been professing his undying adoration and, although she was seven years his senior, she was suddenly emotionally and physically besotted. By the spring of 1791, barely a year after giving birth to Hartington, she was pregnant by her lover.

The last thing Georgiana needed was another scandal, but when the Duke realised that she was pregnant, she made no attempt to convince him that the child was his. His own past behaviour notwithstanding, he was suddenly beside himself with righteous anger. Charles Grey, all adoration now forgotten, was suddenly reluctant to endanger his political career by becoming openly involved with such a famous married woman. And the virtuous Duke, appalled by the possibility of scandal, insisted that Georgiana left the children and went abroad to have the baby.

What followed was an extraordinary demonstration of the unexpected power of late eighteenth-century women, as all the females in the family, Bess included, rallied to support Georgiana. In the autumn of 1791, when a noticeably pregnant Georgiana set off for Montpelier in the South of France to have her baby, she travelled with a small platoon of women – including her mother,

her now convalescent sister, Harriet Duncannon, the Duncannon's daughter, Caroline Ponsonby, Caroline St Jules – and her husband's mistress, dearest Bess. At the same time, back in England, the Duke was drinking heavily and threatening legal separation, while his two daughters, Georgiana and Harriet, were looked after by Miss Trimmer.

Georgiana missed her daughters, but her greatest misery came from being parted from her infant son. In early January in Montpelier, she gave birth to a daughter, who was entrusted to a wet nurse and almost immediately sent back to Grey's family in England, where she was brought up as his baby sister.

Meanwhile, Georgiana and the women stayed on in exile on the Continent until the Duke relented. As they were rich and titled it was no great hardship as, with Bess to guide them, they took a long extended holiday in that final year before war with revolutionary France would change their world for ever. In Naples they were entertained by the King and Queen in their great Versailles-like palace at Caserta. In Rome they enjoyed the carnival, and in Switzerland Bess took them all to visit her old admirer, Edward Gibbon. Finally, the Duke had no alternative but to surrender.

The truth was that he was missing Bess, and the only way to get her back was by extending his forgiveness to Georgiana. He did so, reluctantly, in the summer of 1793. Once the travellers returned to Devonshire House, his relief was obvious to all. As the servants lined up to welcome back their Duchess, it was clear that it was Bess whom they really wanted. The house had been dead in her absence. With her return, life could begin again.

At thirty-six, Georgiana should have been able to count her many blessings and enjoy her family and friends in relative tranquillity at last. She was still the undisputed queen of society and was universally loved. But the evil fortune that accompanied her gambling pursued her. Her 'wild and scrambling life' was claiming retribution and it seemed that there was no escape.

Early in 1795 she was deeply hurt when Charles Grey suddenly married her young kinswoman, Mary Ponsonby, without a word to her of his intentions. The following year her left eye became seriously inflamed. A corneal ulcer had developed, and after 'a dreadful operation which she bore with great courage' – and without anaesthetics – she lost the eye, and with it what remained of her beauty. 'The change is painful to see,' wrote Lady Holland. 'Scarcely has she a vestige of those charms which once attracted all hearts.' Not surprisingly, Georgiana increasingly retired from the world and started seeking consolation in religion. But religion would not pay her gambling debts. Nor would the Duke, and as they went on mounting they added to her misery.

Bess, in contrast, was in perfect health. With the death of her wayward husband she was free to marry, and wasted several years pursuing the Duke of Richmond, who proved to be a male tease. It was hard to believe that she was still in love with Canis, who was growing fat and lazy, but her life was still totally involved with the Devonshires and Georgiana depended on her more than ever. This did not prevent Bess enjoying life. In 1802, during the temporary peace with France, she was among the first English visitors to Paris, where she made a point of witnessing Napoleon review his regiments and was most impressed. In her absence Georgiana missed her frightfully. 'Do you hear the voice of my heart crying to you?' she asked pathetically.

'My dearest,' Bess wrote back in the private language of the Devonshire House set. 'Why are 'oo gloomy? Why are 'oo vexed?'

The answer was obvious – Georgiana's gambling debts and fearful state of health. When war resumed with France, with William Pitt as firmly in charge as ever, the influence of Charles James Fox and the Devonshire House set was over. The patriotic fear of France and its revolutionary principles had completed the work begun by George III and destroyed the unity of the great Whig families, few of whom supported Fox's principles or policies. Georgiana's brother, the second Earl Spencer, had actually become a member of Pitt's government in the war against Napoleon and Canis also offered his support.

Not until Pitt collapsed and died in 1806 did Charles James Fox get into government at last. Georgiana and her political friends and allies had got what they had always wanted, and with Lord Grenville as Prime Minister, Fox at the Foreign Office, Grey at the Admiralty and her brother, Lord Spencer, now responsible for Home Affairs, the new Whig Ministry 'read like a dinner party guest list for Devonshire House'. But the triumph was too late, the party over.

Georgiana did her best, forcing herself out of self-imposed obscurity to give her last Devonshire House supper party for the new ministers and forty-six assorted guests. Her ex-lover, Charles Grey, was there, now called by his courtesy title Lord Howick, and this would be the last time she would see him. Fox was dropsical and clearly ailing, and the Duke, who had been offered any post he wanted in this 'Ministry of all the Talents' had, from lethargy or common sense, quietly declined. This motley combination of Georgiana's friends and relatives had little hope of surviving long, and nor had she.

Despite the spectacles shielded with black crêpe which she wore to protect her failing eyesight, the strain of the occasion brought on blinding headaches, and she was suffering from jaundice, caused by an abscess on the liver. Sick, half-blind and in continual pain, Georgiana now composed herself to meet her Maker.

Her last letter to her mother, Lady Spencer, begged her for a banker's draft for £100 by return of post to pay her latest gambling debts. Her ladyship sent £20, but before it reached her, Georgiana was caught in three days of agony 'more horrible, more killing than any human being ever witnessed'. In the end, Georgiana sank into a coma and on 30 March 1806, at the age of forty-nine, she died. Three years later, Dearest Bess would marry Canis, succeeding Georgiana as Duchess of Devonshire.

Just before she died, Georgiana wrote a letter to her son, Lord Hartington. In it she admitted her faults, and said that she was putting all her hopes in the son she left behind. At whatever cost, and after whatever disappointments, she had at least produced the heir.

'I shall live on in you,' she told him.

CHAPTER 8

The Great Library

George John, second Earl Spencer (1758–1834)

As an example of the perfect late-eighteenth-century aristocrat, it would be hard to better the First Earl's son and heir, George Spencer, who in 1783, at the age of twenty-five, succeeded him as second Earl Spencer. Unlike so many of his recent male predecessors, he had grown up strong and healthy. Fanny Burney thought him 'very handsome with fine blue eyes', and his grandmother Lady Cowper said that he was 'most agreeable'. Most of those who met him thought the same, from George III to the aged Dr Johnson, from Charles James Fox to William Pitt the Younger. He had an air of effortless distinction and was generous and kind. As a scholar he was equally at home in Greek and Latin and spoke excellent French and Italian. He was a faithful husband, a loving father and a man of reasonable but not excessive piety. He gambled moderately and rarely drank too much. A Whig by birth, he was suspicious of the growing power of the Crown, supported American independence and thought the slave trade something that 'no Christian and indeed no man of the least feeling for his fellow creatures can tolerate'. But when war came with revolutionary France, he patriotically joined the government of William Pitt, was appointed First Lord of the Admiralty, ran the navy with extreme efficiency and will always be remembered as the man who picked and promoted Horatio Nelson.

In almost every way the second Earl seemed the embodiment of that good sense which was considered the hallmark of an eighteenth-century English gentleman, which makes it all the stranger that for the Spencer family, his fifty-one year tenure of the earldom proved a period of such decline. While he maintained the splendour and the style of the great nobleman he was, income dwindled, debt increased as the disaster grew from which the Spencers never entirely recovered.

The second Earl had grown up in a family ruled by women and, in the nursery at Spencer House, he had been largely overshadowed by his two dominating sisters, Georgiana and Harriet. With his father often absent or unwell, his closest bond was with his mother, and when he came to marry, as he did in 1784, he chose another strong-willed female in the person of the vivacious and outspoken Lavinia Bingham, daughter of the eccentric newly-created Irish peer Lord Lucan.

It was very much a love match from the start. Early in the courtship he had written to his mother describing an evening with his sociable friend Vesey. 'Best party I have seen there yet; Dr Johnson, Sir Joshua Reynolds, Mr Wraxall, Ly Lucan and Miss Bingham. Over the top. Oh! I am quite distracted. I stayed there till 11 o'clock (talking to the divine Lavinia).Decided to quit gambling and to think of nothing but her, for I can think of nothing else. I am quite out of my senses about her. I got up very late this morning. (I dreamt of her all night.)'

The divine Lavinia responded to the attentions of this handsome heir to one of the great inheritances in England. She was, she said 'mad with pride and happiness, but also with humility whenever I think of his love'. Within two months they were happily engaged and their marriage, at St George's, Hanover Square, was the smartest and grandest of the season.

As a newly married couple they gave every appearance of enjoying a truly enviable situation. Along with Spencer House and Althorp, they also had that great mixed bag of rich estates left to the family by Sarah Marlborough; and George's potentially interfering mother, now the dowager Lady Spencer, was tactfully installed at Holywell, Sarah's old house at St Albans, which was made her dower house.

George's own favourite residence remained 'verdant Wimbledon'. He had been born there and always claimed it was 'the nicest spot on earth'.

The one serious fly in the ointment was financial, despite the £30–£40,000 a year income which the Earl theoretically received. The immense debts which his father had left behind him caused an immediate crisis; George could not even afford to pay his sister Harriet's, marriage portion, and most of the available estates were burdened with mortgages. Normally the Earl would have paid some of these off by marrying an heiress. But Lavinia, with her marriage portion of only £5,000, was by Spencer standards barely an heiress at all. In order to pay off the pressing debts, George began selling some outlying estates, and replaced his father's old agents by Thomas Harrison, a professional administrator, who was assisted by his sons.

Althorp, which he and Lavinia had visited on their honeymoon, needed particular attention. Ever since the tenure of his horse-mad great uncle – Charles, fifth Earl of Sunderland, before he left to become the Duke of Marlborough – most of the money spent at Althorp had been on horses rather than humans and the neglect was all too evident. As George wrote to his mother, it would need a fortune 'simply making the apartment we live in weatherproof, which it really hardly is at present, and saving the house from tumbling down'.

Saving Althorp was an expense that could not be avoided. The great gardener, Lancelot 'Capability' Brown had already cleared away whatever remained of Le Notre's parterres and formal gardens, and the effect, however bare in comparison, was entirely in the eighteenth-century fashion. Being a Whig, the Earl called in the most fashionable Whig architect, Henry Holland, to transform the appearance of the house to match. As a result, at great expense, the wonderful but now decrepit and unfashionable Italianate palace left by Shameless Sunderland was effectively rebuilt by Holland, and given the politest of Georgian façades in greyish so-called 'mathematical' tiles made by a manufacturer near Norwich. When completed, the new Althorp was extremely tasteful and polite and, like the Earl himself, was universally admired.

Back in London, Countess Lavinia, as chatelaine of Spencer House, had taken up her social duties with determination – holding levees, luncheon parties and receptions twice a week, interspersed in summertime with 'breakfasts' for six hundred guests at Wimbledon, starting at around eleven and continuing till dusk. With so much effort, she rapidly acquired a reputation as a social figure, hostess, and something of a wit, but she never could compete with the overwhelming presence of her sister-in-law on the other side of the Park, and increasingly disapproved of Georgiana and the scandalous world of Devonshire House.

The Earl was a tolerant man, who loved his sister and wasn't overly concerned about her morals – or anybody else's. He even got on well with his brother-in-law, the wintry Duke of Devonshire, who positively thawed in his company. Early that year the Duke had called at Wimbledon bearing a live turtle 'which formed the basis for a feast'. But Georgiana did not join them, nor did Lavinia visit Devonshire House in return. 'Your sister,' Lavinia told her husband, 'is quite incorrigible.'

As the first Spencer benefiting from Sarah's great inheritance to be free from her ban upon accepting office, the Earl allowed himself to be politically ambitious. 'I believe that whenever it comes in my way to concern myself in public affairs, I shall be a great politician,' he had written to his father with rather touching immodesty on the eve of leaving Harrow, and nothing since had made him change his mind. As a follower of Fox there seemed little chance of getting into government, but one cannot believe this seriously worried him.

He was the least doctrinaire of men, as his wife was the most vehement of women. 'Do you like Mr Pitt?' she asked him. 'Pray don't, for I cannot. He is so affected, so conceited that he makes me sick.'

In fact the Earl got on very well with Mr Pitt but, as he liked a peaceful life, chose not argue with Lavinia on the subject.

A more serious problem between them was the fact that she was not maternal and deeply resented the sheer waste of time, not to speak of the discomfort, caused by procreation. With time she adjusted to the facts of life, but by then she had formed a life-long antipathy towards her first-born child, Jack. To compensate, George always tried to show his son affection, particularly after his narrow escape when Wimbledon House caught fire in the spring of 1785. While on a trip to Althorp, the Spencers had left baby Jack with his wet-nurse in the nursery at Wimbledon. George was out hunting when news reached him of the fire. Rushing back to Wimbledon, they found that the nursery was the only part of Sarah's house left standing, but that little Jack was safe.

Apart from the nursery, little of Sarah's 'curtseying villa' had survived. 'I had no conception of so complete a demolition of everything combustible,' wrote the Earl. For everything had gone, including Marlborough's state carriage, his marble bust and twenty dozen bottles from his cellar, consumed by the villagers while putting out the fire – this presumably explaining why so little had survived the conflagration.

George took the loss of his villa philosophically, as he took most things in life. However, the house was seriously underinsured, proof of the old regime's incompetence, and the £8,000 insurance money he received was not enough to rebuild it. So it was that, although Wimbledon was the Earl's favourite residence, the family had to camp out in the servants' quarters when they visited until 1801, when he felt he could afford to have Henry Holland reconstruct the large but uninspired new villa called Wimbledon Park House. In the meantime, since Jack was safe he was entrusted to a more reliable nurse when his parents went off on a European tour a few months later.

Like his parents before him, George Spencer did the Continental Tour in style, with a positive convoy of carriages and horses and numerous servants, including two cooks. They slowly bumped their way through Belgium and Germany to Italy, Christmassed in Rome, then travelled on to Naples to meet the spring. George was particularly anxious to see the famous diplomat and collector, Sir William

Hamilton. When they met, Lavinia was not impressed by his young wife Emma, having heard distressing stories of her earlier existence, including a rumour that she had once been a prostitute. But the Earl liked her as he liked all pretty women.

What really impressed George Spencer was Sir William's passion for collecting. Sir William collected almost everything, and the Earl was particularly interested in his library. With Sir William as guide the Earl visited all the Neapolitan booksellers, and was most taken by the splendid books on offer, many of them by the greatest Italian and Sicilian printers. He purchased numerous editions of the classics and it was now that he first contracted the disease that would bring such pain and pleasure to his life. It was now that he became a serious book collector.

The Spencers returned to Spencer House to find Jack looking 'vastly well', despite the fact that, since Lavinia more or less ignored him, he was unresponsive in her presence. The Earl, however, was discovering, as he wrote to his mother, that 'Jack conversed in his manner a great deal with me. I did not understand much of what he said , but more I think than when I went away. He has got one of those swinging hobby horses which he rides extremely well, and is highly delighted with it.'

Apart from playing with his son, the Earl had much to occupy his time. Henry Holland was now hard at work at Althorp, and in London there were the constant demands of politics and high society. But what also occupied the Earl's attention were the books that he had bought in Italy. 'Much occupied by matters bibliographical,' he wrote to his mother, for already he had started adding to what was left of the third Earl of Sunderland's great library at Althorp. As more than half of the books had been removed to Blenheim by great-uncle Charles when he departed to become the Duke of Marlborough, there were more than enough spaces on the shelves that needed filling.

Soon he was writing to his mother of finding 'a jewel of the first water – an early edition of Virgil at a reasonable price'. Then there was even more exciting news: Edward Gibbon was at Althorp visiting his library. The author of *The Decline and Fall of the Roman Empire* was particularly impressed by the Earl's editions of Cicero 'and is very entertaining indeed, tho' nothing was ever as shocking as his figure. He is much pleased with the library.'

This was only the beginning. In 1790, George Spencer heard that the great bibliophile, the Hungarian diplomat Count Karolyi Reviczky, worried by the state of Europe, was anxious for a settled income for his later years and might be persuaded to dispose of his famous library. It contained treasures acquired over many years, including early editions of the Greek and Latin classics, most of them in mint condition. Normally the Count would not have dreamt of selling, but with revolution threatening Europe there were few buyers in the offing and, after some negotiation, Count Reviczky accepted from the Earl a down payment of £1,000 and an annuity of £250 a quarter.

This was probably the one sharp business deal George Spencer ever made. For Count Reviczky died eighteen months later, which meant that for £2,500 the Earl had got one of the great bargains in the history of book collecting. Encouraged by his coup, he determined to persevere with his obsession.

He was interrupted by events in France. As a Whig who still believed in liberty, the Earl welcomed the fall of the Bastille in 1789 but, as the French Revolution gathered strength, it began to worry him just as it had worried the unfortunate Count Reviczky.

Early in 1793, finding Jack 'such good company, and cleverer than many people twice his age', George took him to Dieppe for what was intended as a short holiday; but on reading reports there of 'convulsions at Paris which stopped us going to Rouen', the two hurriedly returned, much shaken, two days later.

Unlike his sister, Georgiana, who was still regarding what was happening in France as a re-run of the great Whig revolution, the Earl feared anarchy spreading from France to England, and when war broke out the following year, his reaction was straightforward: 'God grant we may be successful with it, for I verily believe that our existence as a free and independent country is in the scale.'

Feeling as he did, he was strongly tempted to accept when Lavinia's *bête noire*, William Pitt, with the backing of the King, invited him to join his government. After serious consideration he finally accepted, and at thirty-one found himself appointed First Lord of the Admiralty with overall responsibility for the Royal Navy.

As Pitt had warned, it was a daunting task. Boxing Day found him writing to his mother that 'Yesterday tho' Christmas Day I was ten hours unremittingly at work in this office. I fear I fall far short of what the immense load of business here requires.' He was running the Royal Navy almost single-handed and, along with Pitt and Dundas, was at the centre of the high command directing the conduct of the war.

He proved an exceptional administrator. He was intelligent and hard working, and his planning helped secure the naval victories of Camperdown and Cape St Vincent – just as his sense of justice and good sense helped him settle the naval mutinies at Spithead and the Nore. Had the mutinies continued, the fleet could have been out of action and Britain left defenceless, but, as his wife wrote proudly, 'the sailors have been satisfied thro' Lord Spencer's zeal, activity, judgement and firmness.' Most of their grievances were met and, thanks to the Earl, the threat to the fleet was ended.

But his greatest claim to glory came in 1798 when he selected and supported young Vice Admiral Nelson over the heads of more senior commanders to command the Mediterranean Fleet, and Nelson won his first great naval victory of the Nile in that July.

The Earl regarded Nelson as his personal protégé, but, to start with, his wife was even more enthusiastic about the young Admiral. 'How perfectly he fulfils my notion of a Christian hero!' she exclaimed, and was most concerned about the hero's health. 'His wound is perfectly well, but he complains of a hectic cough, and a state of weakness that goes to my heart. However I trust in the air of Naples doing him good, dear dear creature. Every letter I see of his increases my respect for his character.'

But not for long.

Back in London, Lavinia learned of Nelson's love for Emma Hamilton. Remembering Emma from her trip to Naples she became incensed against Nelson and, when the Spencers entertained the hero and his wife to dinner at Spencer House, she later referred to him as 'that little man between that old fool, Sir William, and his lady wife'. Prig that she was, she could never bring herself to say a good word thereafter for the greatest hero of the age and, although the home that Nelson shared with the Hamiltons at Merton was not that far from Wimbledon Park House, he was never invited to visit. On the very eve of Trafalgar she would write that 'Nelson's disgusting bragging and vanity dyes every friend's cheek scarlet. He makes me vomit.'

The Earl, as usual, made no comment, but by then he had left the Admiralty resigning with Pitt in 1801 over the King's refusal to grant Catholic emancipation. G. M. Trevelyan rated George Spencer as 'the greatest civil administrator of the Navy that ever sat in Whitehall', and according to *The Dictionary of National Biography* his six years in office were 'the most stirring, the most glorious in our naval history, so that for him, more distinctly perhaps than for any other administrator, may be claimed the title organiser of victory'. He remained devoted to the Navy and in 1807 built a family villa at Ryde on the Isle of Wight from which the Spencers used to watch the fleet at anchor at Spithead and sailing through the Solent.

The Earl had accepted the Garter, but seems to have declined a dukedom. Then, when peace returned in 1815 there were more appetising things than politics demanding his attention.

The upheavals caused by the Napoleonic wars had created extraordinary possibilities for rich collectors, and the Spencers were soon off to Italy in search of an ever greater literary treasure-trove. 'When Spencer travelled on the Continent to make purchases for his library, he was accompanied by five coaches, thirteen horses and eleven people in his retinue.'

Never before or since had there been such bargains for a rich book collector. Throughout France and Italy, war and revolution had destroyed palaces and displaced great libraries, throwing treasures of bibliography onto a depressed market. It was one of his buying trips to Italy that produced another of the Earl's most prestigious purchases, the entire library of the Duke of Cassano-Serra, with unrivalled works of all the great Italian and Sicilian printers. By now the Earl was employing the most distinguished bibliophile of his day, Thomas Dibdin, as his permanent librarian, and was constantly buying from dealers and at auction. He was also spending a small fortune on bookbinders.

In London there was great competition between rich collectors, for this was also the great period for aristocratic libraries, the time when, according to the historian of the English country house, Mark Girouard, 'the country house library was at its apogee'. Nowhere more so than at Althorp.

Now that Henry Holland had finished it, the Earl could turn the interior into one enormous library with the entire ground floor to be given over almost totally to books. It was a truly fabulous collection, which finally contained four Shakespeare folios, fifty-eight Caxtons, all the earliest editions of Chaucer, bibles by Gutenberg and Wynkyn de Worde, and unrivalled examples of early Italian printing at its most splendid. It was, according to a modern authority, among 'the most important single collections illustrating the history and development of Western printing ever formed'. Room by room, as the shelves invaded all the available wall-space, the pictures were banished to the higher storeys and books took their place.

But the postwar years, which were kind to the aristocracy as book collectors, suddenly turned against them as land-owners. During the war the price of grain and foodstuffs grew, and new agricultural methods brought increased yields and profits. Peace, however, led to a sharp and unprecedentedly long agricultural depression which would last, with only temporary remissions, for the rest of the second earl's life.

The Spencer estates, inherited from Sarah, remained scattered across a dozen counties and were hard to administer, even when the agents were honest. Thomas Harrison, the Earl's overall manager, and his elder son and successor, were both suspicious of innovations. They were honest but, owing to indifferent health, found it hard to control lazy and dishonest subordinates. Even at Wimbledon and Althorp, the Earl had perpetual problems with farmers, agents and park stewards.

He was reluctant to sell land to pay off debt, feeling that estates were undervalued according to what he felt to be 'normal' standards. Trying to sell Holywell after his mother's death, he dropped the price by a third and still found no buyers.

Yet selling, and, for that matter, buying land for an aristocrat like him was never dictated purely by economics. When the spendthrift squire of the large Harlestone estate adjoining Althorp was forced to sell up in 1829, the thought of the trouble an unfriendly neighbour might cause the Spencers forced the Earl to give £135,000 for it, far more than he felt to be the market rate, and at a time when he could clearly not afford it.

In 1826, he actually undertook a drastic reorganisation of all his estates, replacing the Harrisons with a new self-confident young general manager, John George, Shaw-Lefebre. But the Earl was always hoping for an end to the agricultural depression and went on spending. This continued almost to the day he died, and included wage bills, property repairs, endless entertaining, hunting, political organisation and lavish foreign travel. The Earl was by nature and nurture extravagant. Spending money was part of the role of the aristocracy. There were also, of course, the ever-mounting costs of the library which were not to be denied.

Perhaps there is a book-collecting gene, for his ancestor the third Earl of Sunderland had been another great collector; as was his Blenheim cousin, Lord Blandford, who in 1817 became fifth Duke of Marlborough. With the passage of time, the differences between the Marlborough dukes and the Spencers earls had, if anything, increased. It was probably the effect of Blenheim, but a strong vein of melancholy had started to afflict the Marlboroughs.

The fifth Duke's father, George Spencer, fourth Duke of Marlborough, was a true depressive, who, towards the end of his long life, turned hermit. He refused to meet Nelson when he called at Blenheim and when the celebrated Mme. de Stael arrived, all he could say to her was 'Go away! Go away!'

His son, George, Lord Blandford, was as much of a spendthrift as any of his Althorp cousins, but with far slimmer resources, so that when he outbid the second Earl with the exaggerated figure of £2,600 for an edition of the *Decameron*, the Earl may have suspected that Blandford would not keep it long. Sure enough, a few years later the fifth Duke, as George had now become, went bankrupt. The *Decameron* went up for auction, and the Earl purchased it for £750.

Like all the Spencers, the second Earl loved his hunting and shooting; or, as Lavinia called it, 'the irrepressible spirit derived from sheer pulling the trigger'. But what increasingly occupied his time were the insatiable demands of his ever-growing library.

'While in London, Father spends more and more of his time in book shops and browsing through catalogues,' wrote his daughter, Sarah. While up at Althorp, in his great library, with its eight separate book-rooms, the Earl had built himself the perfect pleasure-dome where, for days on end, he could happily escape from care and worry.

By now he was borrowing heavily to finance his purchases. Buying books on such a scale had become a sort of vice, not unlike his sister Georgiana's compulsive gambling. But with the Earl it was strange to find this obsession in a man who was otherwise a monument of sanity. Increasingly omnivorous in his collecting, all he now demanded of a printed book was antiquity, rarity and, as far as possible, absolute perfection.

At Althorp the result was overwhelming, with what amounted to a series of separate libraries filling the ground floor of the house, culminating in his so-called 'gothic library', built in 1819. Thomas Dibdin described it thus: 'It had a first floor gallery six feet wide, with ample room for chairs and tables; and the studious may steal away from the animated discussions carried out below to the more perfect enjoyment of their favourite authors.'

For the Earl his library was also a place to 'steal away' from the mounting irritations of his life – and particularly from his wife, Lavinia who, energetic and increasingly abrasive, still tried to rule the lives of her husband and their seven children. After the eldest, Jack, Lord Althorp, came Sarah, Robert, Frederick, known as Fritz, Georgiana and the afterthought, George, who was known to everyone as Hodgekin. It was unfortunate that as a clever woman, Lavinia felt obliged to make continual fun at their expense, particularly Jack's. His two brothers, Robert and Frederick, escaped to the Navy as midshipmen, but for Jack it seemed that there was no release from his difficult relationship with his mother.

According to Georgiana's daughter, Harriet, Lavinia's conversation was 'so improving and so very entertaining that I could listen to her forever. She laughs at poor Lord Althorp without mercy and has no compassion on him when he gets bewildered. I love my aunt but would rather be anything but her daughter.'

Another of Lavinia's targets was the royal family. Genial as ever, her husband had come to admire King George III, when he met him during his brief spell as Home Secretary in the Whig 'Ministry of all the Talents'. 'Just returned from the King's drawing room,' he wrote. 'Never saw him looking better, tho' the Queen looks old and ill. They were both, as usual, extremely gracious to me.'

Lavinia would not hear such sentiments and, at King George's golden jubilee in 1810, became incensed when the vicar of Wimbledon called, requesting a contribution to the celebrations, 'just to prove my joy', she wrote with heavy sarcasm, 'at having lived to see the fiftieth year of our victorious, glorious, wise, good and fortunate monarch'. Having contributed five guineas for the poor on condition that it did not go towards the celebrations, she informed the priest that she would not be visiting his church that Sunday 'as pray for the King I cannot and will not'.

But although Lavinia could be intolerable, she adored her husband with a love that grew as they got older. The Earl does not seem to have reciprocated. Instead, behaving like the well-bred gentleman he was, he was kind to her, avoided arguments and disappeared to Althorp and his precious library with increasing frequency.

In middle age, his closest friend was his son Jack who, by now, thoroughly disliked his mother. As a so-called 'Young Whig', Jack was becoming more extreme than his father in his deep distrust of the monarchy, as well as in his belief in fundamental Christianity. The Earl did not agree with him, on either count, nor could he agree with his attitude towards the aristocracy. As a Whig grandee, George Spencer still believed it was his duty to maintain the dignity and splendour of his great position, but Jack was not particularly concerned with either.

In his later years the Earl became increasingly concerned that he was living far above his means, but when he discussed this with his son and heir, Jack was always more than understanding. 'Continue to live as you have been accustomed,' he told him. 'Let the task of retrenchment fall on me; I have no desire to keep up the state of a great nobleman and shall be prepared to live very economically.'

Lavinia, however, was less tolerant of the Earl's extravagance, and sometimes chided him about his library.

'When I consider the heavy charges on your landed estate, and the just and lawful claims your children have to better allowances than they already have, and the frequent opportunities which arrive when an 100 pounds might do them inexpressible good, I have no scruple to say that you have no right to throw away such sums upon an useless fancy, and that as you grow older I earnestly hope you will curtail some of your library expenses.'

He, of course, did nothing of the kind. For if there is such a thing as a libroholic, the Earl was in the final stages of addiction. His wife, as usual, failed to understand and, having lived his life encircled by dominating women, he knew better than to argue with her. But far from being a mere 'useless fancy', his great library had become the centre of his world and he was spending more than ever on his books as the time available to him to buy them lessened. For Lavinia to talk in terms of the occasional hundred pounds showed how little she suspected of the true amounts that he was spending. But her warnings were given point when their straitened circumstances forced them to leave for good the Earl's favourite residence, Wimbledon Park House, in 1826.

The Earl was grateful that, after he was gone, everything would be sorted out by Jack. At least there was the land, including Sarah's vast estates and although some of them would have to go, Jack was not extravagant like his father. The Earl had done his best, but it was now beyond his capacity to change the situation – or himself.

Early in 1814, his mother died. He had written to her every day since he was a boy. Years before she had told him: 'did not the stronger tie of parent and child subsist between us, you are in character, in understanding and in disposition, the person of all others I have ever known (except your father) whom I would choose for a friend.'

Just before she died on New Year's Eve, she had written him a letter of farewell, telling him how much she loved him, and ending 'many many happy years to you my dearest G. and to Lavinia and all your litter'.

During the last years of her life, Lavinia must have haunted her husband. In her letters she increasingly complained about her situation, as he was absent more than ever. She was particularly lonely in the autumn, when the shooting season provided a fresh excuse for him to leave her.

'Plunged, immersed, buried in autumn and all its dreary solitude, I do hate and detest the dreary season . . . I wish partridges, pheasants, woodcocks, snipes and hares all at the bottom of the sea.'

At other times, she would simply say how much she missed him: 'Your Letters are my breath of life,' she told him.

They had a great sadness when their sailor son Robert died suddenly aboard ship off Alexandria. 'He was the best of all of us,' said his brother Jack, who particularly loved him.

Then in June 1831, it was the turn of Lavinia herself. For some time she had been unwell, probably with hepatitis, and throughout her lengthy illness she remained in London, writing the Earl pathetic letters of devotion. While refusing to curtail his hunting and lengthy visits to his library, he was as kind to her as his nature permitted.

Although the Earl was not devout like Jack, he was a believer, and he composed a prayer for the new year following her death. In it he referred to 'God's perfect mercy, unerring wisdom, and strict justice both to her, whom thou hast released from the sufferings and miseries of this world, embittered alas, and too justly, by my own misconduct, and to me by forcing me to a more due attention . . . to all my failings and transgressions.'

What he meant by his 'misconduct' is a mystery. If he kept a mistress, all trace of her has long since vanished. And even if he had, his real mistress was his library, just as his true 'misconduct' was the obsessional love he gave it – at the expense of Lavinia and the children, and indeed the future of the Spencer family through the ever growing debt he created.

He himself died three years later, leaving behind what at the time was the greatest private library in existence. Yet in the process of creating it, he had all but bankrupted the family. On his death in 1834, he left 43,000 priceless volumes and a debt of over half a million pounds.

CHAPTER 9

Reform and After

*John Charles, third Earl Spencer (1782–1845) and
Frederick, fourth Earl Spencer (1798–1857)*

Apart from his mother, almost everyone who came in contact with John Charles, Lord Althorp, ended up loving him. For John Charles was that rare and irresistible phenomenon – an honest, genuinely good man. In his way he was also a great man. Gladstone called him 'the very best leader of the House of Commons that any party ever had'. And Sarah Marlborough's biographer, Frances Harris, believes that in him, 'Sarah's desire to found a great and politically responsible family, endowed with her own fortune, was finally realised'.

He was born at Spencer House on 30 May 1782, and his fate – and with it the fate of several future generations of Spencers – seems to have been dictated by his early reaction to that sharp-tongued, deeply unmaternal woman, his mother Lavinia, second Countess Spencer. Disliking the whole process of human reproduction, she was unable to forgive her first-born child for the discomfort and pain he caused her at his birth. She neglected him during her long trips abroad and when he showed genuine affection for his father she could not forgive him for that either.

Children have a way of turning into what their parents want them not to be and, as he grew, John Charles became what he may have thought would give his mother most displeasure – he was graceless, incoherent, slow of speech and distinctly dull. With his father, he became a different child, but for much of his childhood his father was working fourteen hours a day at the Admiralty, directing the long sea war which culminated in Nelson's victories, and John Charles was more or less neglected. According to family tradition it was a Swiss footman at Spencer House who taught him to read. And at Harrow, where the future lords Byron, Palmerston and Melbourne were already sparkling among his contemporaries, John Charles, Lord Althorp, dull as ever, did the opposite.

Aged twenty-three he showed how much he had rejected the values of his parents' generation when his father, as a former First Lord of the Admiralty, was able to arrange for a Royal Navy sloop to drop him off at Naples for what had traditionally been the culmination of a young Whig nobleman's education – the Grand Tour of Italy. From the days of Shameless Sunderland, a love of Italy and things Italian had almost been an article of faith among the Spencers, but after spending several days in Naples, something must have told John Charles that Italy was not for him. Like many an indignant Englishman before and since, he was soon complaining: 'It appears that there is not a single honest man in this country.' In Rome he thoroughly disliked the Vatican galleries, and in Florence felt much the same in the Uffizi. In him, his family had produced that rarity, a Spencer who positively hated art, so much so that he carefully avoided Paris on his journey back to England, just in case anyone tried to make him visit one more picture gallery.

While abroad he missed his steak and missed his hunting, and could not wait to be reunited with the rainswept shores of England. All he brought back from the Grand Tour was an Aldine edition of Homer for his father, and a Parmesan cheese the size of a cartwheel for his mother.

Back in England he seems to have genuinely wanted to avoid his mother and tried his best to escape from her as soon as possible. Since he was his heir, his father would not to let him join the Navy like his younger brothers, Robert and Frederick, so John Charles did the next best thing, and opted for a life deep in the country. Meeting him at Althorp, his cousin Harriet was shocked to see to what depths he had sunk. 'He has contrived to make himself so compleat a zero in society,' she said. He had become a man 'whose soul is engrossed with one most uninteresting pursuit, and who cares for neither father, mother, brothers, sisters or for anything else on earth but that noble animal, a horse.' In reaction to her own cleverness, his mother seemed to have produced a simple eighteenth-century philistine whose greatest happiness was to spend the whole day hunting.

But John Charles was not quite the 'absolute zero' that he seemed. At his father's suggestion he took over the mastership of the Pytchley at a time when it was dominated by its older members who liked hunting with heavy horses and slow hounds. This did not suit John Charles and, to bring back some excitement to the hunt, he undertook the complicated business of breeding hounds 'for speed and spirit'. He also used his influence to change the hunt membership, and it was always claimed that under his mastership the Pytchley finally attained 'the zenith of it glory'.

His love of the country, and his attachment to the way of life it represented – beef, beer, farming and tradition – became fundamental to the young Althorp's whole existence. But his enjoyment of the hunt was interrupted by the obligation to participate in politics. In 1804, probably to please his father, he had become a member of parliament for what was effectively a Spencer seat at Okehampton in Devon, and soon, through his father's influence, he was given a very junior position at the Treasury in the Ministry of All the Talents. But at this stage he could never be called a dedicated politician. Hunting still came first and, after a late night sitting at Westminster, he would gallop through the night, using relays of horses on the way, to be back in time for the next day's hunting with the Pytchley.

Just as he had been obliged to enter politics, so Lord Althorp felt obliged to marry, but he was not enthusiastic at the prospect. His father suggested his cousin, his Aunt Harriet's unbalanced and glamorous daughter, Caroline Ponsonby who, fortunately for Althorp, married Lord Melbourne instead and later fell in love with the man she called 'mad, bad and dangerous to know' – Lord Byron.

Lord Althorp decided he would please himself and, in the end, he predictably chose exactly the sort of bride his mother would have most disliked – portly, homely Esther Acklom, the daughter of an undistinguished but well-to-do Nottinghamshire squire. Lavinia was heard to say that her daughter-in-law's 'manner of address was so forthright and uninhibited that it rarely failed to cause unease amid well-bred people'. But just as Lavinia came to hate her, so stout Esther soon became the joy of Althorp's life. Once married in 1814, they stayed away from London, settling into her old family house at Wiseton, on the borders of Nottinghamshire and Leicestershire. It was here that John Charles's lifelong interest in farming really started. He always said that these were the happiest years of his life. He farmed, he turned from breeding hounds to breeding cattle. He loved his wife, and went on hunting.

But already the cares of the outside world were impinging on the rural peace of John Charles Spencer. Through parliament he had been meeting a group of rich young aristocrats from Whig families very like his own. There was Lord Tavistock, heir to the Duke of Bedford. There was also his cousin, the youthful Lord Duncannon and, above all, there was his closest and most influential friend, the immensely rich Lord Milton, heir to the great FitzWilliam estates and fortune.

In the reaction to the war with France, the once pro-French Whig politicians of the second Earl Spencer's generation had become increasingly impotent and disillusioned. But this group of young Whig noblemen was quite different from the older generation. All were devout evangelical Christians and, as such, were united by the bonds of serious belief. Devoted to good works, they were kindly landlords and puritan by inclination. They rigidly observed the Sabbath. John Charles himself began reading sermons to his guests on Sundays, and later had paintings removed from Spencer House 'because they were in a state of nakedness without even fig leaves'. At Wiseton he insisted that 'he had no wish to live the life of a grandee' but preferred to 'live like a squire and not a magnate'.

However, while trying to live the life of a simple country squire with his plump wife and his herds of even plumper cattle, Lord Althorp was changing into something different. It was as if, in the person of this devout, country-loving nobleman, the eighteenth century was correcting itself of its excesses, with social conscience succeeding lordly unconcern, earnest belief taking the place of upper-class indifference, and sheer hard work making up for all the years of noble idleness. Simultaneously, in Parliament the same leaven of evangelical Christianity was working on young Whig noblemen like Althorp, in the cause of liberty, justice and the hatred of tyranny.

Politically, what these earnest young men needed was a cause to unite them; and not for the first time in history it was provided by their opposition to the Royal Family. At the time, King George III's son, Frederick, Duke of York, was Commander-in-Chief of the Army and it was revealed in parliament that his current mistress, Mrs Clarke, had been taking bribes from army officers anxious for promotion. Although it seemed as if the Duke himself had also been involved, the older members of parliament were inclined to deal leniently with the matter. Bribery was something of a way of life and a certain level of corruption made the world go round.

But Althorp was genuinely shocked at such an attitude. So were his friends, for whom corruption, from whatever quarter, was a clear offence against the moral code they all believed in. Somewhat reluctantly, Lord Althorp now became their spokesman. Although he had already sat in the House of Commons for five years without speaking, he roused himself to deliver an impassioned attack upon the hapless Duke of York and, although his motion was defeated, his speech helped to make his name in Parliament. Older Whig politicians like his father had been growing tolerant of royalty, but Althorp would have none of this and from this point on would always be suspicious of the monarchy.

One of the few clouds obscuring the sunshine of the Althorp marriage had been Esther's failure to produce a child. Several times she suffered cruel miscarriages, which John Charles endured with her in agony. Finally, in the spring of 1818, Esther discovered she was pregnant once again, and this time she carried the child full term. Hoping for a Spencer heir at last, Althorp wrote happily to his friend, Lord Milton: 'I never saw her better in my life and am therefore very sanguine as to the result.' This time there seemed no cause for anxiety, but to be on the safe side he insisted on taking Esther to London for the birth. On 9 June, after a prolonged and agonising labour, Esther was delivered of the longed-for son and heir but the baby was stillborn. Two days later, John Charles also lost the wife that he had loved so dearly.

Stunned with grief, he longed to join her. Retreating alone to Wiseton in a state of deep depression, he spoke of death as 'the most inestimable blessing a created being can receive'. When finally he felt that he could face the world again, he tried to convince himself that Esther's death had had a meaning, telling himself that it had been God's way to make him stick more strictly to the path of duty. Only thus would he 'fulfil His plans in order to secure eventual reunion with his wife in heaven'. Until that happened, he felt he was on leave of absence from the great hereafter, with his life at best an interlude before the awesome drama of Judgement Day. From now on Althorp craved no frivolous delights. He gave up hunting and wore black at all times, claiming that his only use of this world was 'as a stepping stone to the next'.

His mother naturally had hopes that he would overcome his grief, and finally remarry, if only to provide the all-important heir for the family. But for such a man, the idea of remarriage after Esther's death was quite repugnant. This was the time when his mother could have helped him, but as she had never disguised her hatred for his dead wife, he found it hard to endure his mother's company. Instead of going back to live with her, he chose to make his home with the person who was now his only link with Esther – his mother-in-law, the widowed Mrs Acklom – feeling it his duty to look after her.

Lady Spencer bitterly complained that her son rarely dined at Spencer House because 'he dare not leave that old drunkard of a mother-in-law who rules him with a rod of iron and who having once got him into her town residence will never let him quit it'.

By setting up home with his mother-in-law, John Charles had effectively cut himself off from his mother. More important for the future of the Spencers, he had protected himself against any urge he might have felt at this stage to remarry. Since Esther had been unable to present him with an heir no other woman was to have that privilege, and the succession would inevitably pass to one of his brothers, Robert, Frederick or George. There were enough of them, and he was not worried. He had other matters on his mind.

Still grieving for Esther, he sought consolation in his farms and with his cattle. As he told his father, 'I hope by such quiet pursuits as these to bear the affliction I am suffering under with tolerable patience.' He also began to educate himself by the serious study of divinity and economics. But work was only soporific, life at best a grim alternative to death, which often tempted him.

The outside world could not be so easily evaded, and it was now that, together with a small group of friends in Parliament, Lord Althorp first became involved in the cause of parliamentary reform. Still fearful of a French-style revolution breaking out in England, the Tory government was firmly wedded to repression. On 16 August 1819, a huge crowd that had peaceably assembled at St Peter's Fields in Manchester to hear the Radical 'Orator' Hunt on the subject of parliamentary reform, was fired on by the Yeomanry. The eleven who were killed became the 'martyrs' of what was known as the 'Peterloo Massacre'.

Amid great concern throughout the country, everyone took sides and Lord Althorp found the cause he needed. Following Esther's death he felt he had to do 'that which is pleasing unto God' and, after the horror of Peterloo, was convinced that what was pleasing unto God was to sweep away parliamentary corruption and extend the vote to the rising middle classes and the unrepresented industrial cities of the North. Only serious electoral reform would prevent further Peterloos and the revolution everybody dreaded.

In Parliament he began to make his reputation as one of the most effective leaders of the Opposition. Lacking the distraction of a wife or children, he could devote himself almost exclusively to his duties. But while he was totally sincere in his dedication both to Christianity and Reform, his character remained the same as ever. The least arrogant of aristocrats, this John Bull figure could not have been more unlike the fashionable and elegant Whig noblemen of his father's generation, particularly now that he lacked a wife to keep him clean and tidy. The diarist Creevey describes him in parliament with his 'stout, honest face, and farmer-like figure, habited in ill-made black clothes, his trousers rucked up in a heap around his legs, one coat flap turned round and exposing his posterior . . .' And, according to R.H. Gronow, 'even in the hottest days he was buttoned up to his chin, and no one has ever been able to discover whether his lordship wore a shirt or not'.

Far from arousing disapproval, all of this endeared him to members on both sides of the House. He genuinely did not want to change his manner or his clothes. And, just as he was proud of looking like a farmer, so he remained completely serious in his belief that as a Christian his true purpose in this vale of tears was to fight corruption and 'place the civil liberties of my country in an impregnable position'.

It was this unusual combination of opposites which gave Althorp such influence in Parliament and, thanks to this, in 1830 the Whig Opposition elected him their leader. Another source of Althorp's strength was the fact that he was probably the only man in Parliament who personally wanted nothing out of politics. He was so clearly what he said he was, that no one could question his integrity. And since, as an aristocrat himself, Reform was clearly not in his own interests, none could question the sincerity with which he urged it on his fellow politicians.

Even his lack of polish as a speaker could work in his favour. When he was in government, a particularly persuasive speaker made a strong speech supporting an amendment against Reform. Althorp, rising to his feet, replied that 'he had made some calculations which he considered as entirely conclusive as a refutation of the honourable gentleman's arguments, but unfortunately he had mislaid them, so that he could only say that if the House would be guided by his advice, they would reject the amendment'. And they did.

For as Peel said, 'Althorp only had to get up, take off his hat and shake his head to convince the House that the Opposition's arguments, however plausible, were founded on a fallacy.'

It was in 1830 after the collapse of the Duke of Wellington's Tory government that Georgiana Devonshire's former lover, Lord Grey, became Whig prime minister and invited Althorp to become his Chancellor of the Exchequer.

Before accepting, Althorp had written to his brother, Robert, 'I will not take office unless some great good is to be effected by it. I know it will make me miserable . . . but I have no right to refuse, though I accept at the expense of my own happiness.'

He was not exaggerating. He remained Leader of the House as well as Chancellor, and the next two years his life were dominated by the unremitting labour of dragging the first Great Reform Bill through a reluctant Parliament. His fellow Whig, the future prime minister Lord John Russell, was the Bill's effective architect, but throughout the gruelling committee stages Althorp had the task of controlling the House and dealing, step by step, with the most minute details of the government's proposals.

He never faltered. After a general election in the spring of 1831 had returned a Whig government with an even larger majority, his work went on. With the opposition fighting every detail, Russell virtually collapsed, leaving Althorp to soldier on 'night after night in the crowded, steaming chamber, which stank in warm weather because of its proximity to the Thames eight or nine hours every evening'. Between December 1830 and March 1832, Russell spoke 329 times in parliament to Althorp's 1014.

For although the Bill was passed by the House of Commons it was twice rejected by the House of Lords, leaving the government no alternative but to start its work afresh.

The strain on ministers became intense and particularly on

Althorp. 'Damn Reform,' Lord Grey remarked to him in February 1832. 'I wish I had never touched it.'

Wearily Althorp said he felt the same, adding that he had removed his pistols from his bedroom, just in case the temptation to kill himself became irresistible. Around the same time he was telling Byron's old friend Hobhouse: 'I don't know whether I ought not to make matters easier by shooting myself.'

'For God's sake,' Hobhouse answered loyally, 'shoot anyone else.'

It needed yet another General Election, and the threat by the new King William IV to create as many new Whig peers as were necessary to get the Reform Bill through the House of Lords, but in June 1832, the First Reform Bill became law. And Lord Althorp, who had done the donkeywork to make this possible, had almost had enough. In 1834, his father's death removed him from the House of Commons to what he called that 'hospital of incurables', the House of Lords. Freedom beckoned. 'At all rates, I am the House of Commons Minister who will be handed down to posterity as being the man who only accepted office for the purpose of carrying Reform, and who first has applied the axe to the root of all our evils,' he wrote. He had 'done what was pleasuring unto God and, without regret, he now returned to the country

Now that his father was dead, he could keep the promise he had made to him to deal once and for all with the apparently insoluble problem of the Spencer family debt. As he had told his father, he had 'no desire to keep up the state of a great nobleman', and was perfectly prepared to live economically. As a former Chancellor of the Exchequer he was also used to dealing with large amounts of money, but even he was shocked to discover that the debt was standing at nearly half a million pounds.

It was a strange situation. For Sarah's great inheritance, far from having proved a financial blessing, had ended up all but ruining the Spencers. The existence of such wealth had encouraged the first Earl in cripplingly expensive self-indulgence, way beyond the income the inheritance produced, and with so many great houses, and increasingly mortgaged resources, the Spencers had been living in an aristocratic cloud cuckoo land for the last two generations. If this continued, John Charles could see that the family would soon be ruined. It was a nightmare task for anyone to deal with, and few could have managed it. But thanks to his frugal way of life, and the fact that he had no immediate family, John Charles uncomplainingly set himself to cope with a situation for which he was in no way responsible.

He began by implementing as many personal economies as possible, spending little on himself, closing up Althorp, selling furniture and shares, and disposing of his apartment in the Albany. But none of this made much impression on the debt. Reluctantly he tried to sell Spencer House, which he loved, by offering it, together with some paintings, several adjacent houses and the Marlborough diamonds, in a package for the knock-down price of £60,000. But even a potential buyer as rich as the Duke of Richmond jibbed at the thought of maintaining such a palace, and incredibly there were no takers.

This left him no alternative to what he called 'the Great Operation', which would occupy much of his attention for several years. His principal ambition was to preserve Althorp and the original Spencer lands in Northamptonshire and Warwickshire. These were sacred, and to keep them it was clear that there was only one sacrifice the family could make. The great Spencer estates on the south bank of the Thames in Wandsworth and Battersea would have to go.

He must have guessed that as far as the future was concerned, this would be a serious loss for the family, for much of the land was undeveloped, and soon this whole area beside the Thames would be thick with wharves and factories, and the dense housing developments of Victorian London. Had the Spencers been able to hold onto them, they might not necessarily have made them the 'leviathans of wealth' that Althorp's biographer suggests they might have been, but they would certainly have been spared the worst of the financial troubles that plagued them later in the century.

But this was not possible. The splendid life indulged in by the last two generations of Spencers still had to be paid for. The debts of the dead had to be met by the living, and John Charles, third Earl Spencer, paid them. The £324,000 which the sales of Wandsworth and Battersea produced, brought down the debt to more manageable proportions and, when further land was sold at Wimbledon Park, the Spencers were nearly solvent for the first time in more than half a century.

It is only human for future members of the family to bemoan the loss of all this valuable land so close to the centre of London, but it would be wrong to blame the loss on John Charles Spencer. More important by far is how much he saved for the family. For just as he helped to preserve the country from the threat of revolution through the Great Reform Bill, so he also saved the core of the family possessions for the future; this included Althorp with all its treasures and his father's library, and the family's greatest extravagance of all – the incomparable Spencer House.

As for himself, he made one attempt to remarry by proposing to his old friend, Lady Clinton; but when she turned him down, he went on living alone as he always had in Esther's family house at Wiseton. Although he was one of the greatest of the Spencers, he continued living as a farmer and a country squire and his greatest pride was probably his famous herd of Wiseton cattle.

When he died in 1843 he had given orders that 'the gold heart which I wear round my neck be continued there when I am placed in my coffin. I promised Esther this should be so when she gave it to me.' He also asked that after 'simple and inexpensive rites', his coffin should be placed beside Esther's in the vault at Great Brington Church in readiness for Judgement Day.

John Charles was succeeded by his brother Frederick, always known in the family as Fritz. He was forty-seven years old and, as the third son in the family, had never expected to inherit. He and his older brother, Robert, had both joined the Royal Navy as midshipmen in the heroic days of Nelson and both had distinguished careers as professional naval officers. Fritz's claim to fame came in 1827 when he commanded HMS *Talbot*, at the battle of Navarino, in which the combined fleets of Britain, France and Russia totally destroyed the Turkish and Egyptian men-of-war in the cause of Greek independence.

Since John Charles and Esther were childless, Robert had been the heir to Althorp and the Earldom. He was popular and charming and all the family had loved him. But in 1830, Robert died aboard his ship off Alexandria, and Fritz became heir to Althorp and the title.

In the spring before Robert's death, Fritz had married his homely cousin, Elizabeth Poyntz. They had two daughters, Sarah and Georgiana, and in 1835 a longed for son and heir was born, christened John Poyntz Spencer.

Fritz was a man of serious and settled ways. The most interesting thing about him was the way his naval training enabled him to run the house and the estates at Althorp as efficiently as a man-of-war. Fearful of debt, he kept the family solvent and, after its long period of neglect under the third Earl, Althorp was brought back to life by him and his young family.

But Fritz made a further important contribution to the future of the Spencers. He became a courtier. Prince Albert had been impressed by his efficiency as a naval officer and, after he inherited the Spencer title, Queen Victoria offered him the post of Lord Chamberlain. This meant working closely with Prince Albert and thus becoming instrumental in reorganising much of the Palace bureaucracy. This brought the Spencers ever closer to the court and much of their time was spent in London.

In 1851, Elizabeth died and, although grief-stricken at the time, three years later Fritz married another cousin, Adelaide Seymour, who was always known as 'Yaddy'. Although by now Fritz was seriously overweight and was twenty-seven years older than his wife, she adored him. Soon there were two more children, Victoria and Robert. But after less than three idyllic years of marriage, Fritz died quite unexpectedly in 1857. He was only fifty-nine, and left behind a distraught young widow with an infant son a few months old, her only consolation. Completely unprepared for what had happened, her twenty-two-year-old stepson, John Poyntz, suddenly found himself fifth Earl Spencer.

CHAPTER 10

The Holy Tramp

*The Hon. George Spencer, Fr Ignatius of St Paul
(1799–1864)*

On a February morning in 1850 anyone walking up Westminster's Parliament Street might have witnessed a portly Roman Catholic monk in shovel hat and long black habit entering Downing Street and pausing at the front door of Number 10 to ring the Prime Minister's doorbell. A footman answered.

'Is Lord John Russell at home?' the monk inquired.

The footman may have thought it odd to find a monk asking for his master, but he could clearly recognise the accents of a gentleman, and decided to play safe.

'Yes, sir, but he is at present engaged.'

'Then be so good as to say to him that Lord Spencer's brother would wish to speak with him.'

At which point the footman's manner changed abruptly.

'Walk in, sir. I'll inform His Lordship,' he replied respectfully, and showed his visitor to a waiting room. Soon afterwards the dapper figure of Lord John Russell, the Prime Minister, appeared in person, and asked the monk to take a chair.

'Do you remember me, my lord?' the monk inquired.

'Oh, yes,' said the Prime Minister, recalling a small boy he had seen at Althorp many years before. He asked what he wanted, which involved a lengthy explanation from the priest about his mission to reunite Britain to the faith of Rome, for which he was requesting His Lordship's prayers – and any practical support that he could offer.

Lord Russell heard him out, and although it is hard to imagine the grandfather of Bertrand Russell being particularly impressed by pleas on behalf of organised religion, he listened patiently, and conceded that 'anything that would tend to a diminution of the spirit of acrimony and of the disposition of people of opposite opinions to misrepresent one another's views must be good'.

With this the interview concluded and thus encouraged, Fr Ignatius Spencer of St Paul, previously known as the Honourable George Spencer, youngest son of the second Earl Spencer, and brother of the current Earl, went off about his business.

Although his pastoral work involved him in the lives of many of the poorest in the land, George Spencer never hesitated to approach the great and famous in this manner, hoping to advance his mission. He had done so years before, when he met the future Queen Victoria when calling on her mother, the Duchess of Kent, soliciting a contribution for a Catholic church he was building at Dudley. Although the young princess was non-committal on the subject of belief, George came away convinced that her mother was at heart a Catholic. He was less successful when attempting to enlist Lord Palmerston to his cause, and the statesman 'sarcastically' informed him that he had 'no wish to see England brought once more under the influence of Rome'. But once Palmerston had made his feelings clear on the subject of religion, he went on to say how good it was to see this old friend from the past, patted Ignatius on the back and wished him well.

Most of those who met George Spencer felt much the same about him, for he clearly had an innocence and gentleness of character that made it impossible to dislike him, and even those who disagreed with him seem to have regarded him as a harmless eccentric or a sort of 'holy fool'. One of the few exceptions was his mother, Countess Lavinia, who believed that he was actually insane and went into deepest mourning on the day he was ordained a Roman Catholic priest.

But modern times are treating George Spencer more seriously than did his own. When Princess Diana and Prince Charles visited the Vatican during their visit to Italy, the Vatican Library put on a small exhibition of letters and documents of her great-great-great uncle, George Spencer, describing him as a forerunner of ecumenicalism, and one of the earliest advocates of unity between Catholics and Protestants. Then in 1992 Cardinal Worlock, Roman Catholic Archbishop of Liverpool, began the first step towards his beatification which, if successful, will one day lead to George Spencer being made a saint.

The process of canonisation can be long and painstaking, with no certainty of the outcome, but with George Spencer it is hard to see the Vatican permitting his cause to fail. For, being realistic, no Pope is likely to forego this unique opportunity of one day being able to create a Roman Catholic saint from the family of the future king of England.

So who exactly was George Spencer? And why should the Spencers, who for three centuries had been foremost in the defence of Protestantism, have suddenly produced a potential Roman Catholic saint?

George started life in 1799 as the youngest son of Lavinia and George John, second Earl Spencer, being born in Admiralty House during his father's spell as First Lord of the Admiralty. Within the family he was always known as Hodge, or Hodgekin and the natural humility which was such a feature of his priestly calling started early. In contrast with the older children, he seems to have succumbed completely to his fearsome mother's domination, and soon became her favourite. When he was ten she described him as 'our dearest boy who is indeed so amiable and as truly estimable a creature as ever made parents happy'.

As well as being 'amiable', George was clearly something of a softy – later he called himself 'a chicken hearted creature' – and at Eton he was badly bullied, which made him humbler still, and caused a tendency to melancholy which he called 'the dumps', and stayed with him for life.

As often happened in rich families, it was assumed that, as a younger son, George would become a clergyman in a well-endowed family benefice. He accepted the idea and, to prepare him for the priesthood, he was tutored at Eton by the pious Dr Godley, a fervent evangelical whose influence on the tender-hearted George was all-important. For as well as totally accepting Godley's evangelicalism, George began studying tracts of deep devotion, and indulged in such extreme ascetic practices that his health became affected. Even his parents were alarmed and, after removing him from Eton, entrusted him to what they thought would be the corrective care of the future High Church Bishop of London, the Revd Charles Blomfield.

This seemed to work, for by the time George went to Cambridge, he had apparently become a High Anglican himself and enjoyed his time at university, dancing, shooting, playing cricket, and taking a degree in mathematics. Afterwards he joined his parents on one of their extravagant journeys to the Continent. But already something was at work preventing George from succumbing to the slumberous life of a well-connected country vicar. 'The dumps' still troubled him, and during his time in France he experienced what he later described as his first 'true conversion'. It was somehow typical of George that this happened in the Paris Opera. During a performance of Mozart's *Don Giovanni*, as the Don was taken off to Hell, the vulnerable George was smitten with a vision of his own damnation.

From now on he appears to have existed on two separate levels. With his family and friends he was still the amiable Hodgekin, whose pastimes even included mild flirtations, and who was clearly anxious to remain the son his parents wanted. But at a deeper level, he treated his entry into the church with extreme seriousness, when the following year, at the age of twenty-three, he was appointed to the rich Spencer family living at neighbouring St Mary's Church, Great Brington.

At first George went on living at Althorp with his parents while a new rectory was being built for him, barely noticing that his mother still treated him exactly like a schoolboy, telling him when he was to be home, and giving him instructions over almost everything he did. He also did his best to follow his father's advice when

The controversial Augustus John portrait of Albert Edward John,
seventh Earl Spencer (1892–1975).

Diana's grandfather, Maurice Burke-Roche, fourth Baron Fermoy (left) with his twin brother Frank Burke-Roche.

The maternal great-great grandparents of Diana, Princess of Wales. Frances Burke-Roche (above) and her first husband, James Burke-Roche.

Diana's parents: Edward John, Viscount Althorp, later eighth Earl Spencer (1924–1992) leaves Westminster Cathedral with his bride, the Hon. Frances Roche.

Above: Teenage Spencers: Diana at much the same age as her eldest son, Prince William. William, who is physically more Spencer than Windsor, is pictured here at the Queen Mother's ninety-seventh birthday party in 1997.

Below: The royal in-laws. Edward John, eighth Earl Spencer with his second wife, Raine, mixing with the crowds outside Buckingham Palace after his daughter's engagement to Prince Charles was announced.

Top left: Happy never after. Prince Charles kisses the bride after the Royal Wedding, July 1981.

Top right: After her reconciliation with her stepmother – Diana goes shopping with Raine.

Below: Diana in Bosnia, shortly before her death, surrounded by the media who made her.

Above: The Windsors watch in silence as Diana makes her last journey.

Below: Prince William and Prince Harry mourning the loss of their mother at her funeral, supported by their father Prince Charles and their uncle, Earl Spencer.

Charles
Edward
Maurice,
ninth Earl
Spencer
(b. 1964)
at home at
Althorp.

he told him to find himself a wife once the rectory was finished. He got as far as driving off from Althorp to propose to a girl he admired, when the vision of Don Giovanni appeared before him, and he returned to Althorp without asking her.

This proved a foretaste of what was soon to come. Troubled by 'the dumps' and haunted by his vision of damnation, George felt increasingly obliged to prove his worthiness to God by his zeal within his parish. Soon he was out from dawn to dusk, visiting his flock, tending to their needs and ensuring that every member of his congregation was baptised and acquainted with the Bible. He prayed and fasted, but his permanent concern was with the poor. He did everything he could to help them, from providing them with food and money to attending Northampton Hospital, where he studied elementary medicine and learned to set broken bones.

At first Lavinia was condescending as she watched what she saw as her gentle, rather simple-minded son playing at being a clergyman. 'It is quite comical to see him followed by his flock,' she wrote. 'He don't allow any deviation from the right path . . . and his earnestness is truly persuasive, but when I see his authority amongst them it strikes me in the oddest way, for I can't believe that this excellent and grave character is the boy whom I remember so little a while since as a little ragamuffin hobbledehoy.' But when George's earnestness increased, Lavinia's tolerance did not.

He soon found himself afflicted by the curse of the believing classes – honest doubt. And it was honest doubt that drew George from the spiritual safety of the High Anglican beliefs of Bishop Blomfield, to the quicksands of evangelicalism and Wesleyan Methodism. When his mother heard of this, she dragged him back to Charles Blomfield, who by now was Bishop of Chester, trusting he would bring George to his senses. But George revealed a vein of unexpected toughness, and Lavinia became 'most distressed' at Bishop Blomfield's inability to 'reconvert' him.

She found this difficult to forgive. 'George,' she wrote, was 'entirely immersed in vanity and conceit.' It was, she told her husband, 'a great and distressing evil to have this kind of most awful schism taking place in our hitherto united family'.

During his seven years as Rector at Great Brington, George Spencer tended his parishioners and wrestled with his faith. In terms of doctrine he increasingly inclined to Rome, but towards his parishioners he was equally influenced by the social conscience of the evangelicals. He was faced with a difficult dilemma, which in 1830 he resolved by exchanging the security of Great Brington for the deeper certainties of the Church of Rome.

'There goes three thousand pounds a year,' he wrote light-heartedly, relieved that his doubts at least were over. But his family seemed as shocked as when his ancestor, Shameless Sunderland, converted to Catholicism two centuries earlier.

'My dear and poor, poor brother,' wrote his sister, Sarah. 'What shall I say of him? I mean George, who is become a Catholic, we fear a Catholic priest . . . It is so deep an affliction to my dear Father and Mother, so great a breaking up of our family, so painful a loss at Althorp . . . that it weighs us all down.'

Sarah was in fact exaggerating. For while it is true that Lavinia was behaving as if George had died, donning mourning and refusing to speak to him ever again, the rest of the family soon recovered from the shock and behaved quite sensibly, treating the erring son with an understanding which was rare among rich families facing a similar situation. His father, generous as ever, gave him a lump sum and a stipend of £450, to compensate for the £3,000 he had lost. And it was his sister Sarah once again who best summed up the feelings of the family.

'Poor George,' she wrote. 'His peculiarities are so many and so great. It is a most heavenly mind, but it is not fit for this unheavenly world.'

Thanks to his father's generosity, George could enter the Catholic priesthood by studying at the English College at Rome, which was originally founded to train Catholic 'missionaries' to reconvert Elizabethan England. Closed by Napoleon, the College had recently reopened, and for George's sake his sister was reassured that, as she says, 'the English college is a particularly respectable establishment well conducted by a very clever man, Dr Wiseman.'

It was in fact an optimistic time for members of the College. Nicholas Wiseman, already an oriental scholar of repute, was at the centre of a group of young enthusiastic Catholic activists, and George's 'heavenly mind' was strongly influenced by hopes within the college that England was ripe for reconversion to Catholicism. Although this was sheer wishful thinking, George never gave up hope that unity between the faiths could be achieved through prayer and preaching and his own personal example.

George's conversion came some fifteen years before the so-called Oxford Tractarian movement's failure to reconcile Anglican and Catholic doctrine brought a more celebrated convert over to the Church of Rome in the person of another 'tortured' former Church of England parson, John Henry Newman. But George was content to take a humbler path than Newman. Ordained priest in 1832, George returned to England and was appointed to the large industrial parish of West Bromwich in the Midlands, and continued working with the poorest of the poor, using the money sent by his family to help alleviate the overwhelming local poverty. And just as this work among the Catholic poor was much the same as that with his Anglican flock at Great Brington, so he never wavered in his faith that prayer and goodwill were the surest way to heal the rift between the Churches. During this period he had little contact with the family at Althorp, since his evangelical brother, the third Earl, made it a condition that if he came he was not to try converting any of his former Anglican parishioners to Catholicism. The ban became even stronger when George's strongly anti-Catholic brother, Fritz, acceded to the title.

By now George had started what he called his private 'missions', travelling the length and breadth of the country, preaching his message of union between the Churches, and continuing to work among the sick and desperately poor. But in 1839, when his own health began to suffer after seven years working in his parish, he was appointed to teach future priests in the newly opened Catholic seminary of Oscott College. Here he was regarded as a loveable, eccentric figure who still taught his students cricket along with Catholic doctrine, and continued to proclaim his absolute belief in England's ultimate reconversion. While continuing to tend the needy, it was now that he first began to use his contacts with the great and famous to spread his message. In 1838, he journeyed specially to France and persuaded the Archbishop of Paris to ask all French Catholics to pray regularly for the conversion of England.

But he was dissatisfied with what he felt to be the undemanding life that he was living and in 1845 – the year in which John Henry Newman made his celebrated passage to the Church of Rome – George Spencer, deeply moved by reading the *Spiritual Exercises* of Ignatius Loyola, the founder of the Jesuits, decided to become a monk. He adopted the name Ignatius in honour of his hero. But instead of becoming a Jesuit himself, he felt himself directed to the small missionary order of Passionists, founded in the late eighteenth century by St Paul of the Cross, to pray for the reconversion of England.

By now the contrast between the two clerical converts, George Spencer and John Henry Newman, could hardly be more marked. Newman, the Catholic intellectual and successful churchman, had become a famous author, a great Victorian, and founder of the Catholic 'oratories' at Birmingham and London; whereas George Spencer was to face a life of increasing hardship and abasement as he served the poor and continued his missions through the land.

Now in his late forties, he was far from strong and became seriously unwell from the hardships he inflicted on himself during his noviciate. There could hardly have been a greater contrast than between the world he had forsworn as the son of an Earl and that of the novice monk he had become. Ignatius slept on a straw mattress, rose in the middle of the night to pray, and ate the roughest food. He suffered terribly from chilblains. After tending Irish immigrants from the Great Potato Famine in 1845 he contracted fever and nearly died himself. This was the one occasion when his family came to his assistance. His brother Fritz, now the fourth Earl Spencer, while disapproving as strongly as ever of the Pope and Rome, agreed to pay his doctor's bills. George himself was penniless, having made over his own small income to the Passionists, after swearing himself to poverty as well as chastity.

In spite of sickness, George persisted in his cause and in 1848 took his final vows as a Passionist brother. He was beginning to be regarded as something of a Holy Man and made many converts, less by argument than by personal example.

Once he had taken his final vows as a Passionist monk his life became increasingly occupied with his 'missions', travelling throughout the British Isles. But when he was on foreign journeys on behalf of the Passionists, the self-confidence which had never left him as the son of an Earl, made it seem quite natural for him to call upon Napoleon III in Paris, or the Emperor Maximilian in Vienna, asking them, too, to pray for England's reconversion.

The steadfastness of his belief is staggering, sustaining him through these endless journeys, enabling him to endure the rebuffs, the ridicule and the physical hardship of his self-imposed existence.

'Why do you travel third class?' someone asked him.

'Because there isn't a fourth,' he answered simply.

There was no glory for him, no fame and no applause, and he still suffered periodical attacks of 'the dumps'. And while he went on forcing his presence on as many of the great and famous as would see him, he still travelled like a holy tramp, dressed in a long black cassock, his few possessions carried in a sack and wearing an enormous cape embroidered with the emblems of the Passion.

One member of his family that he saw occasionally was his sister, Sarah Lyttleton, while she was acting as governess to the royal children. But whenever he called on her, she made very sure it was at her private house, rather than at the Palace, since, as she said, she did not want a 'paragraph' in the papers.

In 1857 the death of his brother Fritz ended his long exile from Althorp. He had always missed his old home and the new Earl Spencer, Fritz's son, John Poyntz Spencer, was a more tolerant and kind man than his father. He became genuinely fond of his eccentric uncle, and late in life George would sometimes stay at Althorp. On one occasion he attended a dinner for the local Volunteers, at which he made a patriotic speech referring to his Passionist habit as his uniform.

By now several of the Catholics he had known in his youth had become great figures in the Church. In 1850 Nicholas Wiseman was appointed the first Roman Catholic Archbishop of Westminster. Later, he and John Henry Newman became cardinals and princes of the church. Whereas George, now in his mid-sixties, continued with his solitary 'crusade of payer' for Christian unity. He was feeling tired and unwell, but nothing could daunt him in this self-appointed task.

In September 1864, on a journey to Scotland, he had to wait for a train at the town of Carstairs, and decided to call on a friend who lived nearby. But before he could reach the house, he collapsed with a heart attack and died by the roadside, much as he had lived, 'on a journey and alone'.

At the time, and in contrast with Newman and Wiseman, it must have seemed as if his life had been a failure. But now, thanks to the unpredictable way in which his distant niece, Diana, would one day become the mother of the future King of England, justice could be done and George Spencer, also known as St Ignatius of St Paul, may yet receive the sainthood for which he would never have believed that he was worthy.

CHAPTER 11

The Red Earl

John Poyntz, fifth Earl Spencer (1835–1910)

In the spring of 1905 John Poyntz, fifth Earl Spencer, was showing signs of great excitement, which was not an emotion normally encountered in that venerable figure. Standing six foot four, with much of his face obscured behind what was once a bright red beard, Lord Spencer was so dignified, and commanded such immense respect that to credit him with something as vulgar as excitement seemed almost *lésé majesté*

What could have possibly aroused him so? He was too respectable – and, at sixty-nine, probably too old – to be tempted by the flesh. Besides, he had everything that in theory a great aristocrat could possibly desire – 37,000 fertile acres, Althorp Park and Spencer House, and more than his share of worldly honours. He had twice been the Queen's Viceroy in Ireland, President of the Council and First Lord of the Admiralty under Gladstone, and had twice declined the Viceroyalty of India. Nearer home, he was Lord Lieutenant of Northamptonshire, Chairman of the County Council, three times Master of the Pytchley Hunt and Chancellor of Manchester's Victoria University. He was sometimes referred to as 'King of Northamptonshire', and the Order of the Garter which Queen Victoria bestowed on him in 1863 seemed almost incidental.

One thing alone had eluded him – the premiership. At last it seemed within his grasp. He had nearly made it in to office back in 1894, when the eighty-four-year-old Mr Gladstone, as Liberal prime minister, had told him that should Her Majesty ask his advice about his successor he would be recommending Spencer. In fact,

Her Majesty, to nobody's surprise, was so pleased to be freed from Mr Gladstone's advice that she asked him nothing of the sort. Acting on her own initiative, she had summoned instead Archibald Primrose, better known as Lord Rosebery, to be Prime Minister. But although Lord Rosebery won the Derby twice, he won no prizes at Number 10 as Prime Minister. Lord Salisbury led the Conservatives to victory in 1895 and was succeeded as Conservative premier by A.J. Balfour in 1902. Throughout this ten-year period of opposition for the Liberals, Lord Spencer had stayed on manfully in place at the head of the Liberal opposition in the House of Lords.

With fresh elections looming in 1905, there seemed a real possibility that the Liberals would win and Lord Spencer gain what seemed to be his just reward after thirty selfless years in politics. He had considerable support within the party and the famous journalist, W.T. Stead, was promoting his prospects in the *Morning Chronicle* on the electrifying proposition that 'Lord Spencer is by heredity, by character and by achievement marked out for high position'.

But, on the edge of seventy, age was catching up with Lord Spencer. His health had never been robust and, that autumn, when out shooting over the Spencer properties at North Creak, Norfolk, he had a stroke. Another followed, leaving him so weak that he could play little part in the November election which produced the Liberal landslide of 1905.

Even so, his thoughts were still on the greatest prize in British politics and, for some reason, he had formed the notion that King Edward was about to summon him at last. It was a pathetic moment as the stricken statesman waited for the invitation from the Palace which never came. But when Spencer's friend Lord Haldane saw the King at the Palace on the morrow of the election, he found His Majesty in a state of agitation: 'Who told Spencer that I'm about to call on him to form a government?' he demanded. 'I'm sure *I* didn't.'

It would have been unlikely if he had, for John Poyntz Spencer was in no fit state to form anything very much by now, and to his bitter disappointment his friend and rival, Campbell-Bannerman, became Liberal Prime Minister instead.

With Lord Spencer's illness and this angry reaction from the King, the door slammed shut on the last aristocrat in Britain to have had the chance to lead a government from the House of Lords. After three hundred years it also marked the end of the Spencers as a major force in British politics.

Balfour, ennobled after his electoral defeat, was interesting on the subject of Lord Spencer when later discussing him with the Librarian of the House of Lords, the rising man of letters, Edmund Gosse. 'Gosse,' he said, 'what an amazing example Spencer is of what can be done in this country by a noble presence, a great hereditary position, and a fine personal record, assisted by no intellectual parts of any kind. Such a sweet character, and even such a beautiful character and no ability at all.'

Tactful as ever, Gosse replied, 'Lord Spencer's mind works very slowly.'

'It does not work at all,' said Balfour. 'Lord Spencer has no mind. He has character, but no mind.'

'Character but no mind' – even now the verdict seems distinctly harsh on a man who in his day was immensely popular and in his way entirely admirable. But every upward step in the long distinguished life of John Poyntz Spencer bears out the truth of Balfour's words and demonstrates the remarkable advantages a member of the upper aristocracy could still extract from 'a noble presence and a great hereditary position' throughout the reign of Queen Victoria.

But his long career proves something else which has a particular bearing on our story. There was one area in the Earl's life where brains and foresight were required – over the fate and future of his family. Here, in contrast with the world of politics, a fine presence and a great hereditary position were not enough, and the Earl's incumbency at Althorp saw what seemed like the beginning of the irreversible decline of the House of Spencer.

The key to the fifth Earl's career lies in a strange phenomenon that lasted almost throughout the long reign of Queen Victoria. At a time when electoral reform was busily eroding the political power of the aristocracy, people began to feel a deep nostalgia for the image and the ethos of the old nobility. Even as they clipped their wings, the Victorians seemed to fall in love with them and the aristocracy responded by appearing even grander than they ever were before. Never had noblemen looked more authentically noble than Victorian grandees like Lord Salisbury, Lord Hartington and the fifth Earl Spencer. For although he survived until 1910, in almost everything he did, John Poyntz Spencer unashamedly played the part of an eighteenth-century Whig grandee until the day he died.

It was, of course, a role in life that he was born to. Starting life amid the neo-classical splendours of Spencer House in 1835 there was an effortless quality about him from the start. Thanks to 'inherited position', he became Lord Althorp at the age of ten, when his father, Frederick, succeeded his brother Charles, third Earl Spencer, and the family moved to Althorp.

Like all the Spencers except the great bibliophile, George John the second Earl, John Poyntz made little mark at Harrow. But thanks again to 'inherited position' he entered Trinity College Cambridge, wore the gold tasselled gown of a nobleman undergraduate, and as such emerged two years later honoured with a degree without the vulgar necessity of an examination. Inherited position also gained him a seat in the supposedly reformed House of Commons as member for Northamptonshire, which the Spencers still effectively controlled. Within a year he effortlessly ascended to the House of Lords when his father, the fourth Earl, died in 1857. Father and son had never been particularly close, so John Poyntz Spencer did not have to suffer too much grief when at the age of twenty-two he found himself an Earl and heir to two great houses and one of the greatest inheritances in the country. It was now that he started doing almost all the things – and many more – that a great Whig magnate would have done a century earlier.

First he had to find himself a wife. Shortly after leaving Cambridge he had toured America, but instead of using the opportunity to find himself an American heiress who might have proved the ultimate salvation of the Spencers, he took the line of least resistance and soon after his return to England married his distant kinswoman, his step-mother's cousin, the beautiful but not overbright Lady Charlotte Seymour, who brought no money to the union and, possibly because of consanguinity, would bring no children either. Apart from this, Charlotte played the part of Countess Spencer to perfection. She was good and kind, just as the Earl was serious and rather shy, and the couple settled very grandly into the role awaiting them at Spencer House and Althorp.

In terms of income, the new Earl was better off than any of his immediate predecessors. Thanks almost entirely to the third Earl's self-denying economies and his sales to rid the Spencers of chronic indebtedness, he was not only free from nagging worries over debt, but enjoyed an unencumbered income, chiefly in the form of agricultural rent, which at his accession was estimated at £47,000 a year.

It seemed a lot, and in fact it *was* a lot. But common sense suggested that since this income came almost entirely from land it might not continue so abundantly for ever. The brighter members of the aristocracy were already busily diversifying their resources. The Duke of Devonshire would soon be developing seaside Eastbourne, and the Cadogans were hard at work improving their London property in Chelsea; likewise the Grosvenors in Belgravia and the Bedfords in Covent Garden. Thanks to the third Earl's sales, John Poyntz no longer had the priceless assets of Wandsworth and Battersea to exploit and, in 1871, he would reluctantly relinquish the Spencer's last practical connection with Sarah Marlborough's Wimbledon – the unprofitable manorial rights over the Common.

What really interested the Earl was spending money, rather than making it – and thereby asserting the position of the Spencers in politics, in London Society and in the county of Northamptonshire. In all three areas Spencer influence had been declining during his father's tenure, but the fifth Earl was quietly determined to reassert the traditional position of the House of Spencer.

Because of this there was much on which the Earl could spend his fortune. Althorp had been considerably neglected since the second Earl's death in 1834 and the gardens had all but disappeared as part of the third Earl's economies. But with the new Earl, money was no object, and he was happy when his wife engaged the fashionable French landscape architect, Teulon, to re-create a full-scale formal garden at Althorp.

At the same time the Earl himself was keen to reassert the position of the Spencers in the county. Traditionally, one way of doing this had always been through the mastership of the Pytchley Hunt. His father had not hunted, nor had his uncle, the third Earl, from the day his wife Esther died. When John Poyntz took on the mastership of the Pytchley for the first time in 1861, he was determined to be totally in charge. A forceful rider, as Master he rapidly established his authority over the ill-disciplined 'wild boys', whose behaviour in the hunting field had been bringing the Pytchley into disrepute.

He felt obliged to do this for the simple reason that whoever ran the Pytchley also controlled most of the rural society of Northamptonshire and much of the Earl's authority within the county came directly from his mastership of the hunt. But such authority did not come cheap. According to the social historian Lawrence Stone, at this time 'a good hunter, which would keep its owner at the head of the field, cost anything between £400-£700'. As Master of the Hunt, the Earl kept a stable of over fifty horses at Althorp, and by his own estimation the mastership of the Pytchley never cost him less that £14,000 a year.

Another expense he shouldered was supporting the local Liberal Party organisation, which formed the basis of the political influence of the Spencers in the county. Meanwhile, in London, the young Earl thought it even more important to reassert the position of the Spencers as leaders of society. This meant almost completely redecorating Spencer House which, like Althorp, had also been much neglected. All this activity was soon consuming almost all the young Earl's income, but since he had £47,000 rolling in each year from rents and farming and the world believed that he was very rich, there seemed no reason for the Earl and his sociable young wife to think otherwise.

Once the Spencers were enjoying the splendours of the freshly carpeted, curtained and redecorated Spencer House, the Earl owed the next important step in his career to 'heredity and great position'. Despite attempts to wipe out so-called 'old corruption' in Victorian society, at Court the position of the aristocracy continued much as ever. Senior courtiers still came exclusively from the aristocracy, and since the Earl's father, the fourth Earl Spencer, had been Lord Chamberlain, his son was soon given a position in the court as Groom of the Stole to the Royal Consort, Prince Albert.

With his great height and absolutely perfect manners, the young Lord Spencer might have been bred to be a courtier. Along with the mastership of the Pytchley and attendance at the House of Lords, his role at court was a source of interest and prestige, and he was upset when it seemed that it would have to end, less than two years later, on the sudden death of Prince Albert. In fact the Earl's connection with the court was far from over, thanks to what was tactfully referred to in court circles at the time as 'that dreadful business at the Curragh'.

Twenty miles or so from Dublin was the Curragh Camp, the main British garrison in Ireland. It was here that the nineteen-year-old Prince of Wales was sent on six weeks holiday attachment to the Grenadier Guards. Until now the Prince had led a cosseted and sheltered life, and this was the first time he had been free from his parents and the royal minders. The Prince got on well with the officers at the Curragh and several of them, feeling sorry for a sexually frustrated fellow Grenadier, smuggled a present into the royal quarters in the form of Nellie Clifden, a pretty twenty-two-year-old actress.

As an action it was kindly meant, but the 'soiled rose', as Nellie was called, was indiscreet. She afterwards told someone what had happened, who told Lord Torrington, one of the Queen's gentlemen-in-waiting, who felt it his duty to tell Prince Albert – who was deeply disappointed. 'This has caused me the greatest pain I have yet felt in this life,' wrote Prince Albert to his son. 'You must not, you dare not be lost. The consequences to this country would be too terrible.'

In his anxiety to save his son from moral destitution, Prince

Albert took the royal train to Cambridge, where Albert Edward was finishing his studies at the university. The Prince was contrite, and his father, overwrought and overtired, returned to Windsor and took to his bed with what would prove to be a fatal fever. Rarely absent from his bedside, the Queen was forced to hear her husband's delirious ramblings on the sinful nature of their son.

Prince Albert died some twelve days later from typhoid fever, which he had actually contracted from the royal drains at Windsor before his trip to Cambridge. But the Queen remained convinced that their son's wickedness had helped to kill him. It was a fearful thing to happen and, in her grief, she was desperate for somebody to keep the royal heir in order.

Who better than Lord Spencer? The Queen trusted him implicitly. Prince Albert had respected him; so, it seemed, did their son. As Groom of the Stole to the Prince of Wales, Lord Spencer could fill the gap left by the sorely missed Prince Albert.

To start with, all went well. Spencer was barely six years older than the Prince, and Albert Edward warmed to the idea of inheriting his father's senior courtier. The Queen was also reassured and, if nothing else, Lord Spencer's presence made the Prince a little more discreet about his indiscretions. But Victoria believed that the only real answer for the oversexed Prince lay in marriage. Her firm insistence that her children should marry only into European royalty made this difficult, but in 1863, careful negotiations resulted in one of the dynastic marriages of the century, between the Prince of Wales and the beautiful Princess Alexandra, eldest daughter of King Christian IX of Denmark.

Lord Spencer, who had been suffering from a patch on the lung, and who may have guessed exactly what would happen, tendered his resignation, but the Queen begged him to continue. She also offered him the Garter. He agreed.

Marriage seemed to have an unsettling effect on the Prince of Wales. Instead of calming down and enjoying wedlock with his loving wife, he became obsessively unfaithful and keener than ever on fast society. By marrying, he had freed himself from the royal apron strings, and soon embarked upon the social round which rapidly became his greatest interest. He was indefatigable in pursuing pleasure, in the form of food, sex, bridge and smart society.

Brought up in a European court with a womanising father, Princess Alexandra knew the rules and uncomplainingly assumed her role of mother and the future queen of England. She was beautiful and good and was honoured as the mother of the Prince's children. The Prince respected her and insisted that everybody did the same. And there his commitment to his marriage ended. For Albert Edward also knew the royal rules, which were quite different for princes than for lesser mortals. Traditionally there had always been a double standard which prescribed that while the royal wife stayed faithful, the husband was allowed his freedom, provided scandal was avoided. This was an appealing doctrine for the Prince, and the skill with which he made it work made him something of a role model for the livelier male members of the House of Windsor, even to the present day. But as a royal adulterer Albert Edward had advantages over his royal successors. Television had not been invented; there was no prying mass media; and his friends and the members of the court were terribly discreet.

Soon, the Prince was being called the 'Bismarck of Society', because his power was as absolute as the German Iron Chancellor's, and the more Society circled round him, the less could dignified Lord Spencer hope to influence his behaviour. As a Whig grandee, Spencer was not a narrow-minded man. He was a man of decency and breeding, married to a wife he loved, and his ownership of Spencer House made him a pillar of very grand and highly respectable London society, which had little contact with the so-called 'Fast Set' round the Prince. When the two worlds met there could be trouble, as was shown early in 1866 when something relatively trivial changed the whole pattern of Lord Spencer's life for ever.

An inelegant but fearless horseman, the Prince of Wales had often hunted with the Pytchley and when the Earl arranged a hunt dinner at Althorp, he inevitably invited the Prince as guest of honour. But among his chosen friends and followers, the Prince was becoming increasingly addicted to what was known as 'fun'. Fun was the pastime of the Victorian idle rich, and involved practical jokes like apple pie beds and sewn-up jackets. But for the Prince of Wales, fun came with a difference. Royal fun was generally at the expense of others – never of himself – as the fate of the unfortunate Christopher Sykes demonstrated.

Sykes, the owner of a Mayfair mansion and a stately home in Yorkshire, was among the most slavishly devoted of the Prince's followers. One evening over dinner at the Marlborough Club, the Prince, having nothing better to do, poured a glass of brandy over Sykes's head and watched it trickle slowly down his collar.

How to respond to such an act? Ignore it? Leave the table? Sykes, the perfect courtier, had what appeared to be the perfect answer. Unshaken and apparently unstirred, he simply murmured, 'As Your Royal Highness pleases.'

Everybody laughed; and the Prince, who loved to be the source of laughter, was glad to have invented a new party game. From now on no princely dinner party was complete without the presence of the loyal Sykes as victim for the Prince who, to loud applause, would cheerfully assail the wretched man with soda water, fine Champagne, or hock and seltzer. Finally, of course, the joke wore thin, the Prince grew bored and Sykes, no longer a source of amusement, was abandoned by his friends, sinking into relative oblivion.

Lord Spencer's dignity and rank protected him from anything remotely similar, but on the evening of the Pytchley dinner, the Prince was tempted. He knew how deeply his Groom of the Stole disliked tobacco, but since extremely large cigars were something of a symbol of the Prince's own priapic nature, what fun to make Lord Spencer smoke one. After dinner, with everybody watching, the Prince took out his great cigar case monogrammed in gold, and offered Lord Spencer a jumbo-sized Havana.

The Prince knew – and everybody present knew – that the offer was tantamount to a command. And with unshaken dignity, Lord Spencer responded as a courtier should. He accepted the cigar, cut it, ignited it and smoked it to the bitter end in silence. It was a stylish performance, and nothing more was said. But a few days later Lord Spencer resigned as Groom of the Stole to the Prince of Wales. This time his resignation was accepted.

Resignation left Lord Spencer unemployed, but not for long. There were in fact two things Lord Balfour had omitted from his list of Lord Spencer's virtues – one was courage, the other was a remarkable capacity for sheer hard work. Once engaged he could be enormously industrious. Like most Spencers, he lacked any claims to eloquence and so had little chance to make his parliamentary name through oratory. But when appointed chairman of the parliamentary Cattle Plague Committee, he worked at the subject with such diligence that he caught the attention of the Liberal leader, Mr Gladstone

In 1868, when the Liberals returned to power, Mr Gladstone had difficulty finding anyone suitable for the post of Irish Viceroy. As the Queen's representative in Ireland, the Viceroy had to be an aristocrat with sufficient private wealth to cover his expenses, which were estimated at twice the official salary of £20,000 a year. At the same time, the Viceroy had to be in political sympathy with the government's declared intention of 'pacifying Ireland'.

When Lord Hartington and Lord Halifax both refused the honour, Mr Gladstone turned to young Lord Spencer, who, despite his total inexperience of high political position, accepted with alacrity. He was anxious, as he said, 'to be of use', and when the Spencers took up residence as the Queen's official representatives in Dublin Castle, Mr Gladstone got exactly the loyal and dignified representative in Ireland that he needed. The Countess, although still childless, was as popular and forthright as the Earl was dignified and shy. Hiding behind his bright red whiskers, which earned him the inevitable nickname of 'the Red Earl', John Poyntz Spencer was an impressive figure and he and his wife enjoyed the splendour and prestige of their position, presiding like royalty in St Patrick's Hall in Dublin Castle.

They also enjoyed the less formal side of Irish life, with Lady

Spencer visiting the poor and her husband hunting regularly with the Meath and the Kildare, and doggedly attempting to teach the Irish the rudiments of cricket on the lawns of Dublin Castle.

Politically, Lord Spencer's inexperience suited Mr Gladstone, for it meant that as Viceroy he was perfectly prepared to follow his leader's Irish policy to the letter. So it was not entirely Lord Spencer's fault if Mr Gladstone's plan to disestablish the Church of Ireland produced much argument but little satisfaction both in Ireland and Westminster. It was much the same with Gladstone's highly complicated Land Act of 1870, while his cherished plan of creating a non sectarian university in Dublin caused such a furore in Ireland – even Spencer called it 'a very ticklish affair' – that it helped bring down the Gladstone government in 1874.

It also brought Lord Spencer's five year-stint in Dublin Castle to an end. It had been an expensive and at times a gruelling period, which had cost him something in the region of £100,000, in addition to the expense of maintaining both Spencer House and Althorp in his absence. But the Earl and his Countess had undoubtedly enjoyed the splendour and the adulation of their five years reigning over Irish Society. Charlotte later said this period had been 'the happiest five years of my life', and her husband was proud to be returning to his home at Althorp as what he felt a Spencer ought to be – a figure of acknowledged national importance. If it had cost him £20,000 a year, he undoubtedly considered it was worth it.

The extravagance so evident throughout this period, was undoubtedly connected with the childless state of the Earl and Lady Spencer. Had they had children and an heir to inherit and carry on the line, they would have been forced to pay more serious attention to the future, and worry over who would pay for their extravagances if the economic climate changed and their income faltered. Instead it was now that Lord and Lady Spencer embarked upon the busiest, most ostentatious and certainly the most expensive period of their lives.

On the face of it they now had everything a noble couple could desire – celebrity, prestige, considerable possessions and a great position in society; at the same time the absence of children meant that they were that much more dependent on each other, and had yet more time for friends and politics and entertaining. Spencer himself enthusiastically embarked on a second and triumphant period as Master of the Pytchley which underlined his position as social leader of the county.

Ever since resigning from the court, relations between the Earl and the Prince of Wales had stayed distinctly cool, but Althorp and the Spencers were suddenly enhanced by a more glamorous and dramatic royal presence than overweight Prince Albert Edward. They had first got to know the horse-mad Empress Elizabeth of Austria in the hunting field in Ireland, and the friendship grew – particularly when the Earl appointed as her guide and companion one of the finest riders and most accomplished womanisers in the country, Captain 'Bay' Middleton, who soon became her lover.

Throughout this period the Austrian Empress added enormously to the glamour and allure of hunting with her dashing presence and her hour-glass figure. She also added to the glamour and allure of her friends the Spencers, and it was largely to make Althorp fit to receive Her Imperial Highness that extensive alterations were begun at Althorp by the fashionable architect, MacVicar Anderson. These alterations proved to be the most expensive work the house had seen since the second Earl virtually rebuilt it in the 1790s, and from 1876 to 1878 the Spencers actually moved out and lived at Harleston Hall, which they also owned, while the work was finished.

The South wing was largely rebuilt, the staircase hall enlarged to take what was left of the interior courtyard, the great staircase itself returned from white to natural wood, and Holland's blue sitting room with Pernotin's painted panels was re-sited and restored for the use of the Empress. She duly came and stayed at Althorp, and in 1878 her hosts were rewarded with an invitation back to Hungary as official guests of the Empress and Austro-Hungarian Emperor Franz Josef.

Shy though he was, the Earl was also vain and quietly determined to assert himself. Because of this, towards the end of the 1870s, his expenditure rose to a peak in spite of the great agricultural depression already looming. In addition to all the work at Althorp, he refused to restrict the work in London either, and he and Charlotte felt the time had come to bring Spencer House to the highest flights of Victorian fashion.

The Earl became impressed by the fashionable architect Frederick Sang, who proposed repainting and decorating the entire interior in the style of a baroque Italian palace, complete with coloured Italian marble pavements and painted ceilings. Although the Countess was also very much in favour, they settled instead for the more restrained but equally expensive second Empire-style interior the famous French decorator Barbier evolved for them, with an Earl's ransom in silk damask, French furniture and velvet hangings.

During this period, Spencer House played a key role in the social and political life of London. According to Lord Elcho, the Red Earl had three personal advantages as a politician which he defined as 'station, wealth and a large Whig house in the centre of London'. These were advantages Spencer was determined to exploit, and he and the Countess continued entertaining on the most ambitious scale. This undoubtedly helped his political career and Spencer House became famous for its grandiose receptions. When he was actually in government his house was often used for informal meetings of the Cabinet.

The food at Spencer House was famous – as was the Earl for the 'Spencer appetite'. After a lengthy meal he once devoured a large apricot tart, and for several years in the 1880s he employed one of the most famous chefs in London, Monsieur Beguinot, formerly chef to the Duc de Morny. As late as 1881, there were still twenty-nine resident servants in Spencer House.

By then the series of appalling harvests at the end of the 1870s was affecting the English landed interest like the sudden change of climate which destroyed the dinosaurs. In 1879 the Earl was already being forced to borrow £15,000 to meet excess expenditure. By 1885 his overall income had declined by £20,000 a year, and the decline continued to the end of the century, with Althorp particularly hard hit, its rents dropping from £21,000 in 1890 to £12,000 five years later.

The Earl, with the optimism born of a lifetime's effortless superiority, refused to waste time worrying or trying to solve what, by its nature, was insoluble. Instead he went on borrowing, including a loan for £9,000 in 1887 for just one year's expenses as Master of the precious Pytchley.

He was not in a position to give much personal attention to such mundane matters as debts and mortgages. For in 1882, in the very middle of the crisis, he was once more summoned to the call of duty by the voice of Mr Gladstone asking him to serve a second term in Dublin Castle. And once again, despite the cost, the inconvenience and the danger, the Earl responded out of loyalty to the Chief and longing for political success.

Virtually his first task was to cope with the aftermath of the murder of his friend and kinsman, the newly appointed Irish Secretary, Lord Frederick Cavendish, in Dublin's Phoenix Park. Spencer had actually been riding on ahead when Lord Frederick and his under-secretary, T.H. Burke, were knifed to death by a gang calling themselves 'The Invincibles'. For Spencer it was a murder in the family, and his tears revealed a streak of untypical emotion behind his normally impassive nature.

The murder convinced him of the need to deal with the current wave of violence, and by his ruthlessness and courage he seemed to be getting close to pacifying Ireland by coercion when his period in Dublin Castle ended in 1885. But by now Mr Gladstone had arrived at a somewhat different decision – to grant Home Rule to Ireland. And, as usual, when Mr Gladstone changed his mind, Lord Spencer did the same.

Back in England, debts were troubling him. While he was still in Ireland, his solicitor had reported having trouble raising a £40,000 mortgage and the situation was so serious that Lord Spencer was forced to consider leaving Ireland to take on the more lucrative – and peaceful – Viceroyship of India.

When he murmured something in Cabinet about 'rather liking the idea of elephants and rajahs', Gladstone instantly retorted: 'Of course, Lord Spencer has only to raise his little finger in order to have it placed absolutely at his disposal.'

One wonders why Lord Spencer did not raise his little finger. One reason was almost certainly his wife, who loved entertaining and insisted that she had never been happier than when in Dublin or in London. He also hated the idea of leaving England and his hunting. But his most conclusive reason for continuing to pile up debt by remaining in London was political ambition. With Gladstone ageing, the premiership would soon go begging, and Delhi would have placed it firmly out of Spencer's reach for ever.

In 1885, when Gladstone campaigned actively for Home Rule and split the Liberal party, Spencer almost alone among the Liberal grandees stood with him – even if cynics did remark that since the Spencers had no estates in Ireland, they had nothing personally to lose by giving Ireland to the Irish. Having once made up his mind, Lord Spencer was immovable, and he was at his best as he stuck by his leader and his principles. This cannot have been easy. Irish Home Rule was an emotive issue, particularly among the royal family and the higher reaches of the Establishment. The Duchess of Teck described Spencer as 'a convert – or should I say a pervert – to the cause of Home Rule'. Queen Victoria ceased inviting him to dinner. And as for the Prince of Wales, he solemnly remarked: 'I lose for ever the high opinion I once had of him', and never forgave him.

But with Mr Gladstone's Home Rule plans now splitting the Liberals, Lord Spencer's sacrifice was made in vain, for the Gladstone government was defeated, Ireland failed to get its independence, and staunch Lord Spencer found himself in limbo, facing the twin realities of political failure and financial disaster.

Back from Ireland in 1885, the Earl took on a third term as Master of the Pytchley almost out of habit, but he was not as happy or carefree now as in the past. His thoughts were on finance, not foxes, for with £14,000 going out each year on the Hunt alone, it was clear that if nothing was done, Lord Spencer would go bankrupt.

At Althorp there was one obvious asset – the greatest private library in Europe. The Earl put on a good show of pretending that the very thought of selling it pained him deeply. But one feels that the man who according to Margot Asquith 'had never opened a book for pleasure, and believed Jane Eyre was written by George Eliot' cannot have been totally distraught to see the back of so many books that he would never read.

He wrote to the Librarian at the British Museum, 'It would be a matter of concern for me to be obliged to deprive the house of the books which have such a great reputation, and are a monument of the book learning and collecting industry of my grandfather.' But the agricultural depression was making it 'extremely difficult for me to keep locked up the large amount of capital which the books here represent'.

He did not hesitate too long. By the end of July 1892 the deal was done and the greatest private library in Europe went to the John Rylands library at Manchester University for £250,000.

Writing to his half-brother, Bobby Spencer, the Earl admitted that the sale had left him feeling 'rather depressed', but he had convinced himself that it had been his duty to do it. 'I could not have gone on as I have been doing for the last twelve or thirteen years, and believe me of what at times was intolerable, the feeling that I had no right to go on even in the very reduced way which we have adopted for the some years past, and I saw no way out of the difficulty.'

At less than £6 a volume the sale was less a deal than a steal, and today a single Caxton could fetch more than the Earl received for the whole collection. In the circumstances it is hard to criticise him for the sale – although it is hard to believe that by trying just a little harder he could not have got considerably better terms for such a totally unique collection.

Where he seems to have been genuinely irresponsible was in the way he used the money to continue living much as he had before. A few years later, when the Duke of Devonshire sold Devonshire House to make space for offices and car showrooms, much of the million pound profit was shrewdly invested in the Canadian Pacific Railway. But the nearest Lord Spencer came to investing his own little windfall was to install electric light at Spencer House. The money also permitted Lady Spencer to redecorate the house yet again to make it fit to receive Queen Victoria.

There was a further reason why Lord Spencer still refused to think of serious economies. True Spencer that he was, it was against his nature to be provident. In addition, the lure of power still tempted him and a hint of poverty might have hurt his prospects when Mr Gladstone formed his fourth administration after the election of 1892, and appointed Lord Spencer to the position of Lord President of the Council.

With Gladstone now in his eighties, someone would soon be called upon to succeed him as premier, and Spencer was aware of his chances. For the second time in his life, he reluctantly declined the Viceroyship of India and became instead First Lord of the Admiralty. Ironically it was as head of the Admiralty that Lord Spencer won his greatest political victory, when for the first time in his long political career he disagreed with Mr Gladstone.

This began in 1893 when the collision of two British men of war in the Mediterranean, with heavy loss of life, started a nationwide panic campaign to build more warships. As Roy Jenkins writes in his biography of Gladstone, this campaign was not entirely logical, since 'it was not obvious that the answer to British ships running into each other was to have more of them'. But logic had never been Lord Spencer's strongest point, and when the admirals and *The Times* began an emotional campaign to build more ships, Lord Spencer was converted. And once he had 'swallowed the arguments of the admirals whole', he became a formidable adversary against Mr Gladstone.

When Gladstone was defeated over Lord Spencer's increased navy estimates he instantly resigned the premiership; and thanks to the man who had been among the most loyal of his supporters, the Grand Old Man's long career in politics was over.

As Gladstone had feared, the sudden growth in British warship construction was answered by increased naval building programmes among other nations, particularly Germany, which are often claimed to be among the many causes of the First World War. But Lord Spencer's navy estimates had another unexpected result, which would prove perhaps his most disastrous lasting legacy to the aristocracy, and especially the Spencers, to the present day.

In 1894 the Chancellor of the Exchequer, Sir William Harcourt, finding himself hard pushed to fund Lord Spencer's naval building programme, decided on a novel tax – death duties on a sliding scale, so that on their death the largest landowners were to make the greatest contribution to the Exchequer. Among the hardest hit would be the Spencers.

From now until his death, the Red Earl was never free from money troubles. It was a galling situation, for just when his public role and reputation had never been higher, his private income and the state of his affairs had never sunk lower.

As a young man he had started out as the richest and most hopeful Spencer Earl for a century. Now with age he found himself afflicted by the constant scourge of the House of Spencer which he once believed he had evaded – chronic and persistent debt.

There was not a great deal to be done about it now, but had he been cleverer or less profligate, things might been different. Instead there were more economies, which filled his later years with a sort of nagging sorrow. An Earl Spencer should simply not be short of money, but since he was, he dismissed staff, closed up Althorp for six months every summer, let Spencer House and took Charlotte off to Egypt for the winter. This was something that a childless couple could do – and without the responsibility for children their money worries must have been easier to bear. But it must have been particularly lonely for the childless Earl when in 1903 his wife, Charlotte, died quite suddenly after a cancer operation. This had been performed a few months earlier in Spencer House by one of the earliest female surgeons, Dr Mary Scharlieb.

'Charlotte left us in a sleep of perfect peace and beauty,' wrote her husband, and there is something touching in the last impression of this lonely nobleman keeping up appearances in old age at the end of so long a line. Just as the pre-eminence of the early Spencers had been built on economy and money, so the absence of both was undermining them.

Mounting costs would all but overwhelm the Earl and he had always lacked the foresight – and brutality – that might have eased the situation. Instead, with unerring misjudgement, John Poyntz almost always made the wrong decisions.

The contrast with more successful aristocrats was cruel but telling. With the Red Earl, there had been no heiresses, no mineral rights, no children and finally no premiership. Just as the early Spencers had always been lucky, so he was hit by terribly bad luck. Had he not had the two fatal strokes just before the Liberal victory in December 1905, he might still have been prime minister, making his whole career appear worthwhile. The winner of that particular battle, Campbell Bannerman, was only two years younger and had only two more years to live himself.

As it was, the Earl never entirely recovered from the two strokes and his health began to worsen. When he resigned his Lord Lieutenantship of Northamptonshire in 1908, he received the coolest of replies from his former friend, the King, who had a long memory and had never forgiven him for backing Home Rule for Ireland.

Towards the end, Lord Spencer's mind began to wander. Bobby Spencer, who for many years had been his heir, remained loyally with him at Althorp and was with him when he died. He described what happened: 'He did not suffer at all, I think, though there was a fearful restlessness always to get home . . . Then the idea of hunting, actually insisting on getting up fairly early to be in time to start, and our helplessness to convince him that there was no hunting and that he was in his own house – all this was a strain . . . At last he took to his bed, but his strength was such that even then he tried to dress on purpose to get home. I was with him when the blessed peace came to him and he gently sighed his life away.

'I had the ribbon of the Garter put on him, and later when he lay in the big hall, I covered him with the mantle of the Garter.'

CHAPTER 12

'Dearest Boy'

Charles Robert, sixth Earl Spencer (1857–1922)

Once he had placed the mantle of the Garter over the large recumbent body of his brother, Charles Robert, who found himself now sixth Earl Spencer, had to take stock of his situation.

He was fifty-three, in poor health and without a wife. He did not hunt, he did not particularly enjoy the country, and he did not wish to live permanently at Althorp. In his latter years his brother had let Althorp go, and Bobby had no idea how, if ever, he would sort the problems out, what with the death duties, the condition of the estates and the whole chaotic muddle.

For that matter, how could he possibly live up to that larger-than-life character? His half-brother had been 'King' of Northamptonshire, but Bobby Spencer knew that he could never be a king. He was a courtier, and for several years his life had been totally taken up with his work at court and the lives and activities of Their Majesties. To leave them, and retreat to Althorp, would be like going into exile.

While the Red Earl was alive, he and Bobby had made a most unlikely double act; the Earl so tall and bearded, and Bobby so cleanly shaved and barbered. There was always something birdlike about Bobby with his winged moustaches, high pitched voice and what his friend Eddie Marsh once called his 'deliciously petulant way of speaking'. As a young man he was very vain and something of a dandy. He dressed immaculately and was proud of the sartorial trademark which he had long ago adopted – the four-inch high stiff white collars which were specially made for him by one of London's most fashionable shirt-makers in Jermyn Street.

But the truth was that Bobby's succession to the earldom meant more than just a change of personalities. The gusto and extravagance which the Red Earl had spread so heedlessly around him had departed. With his death an air of sadness seemed to fall upon the family. For behind the four-inch collars and the winged moustaches was a deeply melancholy man. Even the circumstances of Bobby Spencer's birth had been part of a Victorian tragedy.

In 1855 Lady Stanley of Alderley who was staying at Althorp had written to her husband about Fritz's young wife, Yaddy: 'Lady Spencer is delicate. She never comes down in the morning and lies in the evening with her feet up. I suppose she is trying to make a little Spencer.'

She was indeed. Yaddy already had a daughter, Lady Victoria, known to one and all as Va, but Fritz was anxious for a second son and in October 1857 she gave him what he wanted in the shape of Charles Robert.

Bobby's arrival was greeted joyfully. Fritz doted on his young wife, and she on him. He was apparently in perfect health, and the mysterious illness which hit the Earl in the midst of all their happiness on the very eve of Christmas, seemed particularly cruel. Within a few days thirty-two-year-old Yaddy found herself a widow.

In its abruptness, Fritz's death foreshadowed that of Prince Albert four years later, and Yaddy herself now acted much as the widowed Queen Victoria would do. Mourning became her way of life, and the bereft and deeply pious widow saw her delicate son as a gift sent specially from God to console her for the husband He had taken. She treasured him, and for the rest of her life was almost totally obsessed with him. The result was predictable, with Bobby growing up a spoiled and solitary mother's darling. Apart from his sister, he had few companions.

Yaddy was less concerned about her daughter, Victoria, who eventually married Lord Sandhurst. But living her life for and through her son, the moment Yaddy dreaded most was the day he left for Harrow, and his long absences at boarding school became a source of misery for them both. She wrote to him every day, and the correspondence from this lonely widow to her 'Dearest, Dearest Boy', laboriously penned on black-edged paper, is extraordinary. For here in these innocently pre-Freudian times is a classic case of a mother besottedly in love with her beautiful male child who inevitably becomes what, subconsciously at least, she longs for him to be – dependent, delicate and over-sensitive.

Inevitably he learned the art of using illness to get what he wanted out of life and those around him. One sees him doing this already when, at seventeen, he decided he had had enough of Harrow. Towards the end of January 1875, Yaddy was writing anxiously to him at school – 'My Own *Own* Boy, I hope the changes of tonic may do your poor head real good my precious . . . God Almighty bless you and prosper you my own.'

The change of tonic must have worked, for all was well, and it was not until the end of the summer holidays that the threat of school brought a recurrence of Bobby's headaches – and his mother's unhappiness at losing him again.

'My Dearest Boy, I can never tell you, never, what it cost me to send you back last Wednesday – and it was all I could do to do it – and as it happened I had better not as I have only given you more suffering, my poor, poor darling.'

By now Bobby's headaches must have been enough to persuade the school authorities to send him home for good, and soon his mother was writing with the news that they would soon be reunited. 'And so end my letters to you as a school boy my own dearest child . . . Most precious boy. How I do miss you. I'm sure no one has a Boy like mine. Such a good dear contented helpful Boy. God will bless you, my own, for all your goodness to me, my old Darling.'

Robert Charles was just twenty when his mother died without warning and he seems to have bottled up his grief as he always would throughout his life. Freed from the suffocating love of Yaddy, he appeared transformed and positively light-hearted among his friends.

Having loved his stepmother dearly, the Red Earl dedicated the new panelling in St Mary's Great Brington to her memory. He also looked after his younger brother, and it was through his patronage that Bobby, at the age of twenty-two, became the youngest member of the House of Commons, representing what was still effectively the Spencer family seat of Northamptonshire as a Liberal.

Although not a dedicated politician like his brother, Bobby Spencer held the seat for over twenty years and was widely admired in the House for what his mother would have wanted him to be – elegant, witty, and the best dressed man in Parliament.

With his stylish dress and perfect manners he was also a popular social figure, and as such had little difficulty impressing the grandest London hostesses, including middle-aged Lady Holland who liked to have devoted young admirers around her. She was the last of the great Whig hostesses, and when Bobby told her how much he wished he had had a chance to meet Charles James Fox, she replied, 'Believe me, my dear, so do I, but then we should not be alive today, my dear, and the alternative is rather depressing.'

She was a perfect mother substitute for the handsome Bobby. His delicate health attracted her devotion and soon a distinctly arch flirtation had begun between them. Before long she too was writing to him as 'My dearest love', and 'My Dear, Dear Bobby'.

It is intriguing that Lady Holland ended her letters to Bobby using the private language which his distant Aunt Georgiana Devonshire had invented when she wrote to Dearest Bess, and which was still sometimes used in Whig society: 'Take care of yourself, dearest Don Roberto, and I'se 'appy'.

Bobby Spencer seemed so completely in his element as a social figure, that his friends were puzzled when, at twenty-eight, he was struck with a mysterious depressive illness. A note has been preserved from Sir William Gill, the fashionable physician: 'I was unhappy to find you so depressed yesterday. I have analysed the contents of the bottle and find it quite satisfactory.'

His urine sample may have been satisfactory, but something was obviously amiss and Bobby's doctors recommended a period of total rest in the winter sunshine of Madeira. Here he started to recover, but one feels that more therapeutic than the sunshine was the letter he received just after Christmas Day on heavily embossed paper from Marlborough House.

My Dear Bobby,
How kind of you to send me such a charming Christmas present. I envy you spending this season of the year in so charming a climate and trust that you are feeling all the better for it.
I send you a Tiffany cigarette case as my Xmas offering and trust that you will sometimes use it.
From yours very sincerely,
Albert Edward.

This letter from the Prince of Wales and the Tiffany cigarette case that accompanied it mark an important moment in the life of the Honourable Robert Spencer, showing that he had made it to the topmost reaches of society. Early in the New Year he returned to London and five weeks later he received a second letter from Marlborough House in the same unmistakable handwriting.

My Dear Bobby,
Many thanks for writing to tell me that Mr Gladstone has submitted your name to the Queen as Parliamentary Groom in Waiting. I congratulate you sincerely on this appointment which I was very anxious for you to obtain. My only regret is that you form part of a Home Rule group.

Obviously the Irish Home Rule problem was still worrying the Prince, but although the office of Parliamentary Groom in Waiting was a political appointment, which made Bobby one of the Liberal whips in Parliament, it also gave him a ceremonial position in the court.

It was now that Bobby realised the time had come to marry. Living the life he did, he might not have bothered but for a serious misfortune which for the second time within the century had struck the Spencers.

His brother and sister-in-law were childless and with the Countess now in her early forties it seemed they would undoubtedly remain so. Bobby was suddenly expected to provide the son and heir his brother could not.

He might have taken his distant Marlborough cousins as examples. Nine years earlier his near contemporary, Lord Randolph Churchill, had gone to America to find an heiress and returned with the ravishing Jennie Jerome, who provided an explosive boost to the bloodline of the Spencer Churchills by giving birth in Blenheim Palace in 1874 to his cousin Winston. A few years later another of Bobby's distant cousins, the young duke 'Sunny' Marlborough, was to land the richest American heiress of them all – Commodore Vanderbilt's daughter, Consuelo.

Bobby had no intention of going to America to find a bride, so he chose an heiress nearer home, settling for eighteen-year-old Margaret Baring, daughter of Edward Baring First Baron Revelstoke, head of the great banking house of Baring Brothers.

The Barings were no ordinary bankers. Having come to England from Germany in the 1770s, they established the great financial house by lending to the government of William Pitt. The Barings had subsequently married into the aristocracy, and on Margaret's marriage Lord Revelstoke promised his daughter the adequate but not enormous allowance of £5,000 a year.

Homely Margaret was the perfect wife for Bobby, being the sort of gentle, motherly figure he needed, and he grew to love her, as he also came to love her family, whose cosmopolitan, highly civilised life-style, must have seemed particularly attractive after the political and hunting world of the Spencers. In contrast, the exotic Barings could have been a race apart, with their love of music and the arts, their private language, and their obsession with all things French. This included speaking French at meals – a habit which Bobby soon adopted. Indeed in many ways he seemed to be becoming more of a Baring than a Spencer, and although Margaret was twelve years younger he became totally dependent on his loving wife whose younger brother would become the celebrated writer, Maurice Baring, and who, having studied music in Paris with violinist Joachim, would play lullabies to their children on her Stradivarius.

They enjoyed a comfortable rather than a luxurious life together. His brother, the Red Earl, offered them the use of 28 St James's Place, next door to Spencer House, along with Dallington House in Northampton, and the greatly-needed children started to arrive – in 1889 a daughter, Adelaide, known as Delia; in 1892 a son and heir, christened Albert Edward John, but always known as Jack; two further sons, Cecil and George, born in 1894 and 1902; and a daughter, Lavinia, born in 1899.

Although Margaret was a Baring, she and Bobby were not considered particularly rich by the standards of the society they inhabited – especially when Lord Revelstoke, through lunatic investments in the Argentine, all but bankrupted Baring Brothers in 1890. Bobby offered to forego Margaret's annual income. As the Bank of England gallantly bailed out Barings Bank, the sacrifice was not required, but it so impressed one of Bobby's rich banking friends, Baron Ferdinand de Rothschild, that he left him a legacy of £10,000.

Bobby had always been a snob, but one of that refined variety that can find true satisfaction only in the very highest reaches of Society. Baron Ferdinand had presumably belonged there, but the truly favoured recipients of Bobby's admiration were the members of the Royal Family. He knew them personally, visited the Palace regularly, and took care to send them presents every Christmas. By now, he was steadily ascending the royal ladder. In 1895, when the Liberals were again returned to office, he was appointed Vice Chamberlain with the duty of standing in for the Lord Chamberlain during his absences from the court. Then, with the Liberal landslide of 1905, he was tipped for the post of Lord Chamberlain himself.

Although the main courtiers were appointed by the Prime Minister, the court had clung on grimly to the principle that those closest to the monarch had to be chosen from the upper aristocracy, but few Liberal peers were suitable or willing to accept the demanding post of Lord Chamberlain. King Edward was hoping that his bridge-playing friend, Lord Carrington, who as W.H. Smith had founded the famous firm of newsagents, would accept; but knowing what the work entailed, Lord Carrington wisely pleaded ill health and declined.

The obvious candidate was Bobby, but according to King Edward's friend, Sir Lionel Cust, when the new premier, Campbell-Bannerman, suggested him, the King was not enthusiastic. He still suspected him of radical tendencies, like his brother's, particularly over the issue of Ireland. But Cust added that Bobby's obsession with etiquette and protocol weighed in his favour and in the absence of other candidates, he was chosen. There was still one minor problem. Although heir-apparent to the Spencer earldom, he lacked the necessary title, and it had to be arranged for him to be made Lord Althorp in his own right.

With a peerage, a stipend of £2,000 a year and an important court appointment, Bobby was in his element at last, at the very apex of Society. As Lord Chamberlain his finest hour had come, and he was happy.

Such good fortune could not last. Margaret, who had always had a calming influence on her husband's obsession with the monarchy, managed to remain devoted to her family and the children, and when at Christmas she discovered she was once more pregnant, she was perfectly content. By now, her homely sister, Susan, had married Sir James Reid, the royal doctor, and Sir James himself assured Bobby that at thirty-eight his wife was strong and healthy and that there was no cause for worry.

But on 4 July 1906, when Margaret went into labour in the middle of the night, she lost consciousness nearly at once. A healthy baby girl was delivered at 3 a.m., but by then the doctor was so worried about Margaret's health that he called Sir James. When Sir James arrived, however, there was nothing to be done.

'On going into the room I found poor Margaret looking as if she were dying – we did all we could with strong remedies, oxygen, etc., but she never revived and died quietly at 6. It was heart failure, and I think an attack of influenza she had a month ago, which lasted three weeks, had left her heart in a weakened condition. Susan came in just before she died, and Margaret recognised her and said "my boys", meaning that Susan should look after them.'

The unexpected death brought widespread sympathy – ranging from letters of condolence from the King and Queen, to an estimated crowd of 5,000 at Margaret's funeral at Great Brington. In the words of a local reporter, 'It was a strangely pathetic procession from Althorp House to the church on the hill a mile away. Behind the coffin walked the solitary figure of Lord Althorp, who bore up bravely under his unspeakable grief, but how deeply his sorrow was shared became touchingly manifest as the procession passed through respectful crowds that lined the route, for many were unable to control their emotion.'

Somehow Bobby controlled *his* grief and, just as when his mother died, he refused to speak about his feelings. It was somehow typical of him that the one occasion when he did was in a letter to his future King. Thanking Prince George for his letter of condolence he replied: 'I cannot realise it all at present, though I know that my life's object for nineteen happy years has been taken from me, and I have to live on for our children's sake, though the longing to rejoin my beloved Margaret almost overpowers me. Life's burden seems so heavy, but it must be born and such warm sympathy as You Royal Highnesses are showing to me helps me.'

Just as Yaddy mourned Bobby's father for the rest of her life, so Bobby went on mourning Margaret. But however deep his sorrow and however much he may have blamed himself for her death, he always managed to suppress his feelings. He kept his sorrow to himself, and could not bring himself to speak about her. As the children followed his example, none of them really came to terms with their grief at their mother's passing. According to the youngest daughter, who was named Margaret in her memory, 'None of her six children ever recovered from her death or ceased to miss her.'

Bobby was forty-nine when Margaret died and, curiously, her death appeared to set the seal on Bobby's absolute obsession with his life at court, as he tried to fill the gap she left behind her. Helped by the Reids, he brought the six children up as best he could, with his eldest daughter, sixteen-year-old Delia in her mother's role. Delia was kind and caring to the children, but even she could never quite forgive the baby Margaret for having caused her mother's death.

As for Bobby the minutiae of court life now occupied his life completely and helped to fill the place of Margaret. Within two months of her death he was in Berlin, where King Edward was busy visiting the Kaiser and he seemed to have totally recovered from his loss. Writing home Sir James Reid said, 'Bobby is all right, very fussy, but quite in his element and delights us all.'

But the fussiness increased and with it the desperate involvement in all things royal. Along with his other court responsibilities, Bobby was kept busy in his role as theatrical censor, which was part of the duties of Lord Chamberlain. He was soon banning a performance of Gilbert and Sullivan's *Mikado* for fear of offending the Japanese Crown Prince Fushimi during a state visit. In fact there was something almost Japanese in the profundity of Bobby's reverence for the monarchy, which began to show in his letters to the royal personages. When King Edward finally expired in 1910, he wrote as follows to King George V: 'The Lord Chamberlain ventures most respectfully to hope that the heart-stirring though silent sympathy of the vast crowds of Your Majesty's subjects may have somehow helped Your Majesty in his crushing sorrow.'

But the grand climacteric of Bobby's life as a courtier was still to come. In the Windsor archives is a large red ledger marked 'Preparations for the Coronation'. In its neatly-written pages, one sees something of the sheer extent of the Lord Chamberlain's duties and involvement:

Queen's robes – Are they safeguarded from moth in the Tower?
The stole – H.M. to approve of the design.
Queen's crown – H.M. asks for sketch of.
His Late Majesty's robes – request for permission to sketch. (Declined.)
Breeches – Submitting General Greely's application to wear trousers instead of. (Refused.)
Duchess of Coburg to rank as Princess of Great Britain? (Yes.)

By the time a very weary Bobby entered the Abbey in his robes and coronet, bearing his white wand of office at the new King's Coronation his life at court was all but over. He was genuinely ailing now with a heart condition which had already kept this most faithful of courtiers from attending two investitures. When the King and Queen departed for fresh triumphs at the Delhi Durbar, Bobby was not included in the party due to ill health. And on his return from India, the King received another deeply deferential letter from his ever faithful chamberlain.

'The Lord Chamberlain presents his humble duty to Your Majesty and ventures respectfully to congratulate Your Majesty and the Queen on the triumphant success of the whole of Your Majesty's Indian journey.

'Earl Spencer regrets bitterly to have to inform Your Majesty that owing to the state of his health he has been forced by his doctor and his surgeon to consider the necessity of a somewhat prolonged rest abroad. Lord Spencer would not have considered this, only it appears from the doctor's report that his health, for the remainder of his life, depends on his taking this long rest. Under the circumstances Lord Spencer reluctantly has come to the inevitable conclusion that he must respectfully ask Your Majesty to be graciously pleased to allow him to hand in the resignation of his office of Lord Chamberlain.'

With this most courtly of letters, Lord Spencer's career as a courtier, which had been the glory of his life, was over. True, the King had given him the Garter, and Althorp was awaiting his attention, but neither took the place of the splendour and excitement he had known in the service of his royal masters. His health was doubtful, his children were growing up, and he was bored and ill and lonely.

Just occasionally he still had contact with the Royal Family. In 1913 when the King and Queen attended military manoeuvres in Northamptonshire they stayed two nights at Althorp, and for those two brief days Bobby was a courtier again. Between rain showers, a group photograph was taken of them all sitting in the garden, and that night His Majesty was by royal standards positively effusive when writing up his diary: 'Back to Althorp. Dined at 8.30. Looked at Bobby's lovely rooms full of beautiful pictures. Bed at 11.00.'

In 1914, shortly before war broke out, there was just time for a twenty-first birthday party for his son Jack before he joined the First Life Guards and went to fight in France, where he was seriously wounded in the leg, and rescued from no-man's-land by a fellow officer. He was invalided back to England and was home by Christmas.

Bobby had never liked the House of Lords which, in contrast with the House of Commons, he found boring and unpleasant. But in the library he discovered a congenial spirit in the person of the man of letters, Edmund Gosse, who had recently published his masterpiece *Father and Son*. Gosse was clearly flattered by Lord Spencer's friendship, just as Lord Spencer, as a proudly intellectual man, liked discussing literature with a congenial writer such as Gosse. Soon they were writing regularly to one another and every week, from now until his death, Bobby would start his letter to Gosse with the two words, 'Cher Ami', and end it simply, 'Spencer'.

It is strange how alone he always seemed to be and how in need of friendship. Apart from his youngest daughter, Margaret, his family all had their own lives to lead, and had little time for the sick old man he was rapidly becoming. Money worries plagued him. He described himself as 'living in a small way and somewhat paralysed by financial difficulties, not of my own making.' He was right, of course. None of the debts was self-inflicted. He had inherited them from his brother, and before that from generations of the family who had so often overspent and failed to recoup or change their habits.

In 1915, to his infinite regret, he was forced to sell one of the gems of the Althorp collection, Rembrandt's *Portrait of a Boy*, for £35,000 in settlement of the most pressing of his debts. But the financial worries continued and, four years later, his collection of etchings followed the Rembrandt to the sale room.

One can appreciate the fearful emptiness of Bobby Spencer's

whole existence as the years passed. It seemed part of an overall decline within the family. After almost four centuries of extraordinary wealth and power the pre-eminence of the Spencers seemed to be drawing to a close in the person of this ageing aristocrat marooned among his pictures, with only his youngest daughter and her governess, Miss Wells, for company.

In 1921 he was sixty-three, and in the letters that he wrote to Gosse from Althorp he was lonely, sick and short of money. May had come, but he was physically cold, for, as he told his friend, there was insufficient fuel to keep the house warm, and 'the east wind seems to penetrate every cranny'.

Troubles were mounting up around him. 'There is an overdraft at the bank of "thousands and thousands". I sold another piece of property the other day, but the mortgagers at once took £9,000 of the purchase money. Of course quite right, but it was a blow.'

At the same time, his heart had weakened and he was having trouble with his teeth. 'A big tooth dragged out on Tuesday. So it goes on . . . How long I shall be "toothless Bob" I know not.' He was relying on laudanum to dull the pain. But his financial worries were a pain that would not go away.

Bobby could see no solution. As he saw it, the Spencers were finished, just as the landed aristocracy in general seemed finished. All he could think of doing was to close up Althorp but, as he told Gosse, 'preparations for shutting this house up more or less fill me with despair'.

He relied increasingly on his friendship with Gosse for company and support. In a moment of despair he begged Gosse, his 'cher ami', to come and see him. When Gosse said that he would come, Bobby's first reaction was delight, and the following week he wrote, 'What talks we will have. We will *retremper* [soak] ourselves in the gorgeous past.'

But a few days later came a note of caution as he warned his friend about the dullness of Althorp. Besides, he wrote, 'I am rather a feeble companion, as I do not walk much, and am rather a senile bore.'

Gosse arrived, stayed for a few days, and seemed to cheer him up. But soon after his departure, Bobby suffered two serious heart attacks within four days 'which shattered me'. He had been planning to go to the unveiling of King Edward VII's memorial, 'but there it was. I could not travel.'

He was cheered by news from his youngest son, George, now a midshipman on HMS *Hood* at Invergordon, who promised to spend a weekend at Althorp. But by October 1921 Bobby could no longer cope with the discomfort of another Althorp winter. He closed the house up and went to London. 'I left my dear home last Friday and am relieved at having got over the terrible wrench.'

He was annoyed when a newspaper reported him 'pleading poverty'. He retorted: 'I plead nothing except that owing to financial difficulties, I cannot go on at Althorp.' Others asked him if Althorp was for sale – 'A question of such impertinence that it deserves no answer.'

He remained the social snob he always had been to the end, telling Gosse that he had been reading Byron's letters, but 'the sadness is that Lord Byron was not quite *gentilhomme*, which comes out so dreadfuly in his letters.'

Later, he planned a three-day trip back to shuttered and deserted Althorp. 'I can do little there,' he wrote, 'but I shall have the pictures as companions, so I shall be quite happy.' In fact, he was not happy at all. Back at Althorp he was once more overwhelmed by money worries and the omnipresence of the debt. 'No reduction in the income tax, I fear. Soon I shall have to take to Nebuchadnezzar's very cheap nourishment.' (Nebuchadnezzar had eaten grass like a beast of the field.)

So it was back to London, from where his last letter to Gosse mentioned that 'the bronchitis affected my heart so I am what old fashioned doctors call "much reduced".' On 26 September 1922 came a final heart attack, and the saddest of the Spencer Earls found peace at last.

CHAPTER 13

'Jolly Jack'

Albert Edward John, seventh Earl Spencer (1892–1975)

One will never know how deeply Bobby's eldest son, Jack Spencer, was affected by his mother's sudden death, for he never talked about it. But what seems clear is that after Margaret's death, Jack's life was ruled by a conscious effort not to succumb to the weaknesses which had made his father's life a misery.

This made him very much his father's opposite. He lacked his father's good looks and his father's vanity. Distrusting charm in others, he was virtually devoid of charm himself. He despised uncertainty, and throughout his life infuriated others by his conviction that he was always right. He also despised weakness, which could make him something of a bully.

He was the first of the Spencers to break with the Whig family tradition and openly declare himself a Tory. He was also at heart an intellectual, although this was something else that he kept hidden – possibly because his father had rather prided himself upon his intellect. Jack Spencer would probably have been the last man in London to have made a friend of Edmund Gosse – and *vice versa*.

He was still a serving officer in the First Life Guards in the summer of 1922 when he took over Althorp as seventh Earl Spencer, and it was through military eyes that he surveyed the wreckage. In certain ways the situation was not quite as bad as his sick and lonely father had convinced himself it was. Bobby may have been defeated, but Jack had no intention of surrendering.

*　　　*　　　*

As an undergraduate at Cambridge Jack had been a droll, rather prickly character, and it was there that he earned his nickname 'Jolly Jack'. Like a true Spencer – and again unlike his father – he was a passionate horseman. According to his friend, Sir Alan Lascelles, he 'rode well and was genuinely *philotheros* [fond of hunting]' – so fond that during term time he insisted on taking the train from Cambridge to Northampton twice a week to hunt with the Pytchley.

Towards the end of the war, as a captain in the Life Guards, he came into fairly frequent contact with the monarch and the court in the course of duty. He had absolutely no wish to become a courtier, but as an accomplished ballroom dancer and heir to an earldom, he was in considerable demand at royal balls and parties. At one point it was being hinted that he might marry George V's daughter, the Princess Royal. Instead he married the Duke of Abercorn's considerably prettier daughter, Lady Cynthia Hamilton – who in turn had once been rumoured as a possible bride for the Prince of Wales. Their first child, Lady Anne, was born in 1920, shortly before her grandfather died. Two years later the family moved to Althorp.

It took some time to get to know the house and assess the situation, but it was clear from the outset that Jack's first priority was financial. Along with the outstanding debts and mortgages, many of them dating back to the Red Earl's day, tax was owing and death duties needed to be paid. But during these early months when the Spencers were living at Althorp and at Spencer House in London, Jack came to a decision he would adhere to for the rest of his life. Whatever happened, he was staying put. He would do whatever was required to pay off the debt, but, as far as possible, he would 'maintain the acreage' of Spencer land, and avoid the sale of property. This left him no alternative but to turn, like many a hard-pushed aristocrat in the 1920s, to the intolerable but invaluable Joe Duveen.

Joseph Duveen, who ended life in 1939 as Lord Duveen of Millbank, was the merchant prince of European art dealers. As his biographer S.M. Behrman put it, his 'entire astonishing career' was the product of 'the simple observation . . . that Europe had plenty of art, and America had plenty of money'. Accordingly he gained his fortune and his title by the wholesale marketing of old master paintings from impecunious European aristocrats like Jack Spencer to very rich Americans. He visited Althorp in person and, while there, helped Jack select six of his most saleable masterpieces for America – a pair of full length portraits of Georgiana Devonshire, one by Reynolds, the other by Gainsborough, two further Reynoldses, one of Lavinia, second Countess Spencer, the other of Lady Camden, a Franz Hals portrait of an unknown man, and Van Dyck's ravishing *Daedalus and Icarus*.

Duveen was excited by the pictures, which as he predicted duly produced £300,000 when sold in New York. And while Jack was sad to see them go, there are worse things in life than selling paintings and war had taught him to regard casualties philosophically. As he explained to a reporter from *The Times*, 'The fact of the deaths of the two previous earls occurring within a comparatively short period has compelled the sacrifice.' When asked if he was satisfied with the £300,000 he received for them he felt obliged to add, 'I do not touch a penny of whatever I receive for the pictures'. This was true as far as it went, but rather missed the point about the sales. The fact was that, for the moment at least, the paintings had saved Althorp for the Spencers and that their 'sacrifice' permitted them to go on living in the house of their ancestors.

With Althorp safe for now, Jack began to organise a way of life as far as possible within his means. This was very different from the lavish life-style of his predecessors. National politics were out, and he rarely bothered to attend the House of Lords. He continued to hunt throughout his twenties and thirties, but could not possibly afford the Spencer earls' traditional mastership of the Pytchley. The sale of the paintings had saved Spencer House as well as Althorp for the family, but as they could not afford to live in both he sold a long lease on Spencer House to a ladies' club, and rented a flat in Grosvenor Square instead.

At Althorp he was probably the most economical of the Spencers since the Tudors. He was extraordinarily careful over money, and permitted neither himself nor his wife anything that he considered self indulgent. Staff were reduced to a minimum, the only exception being in the kitchens where he always spent above the odds on a first rate cook. He had inherited the famous Spencer appetite and since he loved his food he and Lady Cynthia employed a local girl and trained her to cook the classic English food they both enjoyed. They had one foreign holiday each year which cost them very little, as they spent it aboard their friend Lord Fairhaven's luxury yacht in the South of France. Jack's great indulgence was to own two second-hand Rolls Royces. They cost him £750 and he had the Spencer crest painted on the doors.

Having sold the paintings, Jack allowed himself one more extravagance. He commissioned Augustus John to paint his portrait, wearing his Life Guard's uniform. Here he was taking a considerable risk, for John was drinking heavily by now and, according to his biographer Michael Holroyd, had a tendency to caricature his male sitters. Jack's portrait is in fact something of a caricature of a pantomime guardee, and was criticised as such when exhibited in London. Even John himself admitted that 'he should have probably been hung [sic] rather than his picture'.

But Jack seemed entirely happy with his portrait, apart from complaining about a crease that John had painted in his guardsman's tunic, and the minor matter of being charged for a full size canvas rather than the smaller one which he insisted was all he could afford – and all that he ultimately paid for.

Edward John, the son and heir and future eighth Earl Spencer, was born in 1924. A pretty and affectionate small boy who was always known as Johnnie, he had clearly inherited all his mother's charm. It was through his mother's close friendship with the Duchess of York that the future eighth Earl made his own first royal appearance, as page to his great uncle, the Earl of Lucan, at the 1937 coronation of King George VI. Shortly afterwards Lady Spencer was herself appointed lady-in-waiting to her friend, now Queen Elizabeth.

But although the Spencers were keeping up distinctly grand appearances throughout the 1930s, it was becoming doubtful how much longer this could be maintained. They lacked serious capital investments, agricultural land had slumped in value and, despite all Jack's economies, with agriculture in the state it was, they were still living way above their income. This meant that, in the same year as the coronation, yet another major painting had to go – Holbein's magnificent portrait of Henry VIII, which had been hanging in the small dining room at Althorp for as long as anybody could remember. The fine art market was depressed and King Henry was purchased by Herr von Thyssen, the German steel magnate, for the ridiculously small – but very welcome – sum of £10,000.

It was now that Jack's distant Spencer Churchill cousin, Winston, spent some days at Althorp researching his full-scale biography of their joint if far-off ancestor, the Duke of Marlborough. Discredited by now, and out of office, Winston was in his 'Wilderness Years', and dreading the approaching European war which he was powerless to avert. He found writing his life of Marlborough a diversion and an inspiration, for alone of all the Duke's descendants, Winston would always look to Marlborough as a hero, and indeed as a model when, like Marlborough, he was called on four years later to command the nation's forces in a full-scale European conflict.

By the time of Winston's visit Jack was gaining a reputation for irascibility, and a story went the rounds that he had been so incensed at finding Winston smoking in his library that he snatched the offending large cigar from the statesman's lips and stamped it underfoot.

Jack was disappointed when war broke out in 1939 and he was officially informed that at forty-seven he was too old to rejoin his regiment. Soon enough, however, he had another battle on his hands – defending Spencer House against the German Blitz in the spring of 1941. The ladies' club had closed, Spencer House stood empty, and Jack was there one night on fire-watching duty when the house next door was hit by incendiary bombs and almost totally destroyed. On this occasion Spencer House lost only its windows, but with the raids continuing, it seemed likely to follow the fate of its next-door neighbour.

Worried about the priceless eighteenth-century fittings in the house, Jack made a snap decision. He would evacuate all the remaining fixtures and fittings from the house, before bombs destroyed them or someone stole them. He brought workmen up from Althorp and supervised the work in person.

It must have been like pillaging a palace in the face of an advancing army, as everything was hurriedly removed – exquisite eighteenth-century chimney pieces specially designed for the first Earl by John Vardy and Athenian Stuart, mahogany doors and elaborate door frames, marble busts, and the great bronze-gilt lantern in the hall. Once he had begun, Jack became determined to leave behind as little as possible and was soon having chair rails and skirting boards prised from the walls, together with the decorated inset panels in the Painted Room. He even rescued the enormous Spencer House doormat inscribed with the one word 'salve' (welcome) in black capitals, which must have wiped the feet of many of the greatest figures in over a century of English history.

By 12 May 1941 all was finished. Spencer House stood gutted and, after driving through the night, Jack supervised the stacking of its treasures in Roger Morris's great stables back at Althorp. Here they would remain for what was known as 'the duration'. At this stage, having preserved this remarkable collection of antiquities, Jack was planning to return them to Spencer House when the war was over, should it still be standing, which in 1941 seemed most unlikely.

War was a gloomy time for the owners of great houses. Repairs were impossible, staff unavailable, and by 1942 Jack Spencer came to the decision over Althorp which he had been trying to avoid for nearly two decades – concede defeat. Rather than let the house destroy him as it had his father, he would pass on responsibility for it to the National Trust.

Early that year, he reluctantly allowed the Trust's local agent to make a full inspection of the house, and when the agent had finished his report, the Trust's Historic Buildings Secretary, James Lees Milne, came up to Althorp to discuss the terms of the surrender.

Lees Milne warmed instantly to Lady Spencer, like everyone who met her, describing her as 'like a goddess, distilling charm and gentleness around her'. Not so her husband, who was barely civil. Lees Milne soon discovered why. The local agent for the Trust had had the impertinence to 'depreciate' Althorp. Like a doctor telling a patient the worst, he had explained that Althorp House was suffering from almost every ailment known to ancient buildings. The roof leaked, the foundations were unsatisfactory, the centuries-old timbers were suffering from wet rot, dry rot and the death watch beetle. This was bad enough but, in addition, the National Trust required a large endowment to keep a house like Althorp going before they would accept it. Not only would the Spencers have to leave the house they had inhabited for nearly four centuries, but yet more land and works of art would have to go to pay for their departure.

As they discussed this, it was not surprising that Jack became increasingly 'huffy', and that Lees Milne left for London feeling deeply pessimistic. As he wrote in his diary that evening, 'Certainly I appreciated Althorp. But the difficulties will be infinite before we get it.'

In fact it was the sheer 'infinity' of the difficulties that finally saved Althorp for the Spencers. Seeing no way round them Jack refused to give the Trust his house, just as the Trust decided it could not accept it. Thus was Althorp saved – and in the process 'the Curator Earl' came into being.

No one knows who first called Jack the 'Curator Earl', but with the ending of the war, the care and preservation of Althorp started to become his true obsession. Since the National Trust was not an option, he had to rescue the house on his own and find alternative means of paying for the extensive restoration. The wartime need for food had boosted agriculture, and government support for farming continued into the post-war period. For Jack this alleviated the disastrous pre-war fall in income, and as far as Althorp was concerned, he was now helped by the advice of his friend, the architect Lord 'Gerry' Wellington. At his suggestion he employed Stephen Dykes-Bower, the surveyor of Westminster Abbey, to inspect the house and it was he who told him how he should obtain official grants for Althorp's preservation.

By now, central government was beginning to accept an obligation to preserve what was known as 'the national heritage'. Jack would have deeply resented the suggestion that Althorp was the heritage of anybody but the Spencers, but, as curator, and in order to save its fabric, he was perfectly prepared to accept money from the government and therefore had to accept the penance of opening the house for sixty days a year to the general public. Starting in 1957, he received six separate government grants to finance the restoration of Althorp.

At times it seemed an endless labour of rebuilding walls, repairing roofs and replacing rotten timbers with immense steel girders, but by the end of it Althorp House was probably in better condition than ever in its history. He also re-created the seventeenth-century state room on the first floor, which had been divided into bedrooms by the second earl in the later eighteenth century, and lovingly restored one of the minor gems of Althorp, the elegant Palladian gardener's cottage in the park.

By now Jack had renegotiated the lease on Spencer House to be used as offices, and since no one seemed to care about the absence of John Vardy's doors or Athenian Stuart's chimney pieces, he decided he was perfectly entitled to use them at Althorp instead.

Jack had a well trained eye for architecture and furniture and could see behind the Red Earl's Victorian restorations to the house which Henry Holland had created for the fifth Earl Spencer. Having so many treasures from Spencer House at his disposal, he was at liberty to do things that not even the second Earl had been able accomplish. Starting with the Sunderland Room, he installed two magnificent chimney pieces in carara marble which had been 'stolen' from Spencer House, one by Athenian Stuart, the other by John Vardy. Impressed by the result, he moved on to the Marlborough Room where he replaced two Victorian chimney pieces with another pair from Spencer House, one by the celebrated Dutch sculptor, Scheemakers. Next he improved the appearance of the South Drawing Room by giving it a mahogany door case, *circa* 1740, by Athenian Stuart. The big 'salve' doormat went perfectly in the entrance hall with Vardy's bronze-gilt lantern from Spencer House above it. As he went on finding places for the treasures hoarded in the stables, Jack was acting like some immensely rich curator, drawing on his private source of authentic masterpieces to enhance his treasure house still further.

Jack was now in his mid-fifties, and over the years had become a considerable historian. He started taking on trusteeships and advisory positions on the boards of museums like London's Wallace Collection and the Victoria and Albert Museum. He grew ever more fascinated by his ancestors and took vast trouble establishing a proper muniment room at Althorp to house his great collection of Spencer papers.

With Spencer House still leased for offices, he treated Brooks's Club in St James's as his fiefdom, relishing the part his ancestors had played in its early history. It pleased him that the dining room at Brooks's was called the Spencer Room, and when lunching there he always tried to sit beneath the portrait of the man he familiarly referred to as 'my great-grandfather' – George John, the second Earl and friend of Nelson.

Jack had never been an easy man. As the years passed and he became ever more obsessed with Althorp, people wondered how his charming wife, Cynthia, put up with the situation. The truth was that they were living very separate lives. Apart from his work at Althorp, he was also deeply involved in the county, as Lord Lieutenant of Northamptonshire, and one of the longest serving members of the county council. He was also an active member of the Northampton Hospital Committee.

Lady Cynthia's world was different. She was a loving mother who would later be adored by all her grandchildren. She was extremely kind, and spent much of her time helping the sick and needy. But she also had another escape route from the strain of her life at Althorp. In 1936 Queen Elizabeth had offered her a place at court, as a Woman of the Bedchamber, and she was later to become a lady-in-waiting to Queen Elizabeth II.

It seemed as if the grief created in the family by Margaret Spencer's untimely death had genuinely scarred all Bobby's children. Jack had come off best, but both his brothers ended sadly. Cecil was killed in a riding accident and sailor George – who was dismissed from the Royal Navy for an 'unspecified offence' – had a lifelong drink problem. In their different ways, Jack's sisters all had unsatisfactory lives as well. Motherly Delia married a much older man, the banker Sidney Peel, who was very much on the rebound after Cousin Winston had stolen the true love of his life, Clementine Hosier. They never had the children she desperately wanted. Pretty Lavinia married the war hero, Lord Annaly, only to discover later that he was homosexual, and they lived apart. Margaret, the baby of the family, had a difficult life, including a marriage which ended in divorce, which was made no easier by her abiding sense of guilt over the death of her mother.

But however unsatisfactory their private lives may have been at home, all Jack's sisters followed Cynthia's example and found a second, more exciting life at court: Delia as lady-in-waiting responsible for Princess Elizabeth and Princess Margaret; Lavinia joining Cynthia as lady-in-waiting to the Queen; and Margaret becoming governess to Princess Alexandra.

So, while Jack's wife and two sisters found another, more exciting world at court, he had Althorp to occupy his time. Now that he had saved it for the Spencers, it was time to restore the house to something of its former glory. The roof was watertight, the timbers sound and the house had a spare elegance about it, with its unrivalled works of art, and centuries old oak floors. He would take enormous trouble discovering exactly what colour paint had originally been used for a particular picture frame or surround. His aim was now perfection – to recreate the house as closely as possible to an eighteenth-century ideal of what a great house like this should be. It had now become the house of a highly discriminating and immensely knowledgeable old curator.

And it was essentially *his* house. It was Fortress Althorp, and he did not really want to share it with anyone. He would tolerate historians, although he liked to check them at work to make sure that they were not stealing any of the family papers. It was irritating that the house had occasionally to open for the public (he particularly objected to stiletto heels). He began embroidering seats for a set of eighteenth-century chairs and, together with Lords Bearsted and Ancaster, 'became one of the three great post-war needle-working earls', often working away in the evening at *gros point* or *petit point* in his own small sitting room, its dark green walls lined with paintings of the third Earl's famous shorthorn cows. He became so expert at his hobby that he ended up chairman of the Royal School of Needlework.

According to the Duke of Devonshire, 'Althorp had become his pride and joy. It was the one true passion of Jack Spencer's life. He was in love with it.'

But it can be dangerous to fall in love with a house, especially a house as beautiful as Althorp. For the moment comes when one grows old and must accept that one is a tenant, not an owner, and that someone else is going to succeed you in the place you love. So you must have confidence in your successor and not resent him. At a certain point Jack Spencer realised he had no confidence in his son, Johnnie. He could have borne the thought of dying if he had been able to entrust the house to almost anyone other than his son.

Johnnie, who was charming and feckless, was not remotely like his father. Sir Roy Strong remembers him as 'absolutely sweet, but there was always a touch of a P.G. Wodehouse peer about him'.

None of this impaired his prospects as a courtier. As a Spencer, with a mother who was a friend and a lady-in-waiting of the Queen, he too had close connections with the court. At eighteen he had joined the Royal Scots Greys, saw service in France and Germany, and was then appointed equerry to George VI.

As Viscount Althorp he enjoyed a busy social life in London. He always remained close to his mother but relations with his father steadily deteriorated. Jack transferred North Creake House in Norfolk to his son to avoid death duties. It had been the scene of happy summer holidays when the children were little but the house was now fairly dilapidated after having been used by the R.A.F. in the war, and Jack was hurt and angry on hearing that Johnnie had had it demolished.

Johnnie then did something that his father found still harder to forgive.

By now he had earned a reputation for falling in and out of love too often. He was one of the most eligible young bachelors in London, and in June 1951 he became unofficially engaged to the Earl of Leicester's daughter, the seventeen-year-old Lady Anne Coke. But Jack had strong personal reasons for disapproving of this match, and finally made Johnnie break off the engagement.

Johnnie did not remain love-lorn for long. He was soon to fall in love with another seventeen year old – Frances Roche, the cool and remarkably determined daughter of Lord and Lady Fermoy, who were close friends and neighbours of the Royal Family. Friends remember Johnnie being 'completely infatuated' with Frances, and before long this would bring yet further discord to the house of Spencer.

CHAPTER 14

The Fermoys

Jack Spencer disapproved of the Fermoys. With his deep concern for families and antecedents he could 'place' almost anyone according to his or her social standing, by which standards the Fermoys were little more than rich Irish *parvenus* from America. He was irritated, therefore, by the favoured position Lord and Lady Fermoy had come to enjoy as friends of George VI and Queen Elizabeth, and he muttered darkly of the 'bad blood' of the Fermoys. As a family they were certainly different from the Spencers.

As he had discovered, these Fermoys had no connection with the ancient Irish family of that name. That illustrious title had been long extinct when in the 1850s Edmund Burke Roche, a landowner and politician from County Cork adopted it on being awarded an Irish peerage for political services. After this, the first Lord Fermoy had suffered badly from the disorder in Ireland. Having lost his large estates in Cork and Limerick, he moved to London, and became Liberal MP for Marylebone. He was succeeded by his spendthrift son, Edward FitzEdmund Burke Roche as second Baron Fermoy.

The second Baron was a gambler, who apparently lost his home in one single night at the tables. By 1881 the Norwich Union, as principal mortgager of what were left of his Irish lands, had put them up for sale. Since they failed to reach the asking price, the offer was withdrawn, and they were sold privately a few years later. Soon afterwards the second Lord Fermoy went bankrupt. But before disaster finally engulfed the family his younger brother, James Burke

Roche, had sailed for America to seek his fortune. Contemporary photographs show James to have been a handsome man with a memorable profile. He chose as a companion one of the great Victorian no-hopers, Moreton Frewen (otherwise known as 'Mortal Ruin'), who was always on to something new to make his fortune, which he never seemed to find. He and James Roche tried prospecting for gold in the Yukon and cattle-ranching in Wyoming. Tiring of Wyoming, they ended up in New York City.

Here it was open season for Europeans in pursuit of heiresses. Frewen soon found and married pretty Clara Jerome, daughter of the financier, Leonard Jerome, whose other daughter, Jennie, had recently married young Lord Randolph Churchill. Soon after the Frewen marriage, Leonard Jerome went bankrupt, leaving Frewen with little but a pretty wife and the honour of becoming uncle to the future Winston Churchill.

James Burke Roche must have thought that he was being smarter than his friend when he picked on vivacious Frances Work, whose father, Frank Work, a former dry-goods clerk from Dogsburg, in the town of Chillicothe Ohio, had made himself the millionaire stockbroker to the Vanderbilts. A man whose prejudices matched his fortune, Work strongly disapproved of idle foreigners preying on American womanhood for financial gain and, on first hearing of his daughter's involvement with Burke Roche, informed a reporter that 'international marriages should be a hanging offence'. So when strong-willed Frances continued with her plans to marry, her equally stronger-willed father promptly disinherited her.

Undaunted, James Burke Roche brought Frances back to London, and in 1881 they married, took up residence in Pont Street, Knightsbridge, and a year later Frances gave birth to identical male twins, Maurice and Frank, soon to be followed by a daughter, Cynthia. But the former dry-goods clerk had not been wrong about James Roche. All he had really wanted from Frances was the means to lead a life of leisure and, since she wanted much the same, when the money ended so did their marriage. Since Roche by now was treating her 'abominably', she felt the time had come to return to father.

Legend has it that James Burke Roche accompanied his wife and children to New York, then dumped the twins on his father-in-law's fashionable doorstep on 74th Street. Shocked but not surprised at such behaviour, Frank Work helped his daughter secure a divorce, then reinstated her and all three children in his will – on strict conditions. The children were to be raised in America as good Americans, and provided they remained there, they would inherit their share of his substantial fortune when he died. Should they return to Europe or renounce their U.S. citizenship they would be instantly disinherited. The same applied to Frances.

The twins, Maurice and Frank Burke Roche, grew up much as was to be expected as grandsons of a New York multi-millionaire. They were educated first at the fashionable St Paul's New Hampton, then at Harvard, and became rich young men about town who also dabbled on the New York Stock Exchange. When Frank Work died in 1911, he left sufficient money in trust for both of them to live the rest of their lives in considerable comfort on the income.

They came to Europe once – in the First World War, with the U.S. forces – but this was not considered grounds for disinheritance, and in 1918 they returned to their happy bachelor existence in New York.

It was there that in 1920, they heard that their uncle, Edward FitzEdmund, second Lord Fermoy, had died in darkest Bournemouth, leaving their long-estranged father, James Burke Roche, to assume the title of third Baron Fermoy. But not for long. Five months later, early in 1921, the old man died and his title was suddenly going begging.

It was a curious situation. As American citizens neither twin was eligible for the title, and if either surrendered his citizenship to adopt it, he would forfeit his inheritance. As first-born twin, Maurice had first call on the title should he want it, but he was not sure he did and reputedly offered it to Frank. Only when Frank declined did Maurice finally decide that, despite his love of America, and despite the risk of disinheritance, he could not resist the lure of returning to England and picking up a peerage – even if it was an Irish one.

He must have discussed this with his lawyers, and also with his sister Cynthia, for soon afterwards he and his brother both left America for Europe, and launched a case in the U.S. high court to set aside the terms of their grandfather's will as being 'both unreasonable and unjust'. Since none of the other beneficiaries to the will objected, the request was granted, leaving them free to live where they wanted on the income from the grandfather's trust funds which were over a million dollars each.

By now their mother Frances was also back in Europe, having also broken the terms of her father's will by marrying Auriel Batonyi, *ne* Cohen, a Hungarian riding master. As this marriage also ended in divorce, she was no great social asset to her son, who was enjoying his role as Lord Fermoy. Frank went to live in Paris and worked in a leisurely manner for the bankers, Morgan Guaranty. According to a member of her family, he was highly anxious and neurotic, and remained unmarried.

Maurice was more personable and ambitious. Being rich, titled and good looking, he spent several years enjoying life and numerous love affairs, living between Paris, London and New York. Then in 1931 at the age of thirty-six, he married the twenty-year-old pianist Ruth Gill from Aberdeen, who had been studying music at the Paris Conservatoire. He decided it was time to settle down in England. Someone advised him to go into politics 'as a means of integrating with the country'. Because of his Irish title, he was free to stand for the House of Commons and, having failed to get himself elected as Conservative for the Liberal seat of Woodhall Spa, he rented Hillingdon Hall in Norfolk in order to contest the next election at neighbouring Kings Lynn. He was duly elected and would represent Kings Lynn until the war. But for the future of the Fermoys what mattered was not so much his role as an MP as the fact that Hillingdon Hall was on the edge of the royal estates at Sandringham.

It has been said that it was 'not entirely fortuitous' that the Fermoys got to know the Duke and Duchess of York so quickly, and that they had moved to Norfolk in the first place with the intention of getting to know the Royal Family. If so, they must have been extremely smart and certainly made the most of their opportunities to get to know their royal neighbours. Like the Duke of York, Lord Fermoy was a first-class shot, and his *bonhomie* and Irish charm partly explain the friendship that grew up between them. But only partly. Rich Americans, even titled rich Americans like Lord Fermoy, were not the sort of company the Yorks normally enjoyed and the true strength of the friendship undoubtedly came from the close rapport developing between the two strong-willed and in many ways like-minded Scottish ladies, the former Elizabeth of Glamis and the former Miss Ruth Gill of Aberdeen.

When the Yorks became King George VI and Queen Elizabeth, most of their friends at court tended to be traditional grandees like Lords Radnor, Stair, Scarborough, and the Duke of Portland, making the continuing close royal friendship with two relative outsiders like the Fermoys all the more remarkable. With the birth of the three Fermoy children – Edmund, Frances and Mary – the King and Queen invited the Fermoys to become their tenants at Park House, a twelve-bedroomed mansion in the grounds of Sandringham.

Lord Fermoy died a year after the marriage of his daughter. Almost at once, the Queen Mother offered his widow a permanent place at court by making her one of her Women of the Bedchamber. Hew new role at court and her enduring friendship with the Queen Mother now became the mainspring of her life. It was a friendship that would be of great importance in the life of her granddaughter, Diana Spencer, forging a further link in the chain that would one day draw Diana to the very centre of the House of Windsor.

Ruth Fermoy could be extremely charming, and particularly to Jack's wife, Cynthia, who became a close friend through the court. So did young Lord Althorp, who after the war was appointed equerry to George VI. Good-natured and amusing, Johnnie was a successful courtier and rumour has it that Princess Elizabeth herself was particularly fond of him before she fell in love with Prince Philip, and had written to him regularly while he was on active service in Germany.

It is hard to tell what part the ambitious Ruth Fermoy had played in bringing the twenty-eight-year-old Lord Althorp into such constant contact with her seventeen-year-old daughter, Frances. Certainly he fell deeply in love with her. Lord Leicester's daughter was forgotten and a year later Johnnie Spencer and his child bride were married at Westminster Abbey, with the Royal Family in full attendance.

It was a very grand affair indeed, but instead of improving father and son relations, the marriage seems to have made them worse, partly because of Jack's dislike of the Fermoys and also because of disagreements over where the newly-weds should live. Finally Jack did lend his son a farmhouse on the Althorp estate, but after constant disagreements, many of them involving Frances, it was clear that this would never work. At which point, Lady Fermoy came to her son-in-law's assistance.

As Lord Fermoy had died in 1955, she suggested that Johnnie should take on the lease of her old home, Park House, Sandringham, and she actually lent him the furniture as well, since Jack was disinclined to let his son remove anything from Althorp.

It seemed that Ruth Fermoy was taking Johnnie from the Spencers and bringing him yet closer to herself and the Royal Family. From then on, Johnnie rarely went to Althorp or saw his father. As a friend said, 'They were barely on grunting terms by now', but Johnnie remained close to his mother. To occupy his time he decided to farm in as undemanding a way as possible and, after enduring the so-called 'gin and tonic course' at Cirencester Agricultural College, he started farming 600 acres near Sandringham, with the aid of a £20,000 contribution from Frances.

To start with it was a happy marriage. A daughter, Sarah, was born in March 1955, followed by another daughter, Jane, two years later, making it a matter of importance for Frances to produce a son to inherit Althorp and the title. In 1960 the longed-for heir was born, only to survive a brief ten hours. Johnnie's dreadful disappointment lifted only when Frances was once more pregnant.

But once again Frances gave birth to a daughter. She was born at Park House on 1 July 1961 and christened Diana Frances.

Diana's arrival was the point at which the marriage faltered. For although Johnnie soon became extremely fond of his new daughter, he remained desperate for an heir. Frances was persuaded to submit to examinations by specialists to see if there was any reason why she had only daughters. She found this humiliating and, although in 1964 she did give birth to a boy, who was christened Charles Edward Maurice, with the Queen as godmother, the arrival of the heir to the Spencers failed to bring back his parents' love for one another.

Now that Johnnie had his heir he seemed to lose interest in his wife. The marriage dragged on four more years, with Frances becoming increasingly bored with Johnnie and with life in the country. Having money of her own, she was free to please herself and spent more time in London; it was only a matter of time before she met the charming but already married Peter Shand Kydd, and fell deeply in love with him.

Their love affair was too intense to remain secret for long, and when Johnnie learned about it he was deeply shocked, and at first could not believe that Frances seriously wished to leave him. Upper-class divorce was still deeply frowned upon at the time, especially in royal circles, where the stigma was enough to banish divorcees from the court and from the Ascot royal enclosure. But in Johnnie's case, divorce seemed unavoidable once Shand Kydd's wife named Frances in her own divorce petition. With considerable reluctance, Johnnie began proceedings too. As the rich owner of his own wall-paper business, Peter Shand Kydd made it clear that he would marry Frances and provide a home for her and all her children.

The news that his son was divorcing Frances upset Jack Spencer, for however deep his disapproval of his daughter-in-law, he disapproved still more of the whole distasteful business of divorce. He would not deny that he and Cynthia had had their troubles, but they had soldiered on. His son should do the same.

But in spite of the Earl's disapproval the divorce took place, and

Frances got her freedom. At this point Frances was still hoping for an amicable arrangement over the children, and she and her lover had made arrangements for the children to live with her in London, visiting their father at weekends and in the holidays.

At first Johnnie had agreed, but after the Christmas holidays he changed his mind, and abruptly insisted that the children were to stay with him. Since Sarah and Jane were now at boarding school this would make little difference to them, but he wanted Diana and Charles to remain with him at Park House and attend day school in Kings Lynn.

At first, Frances could not believe that he was serious, but when she realised he was, a legal battle began for custody of the children. Since Frances was generally regarded as a good and devoted mother whose children loved her, it seemed inconceivable to her that she would lose them. But the easy-going Johnnie suddenly revealed a very different side of his character. Having grown extremely bitter, he was determined he would keep his children at whatever cost, and persuaded a number of impressive friends to testify in court on his behalf.

Although judges had been known to side with the aristocracy over questions of custody, particularly where an heir to the property was involved, everything finally depended on Frances's fitness as a mother. To start with this was not disputed, but then a devastating witness took the stand against her. Her own mother, Ruth Fermoy, courtier and friend to the mother of the nation, told the judge that in her opinion her daughter, Frances, was not fit to have custody of her children.

It was typical of Ruth Fermoy never to give her reasons for her action, but she was clearly determined to do anything she could to ensure that her precious grandchildren were brought up by an Earl rather than a wall-paper manufacturer, however rich. But she had more important reasons still. Having taken so much trouble to advance herself and her family into the royal circle of Sandringham and the court, she had no intention of losing all that she had gained because of divorce within the family. All too conscious of the traditional royal disapproval of the stigma of divorce, she intended to make it clear that she was renouncing her own daughter and everything she stood for.

By doing so, she ensured that the blame for the divorce could be safely heaped on Frances, leaving Johnnie more or less unsullied in the eyes of royalty. So it was really thanks to his mother-in-law that Johnnie's name at court remained untarnished, and he and the children could remain together at Park House, Sandringham. The marriage may have broken, but due to Ruth Fermoy the close connection with the House of Windsor had not.

CHAPTER 15

Raine's War

Lady Fermoy had much to answer for when she helped her son-in-law to win his custody case, for Johnny was not cut out to be a single parent and the children would almost certainly have been happier and more settled with their mother after she remarried. Johnnie still missed his wife as much as he professed to hate her, and winning custody of the children had not made him happy.

He did his best with them. Nannies and then a governess were engaged; the two elder girls were now at fashionable West Heath School near Sevenoaks in Kent, and he tried to keep the family at Park House happy.

But divorce had hit the children hard. Their weekends with Frances would usually end with her in tears. At home six-year-old Charles would sob himself to sleep with Diana doing her best to comfort him. And when Frances had married Peter Shand Kydd, their loyalties were split between the two separate homes. There were the usual problems of a broken family – divided loyalties, children journeying between separate establishments, and 'the two younger ones terribly spoiled by both sets of parents vying for their love and affection', as one of their relations put it. Soon they discovered how to get exactly what they wanted by playing one set of parents off against the other.

By all accounts Johnnie's private life was far from satisfactory, nor was it even very comfortable once Frances had removed her furniture from Park House. Without Frances, he was also rather short of money. He had girl-friends in London, but none of these relationships lasted and, now that he was in his late forties, he was beginning to appear a touch pathetic, somewhat bowed and looking older than his years.

Although Jack had disapproved of Frances, after the divorce its stigma would not go away, and Johnnie's relations with his father remained as fraught as ever. Because of this Johnnie hardly ever took the children to Althorp, and they lived in virtual ignorance of the house and all it stood for. Even Christmases were spent apart from the rest of the family. Johnnie's sister, Lady Anne Wake-Walker, and her husband were close to the old man, and would take their three children to Althorp for a traditional Christmas with her parents, while Johnnie did his best to entertain his children on his own at Park House. On Boxing Day they would be invited over by the Royal Family where the children were shown the film of Ian Fleming's *Chitty-Chitty Bang-Bang*. This happened every Christmas and they came to hate it.

Then the situation at Althorp changed abruptly. Lady Cynthia was taken ill with what proved to be a tumour on the brain, and Jack became the most solicitous of husbands. When Cynthia died in 1973, he was broken-hearted. Now in his early eighties, he was no longer the dominating figure of his prime and it was now that he came beneath the spell of one of the most extraordinary women in the country.

As a pretty teenager, Barbara Cartland's daughter, Raine, like one of the heroines in her mother's historical novels, had decided that one day she would marry a duke, or, failing that, an earl. Her own origins were firmly middle class, being the daughter of Barbara's first husband, Alexander McCorquodale, who was not even a baronet, but the wealthy owner of a firm of Scottish printers.

But while Raine may have seemed like a Cartland heroine, this was deceptive. Feminine she was, but soft she was not. She once said of herself, 'there's pure steel up my backbone', and she was not unlike her mother in her determined attitude to life and her extraordinary capacity to get exactly what she wanted. At the same time, her obsession with the aristocracy was rather like that of the actress Maxine Elliott, who once advised Winston Churchill to 'always remember that a lord is just that little bit better than anyone else'.

Putting this into practice, Raine married – for the first time – the Hon. Gerald Legge, the so-called 'never-never Earl', who, after years of waiting for his inheritance, finally became the fifteenth Earl of Dartmouth, making Raine a Countess. In the meantime, Raine had poured her considerable energies and ambitions into local government and bringing up her children. But when she was elected to the Greater London Council her interests widened, as she concentrated on the heritage and preservation lobby, chairing the council's Historic Buildings Board. She wrote a book entitled *What Is Our Heritage?*, and in 1975 became the heritage queen of England as head of the UK Executive on the European Heritage Year.

This involvement in preserving Britain's architectural legacy may have made her conscious of a certain lack in Gerald. He was a kindly, witty man, but he did not have a stately home. Through her involvement with English Heritage she naturally knew all about Althorp and its treasures, so that when she met Johnnie Spencer, as a friend says, 'it certainly helped that his father was already in his eighties, and that he was heir to a stately home'.

By now, Raine had become a regular visitor to Althorp, where she used her considerable charm upon the octogenarian earl who was feeling sad and lonely after the death of Cynthia. Raine finally arranged a reconciliation between him and his son.

Within the family, bearing in mind what she did to Althorp after he was dead, her friendship with Jack Spencer while he was alive will always be a source of bitterness. She flattered him and made a fuss of him, she brought him expensive chocolates which he loved and antique walking sticks which he collected. Being knowledgeable about old buildings, she was the perfect audience for the Earl to talk to about the overriding passion of his life, his house, and he came to feel that in this feminine, decisive woman, he had found somebody at last who truly sympathised with all he had done to save Althorp from disaster. He came to believe that with her deep involvement in the nation's heritage she would use all her influence to protect and preserve the house in the future. He seems to have hoped that she and Johnnie might marry, believing that with Raine installed as chatelaine of Althorp, the house and the treasures it contained would be safe for ever, and he could die content.

In April 1975 die he did, at the age of eighty-three, disappointed to the last that he was the first Spencer Earl for many generations not to have received the Garter, and Johnnie succeeded him as eighth Earl Spencer. Johnnie's son and heir, eight-year-old Charles Spencer, became Lord Althorp; and the family decamped from Park House, Sandringham to take possession of their lost domain which the children barely knew and had rarely visited.

Charles has put on record how much he hated Althorp as a child: 'it was like an old man's club with all those clocks ticking away'. He has said that for him, as an impressionable child, he had at first found it a 'nightmarish place'. But the fact is that together with governesses and servants and a large flat in Grosvenor Square, the family soon adjusted rather well to the ancestral world of Althorp with its air of melancholy and all the treasures the Curator Earl had left them. Johnnie had inherited the house and its possessions, while the land was left in trust to Charles. Death duties came to £4 million, but they could be dealt with by the judicious sales of land or property.

Soon, the children came under the spell of Althorp, so that in retrospect this came to seem a sort of golden interlude when they had their father and the great house to themselves, with the old family servants still present to look after them.

All this was soon to change. Despite the children's opposition, Johnnie's affair with Raine continued. And once she was divorced Johnnie married her at Caxton Hall in July 1976, without informing the children in advance or having them at the ceremony. Almost overnight the children discovered that they had a stepmother. What they already knew of Raine they hated. War began in earnest.

Any woman entering Althorp as stepmother to the four children would have had a tough time of it, but someone as positive as

Raine was clearly in for trouble. Both sides were well-matched, and neither would tolerate defeat. The children's advantage lay in numbers, mendacity and the inborn ruthlessness of the English upper classes, while Raine relied on will-power, Johnnie's total adoration, and the well-established fact that in the end she always seemed to get her way. As for gentle Johnnie, there was little he could do except watch the battle from the sidelines like an ineffectual referee.

At first Raine did her best to win the children over, supplying Diana with quantities of Barbara Cartland novels, which she loved. This did not work for long, and all four children made it very clear that Raine was not their mother and that they deeply resented her. The fight continued with no quarter given or expected.

Instead of improving with time, the situation at Althorp steadily grew worse, particularly for the adolescent Diana and her younger brother Charles. Their hatred of their stepmother and all she represented became unrelenting. For them there was something quite horrendous in what they saw as a take-over of their father and their home by their stepmother.

In some ways Raine was a considerable help to her husband, especially over the running of the estate. The easy-going days of Jack's reign were past and she encouraged Johnnie to hire a new agent, Richard Stanley, and dismissed a number of old employees.

'As far as running the estates was concerned,' says Stanley, 'I'm afraid I had to blow the whistle, signalling that the party was over. So they ran to Johnnie, but Raine made him do what was necessary. She was a ruthless woman, and I say that admiringly.'

Within the house, Raine also made her presence firmly felt, taking charge of the kitchen, insisting that the bed-linen was changed every day, sacking any member of the staff who failed to meet her rigid standards, and making every servant sign a confidentiality agreement. The children proved less amenable than the servants and never succumbed to Raine's attempts to gain their affection. Twelve-year-old Charles was outraged to return from boarding school to find that Raine had consigned him to a box-like bedroom in the attic.

Raine has a strong sense of decorum, with clear ideas of how she thinks the upper classes should behave. Being fairly besotted with his wife, Johnnie generally agreed with anything she said. Not so the children. They emphatically refused to change for dinner; they never had before and had no intention of doing so now. Nor would they be taught manners by what they saw as this overdressed middle-aged outsider who happened to have become their stepmother. Mealtimes became a nightmare. When Sarah burped in front of Raine at dinner Johnnie felt the time had come to send her to her room. Out of solidarity Diana accompanied her sister. For long periods, the children refused to address a single word to Raine during meals and Johnnie was too weak to make them.

By now Raine must have needed all the steel in her backbone to survive. She particularly hated it when the children tried to treat her as a joke. Their appalling behaviour was the reverse side of something which Diana herself demonstrated frequently to others, and was in contrast with the show of perfect manners which is normally the aristocrat's reaction to inferiors.

One of Diana's closest friends from West Heath School, who was invited several times to stay at Althorp, was shocked by the way the children treated Raine. Both were then fourteen, and she says that, coming from a thoroughly middle-class family, she felt so overwhelmed by her first sight of Althorp and the Earl that when she was introduced to him, she curtseyed: 'but he was so very nice that he didn't make me feel that I'd done anything ridiculous. He was in fact a lovely, lovely man. He may have been stupid. Certainly as far as Raine was concerned he was. But to me he was extraordinarily kind, and I remember him writing to my mother after my visit saying what a perfect guest I'd been.'

At school, she says, she had found Diana 'a very likeable but insecure character. She could be so funny and was always a great disobeyer. We were both good swimmers and we used to go on midnight swims in the school swimming pool, which was very much against the rules, but she loved the naughtiness of it all.'

She says that at Althorp she found Diana made a show of being very offhand about everything, but soon she realised how very proud she was of the house and all it represented.

'During my first visit, Raine had only recently married Johnnie, and Diana absolutely hated her. She hated what she was doing to her father and to Althorp. Being Diana's friend I naturally thought Raine was dreadful too. Even to me she seemed manipulative, and with all her frills and flounces seemed terribly overdressed in the understated world of Althorp. But for Diana what was absolutely unforgivable was the fact that her father clearly loved her.'

Thanks largely to the insecurity caused by her parents' divorce, Diana remained deeply possessive of her father and it seemed that this would be a battle which even Raine could never win. But suddenly she benefited from a quirk of fate which came disguised as an absolute disaster.

One Tuesday morning, early in September 1978, Johnnie woke with a bad headache, which was something he almost never did. In fact he was overweight, with high blood pressure – which the tensions between his wife and his children cannot have helped.

Raine was going up to London to lunch with her mother, but offered to put her off and stay at home. Johnnie would not hear of it, but his headache worsened during the morning, and just before midday, while talking to Richard Stanley, he was violently sick, collapsed and was rushed to Northampton Hospital. By now he was unconscious, and a major brain haemorrhage was suspected. Raine and all four children were summoned to his bedside and were told by the doctors that his chances of survival were slender.

Although no one would have admitted it, it must have been obvious to everyone gathered round his bed how much was at stake. Should fifty-four-year-old Johnnie die, as seemed extremely likely, fourteen-year-old Charles Althorp would instantly become the ninth Earl Spencer and Raine would disappear from Althorp and the children's lives for ever. None knew this better than Raine herself.

But all was not lost while Johnnie clung to life, and Raine did everything in her power to make sure that his grip on it was not allowed to weaken. If any wife could force a husband to recover from a stroke by will-power, it was Raine.

With time running out, and Johnnie's life at stake, she felt that there could be no question of consulting the four children over what should be done. The hospital doctors had warned that it would be dangerous to move their father. Raine disagreed. She was convinced that if he was left at Northampton he would die, and on her sole authority she took the risk of having him driven to London by ambulance to the Hospital for Nervous Diseases in Queen Square. She then took the decision of asking the doctors to operate – which they did.

Johnnie lived, but he was very weak and soon developed complications which kept him in hospital for many weeks, during which Raine rarely left his bedside. After the first shock, the children, not unnaturally, began to feel totally excluded and, had their father died, as at times it still seemed likely, they would undoubtedly have blamed his death on Raine. But Johnnie did not die. After a serious relapse, Raine mounted an extraordinary campaign to save him. Believing in the power of prayer, she asked everyone she knew to pray for him. Even her obsession with titles came in useful now. She happened to know the Duke of Portland who was head of a German drug company, and with difficulty the Duke found Johnnie an experimental drug called Aslocillin, which may well have saved him.

'Don't say, "Johnnie, please get well",' her mother told her. 'Say, "Johnnie, you *will* get well."'

And Johnnie, obedient to Raine as ever, *did* get well.

Within two months, though wobbly, he was on his feet and back at Althorp. He was now in debt to Raine for ever.

In most families this sort of miracle recovery would have brought them all together, but not the Spencers. Feeling excluded during the long weeks Johnnie spent in hospital, the children were resenting Raine as much as ever. For it seemed that she had taken over everything. They all felt that the illness had changed their father. As Diana said: 'he was one person before and was certainly a different person after.' She described him as being 'estranged but adoring'. The illness left him very weak and more grateful and dependent on his wife than ever.

Since he was unable to cope with the daily running of Althorp and the estates, Raine took over. A trust was formed with her, the family lawyer Hugo Southern and the estate manager Richard Stanley to make the decisions Johnnie could not.

Raine was not the one to waste a chance like this, and it was now that she made two important decisions. The first was to plan for her own future. Being nothing if not realistic, she knew that Johnnie could have a second stroke at any time, and his recent brush with death had taught her that she could expect absolutely nothing from the children if he died. From now on it was up to her to look after her own interests. Secondly, she realised that she finally had the chance she had always wanted to leave her mark upon a stately home. For the now convalescent Johnnie was only too happy to let her have her way – believing that everything she did was perfect and that, whatever happened, Raine knew best.

To achieve these two ambitions Raine needed money, and there was one obvious way for her to get it. Two years before, Johnnie had already sold two van Dycks to help pay death duties and the cost of running Althorp. While Johnnie lacked ready money, as lord of Althorp he was actually the owner of a treasure chest crammed with potential capital in the form of masterpieces, paintings and antiquities for which the London dealers would pay fortunes. Legally they all belonged to him, to do with as he wanted.

Despite the earlier sales of paintings by Bobby and Jack the core of the great collections was intact: there were the pictures that had come from Spencer House; the Duke of Marlborough's unrivalled gold and silver collection; statuary, priceless porcelain; and endless objects of value accumulated over four centuries. One might have thought that Johnnie would hope to preserve as much as possible of this Spencer patrimony for his son and future generations of Spencers. But if he wished to dispose of any of his possessions, however historic or important to the family, it was his decision and his alone to do so.

Shortly after his illness, when Johnnie and Raine began a selling spree together, Johnnie appeared, if anything, more enthusiastic to be selling the family heritage than Raine. His son Charles believes that 'my grandfather's compulsive devotion to the house caused great resentment in my father. By selling off the art, my father may have derived pleasure in the knowledge that the seventh Earl would be spinning in his grave. It was his revenge for not feeling loved as a child.'

This seems possible, and, if true, Johnnie must have particularly enjoyed selling Jack Spencer's pride and joy at Althorp, his famous muniment room which he had carefully created and helped to catalogue and which contained the great Spencer collection of documents and letters relating to the family. Without a qualm, Johnnie sold the entire collection for a million pounds, leaving the archive to be split between the British Library in London and the County Records Office in Northampton.

This was only a small part of what was now disposed of. One of the family's proudest possessions, the two solid gold wine coolers reputedly given to the Duke of Marlborough by Queen Anne after the Battle of Blenheim, went to the British Museum for around one million pounds, and barely was a convalescent Johnnie back at Althorp than a pair of great paintings which the first Earl Spencer bought in Rome in 1761 for Spencer House were sold privately to the London dealers Wildenstein, for a fraction of their value. These were *Apollo Crowning the Musician Marcantonio Pasqualini* by Andrea Sacchi, and *Liberality and Modesty* by Guido Reni, both in elaborate frames which Athenian Stuart originally designed for them at Spencer House. (Wildensteins paid £40,000 for the Sacchi, which later went to the New York Metropolitan Museum of Art for £270,000.)

The departure of the paintings from Althorp was the signal for a selling frenzy, as treasures great and small were eagerly disposed of, generally in secret, to the Bond Street dealers. Throughout the eighties a stream of silver, furniture and paintings flowed from

Althorp to the London market. The sales were haphazard and on such a scale that to the present day no one is absolutely sure what went. According to Charles Spencer's own calculations, possibly a fifth of the contents of the house vanished for ever, usually in private sales to individual dealers.

This was curious behaviour from Raine, given her previous commitment to English Heritage, and her normally acute business instincts. Part of the trouble came from her belief that, as always, she knew best, not realising quite how sharp the dealers were.

One of the saddest losses was John Wootton's painting of Sarah Marlborough's dogs, along with six unique chairs designed by Athenian Stuart for the Great Room at Spencer House, which Johnnie presented to a London dealer in part payment for restoration work at Althorp. And sometimes objects would be sold to finance a particular extravagance, or to meet a particular need for money, as in 1983 when Johnnie bought Raine a Rolls Royce Silver Spur for £64,000.

Timothy Clifford, director of the National Galleries of Scotland, called the rape of Althorp 'one of the great tragedies of the eighties', while Robert Simon, editor of the connoisseurs' *Apollo Magazine*, thought it 'the worst scandal that has happened to a country house in the last century. No one has put their hands on a collection and dealt with it so ruthlessly.'

It was now that Raine moved into action, and began using part of the proceeds of the sales to transform the house in accordance with her own decided views of what she felt a stately home should be.

Admirers of Jack Spencer insist that, thanks to his taste and the hefty restoration grants paid for by the tax-payers, Althorp had been left to Johnnie Spencer in near perfect condition. But Raine had recently reached a very different conclusion. 'She is', in the words of Roy Strong, 'a monument to the creature comforts', and since Jack Spencer's Althorp was too spartan for her sybaritic nature, she began to change it into a place fit for herself to live in and her friends to visit.

Few could seriously object to *en suite* bathrooms and better central heating. But, as one of Raine's admirers says, 'at times Raine overdid it, such was her nature'. Once more she was doing what she wanted, and there was something quite extraordinary in the assurance with which she imposed on Althorp what one purist called 'her own profoundly suburban view of what a great aristocratic house should be'. This included double glazing to cut out the draughts from the eighteenth-century windows, oatmeal coloured close carpeting laid over ancient floorboards in the Gallery, and orange coloured dralon to replace Jack Spencer's own *petit point* chair seats. Someone calculated that Raine had over two thousand separate items of furniture at Althorp restored or re-gilded.

Depending on one's taste, the result of all these changes was excessive or spectacular. One neighbour called Raine's Althorp 'fairyland', and it reminded Alan Clark of the Schloss in Pontresina – 'a beautifully furnished hotel reserved for grand German tourists'.

Unsurprisingly, the children hated it without exception, and particularly resented having the portrait of Robert, first Lord Spencer, which had always been at the top of the grand staircase, replaced by a full-length portrait of a very youthful Raine by Carlo Sanchez.

Johnnie's illness had a curious aftermath which would also play a fateful part in Diana's future. Early in 1980, to celebrate his recovery, he took Raine off for a very special weekend, staying at the Ritz Hotel in Paris. During their stay the hotel's public relations person approached them and said, 'Lord and Lady Spencer, our new proprietor would like you to join him for a drink. He loves members of the British aristocracy and is anxious to meet you. His name is Mr al Fayed.'

The Spencers accepted the invitation, and thus began a most unusual friendship, partly based on the fact that, as Lady Spencer must have realised, friendship with the owner of the Ritz Hotel could bring tangible benefits, like upgrading, and all those extras hotel managements can offer their favoured guests.

The friendship between the Spencers and the al Fayeds flowered when Mr al Fayed purchased Harrods two years later. One of Johnnie's greatest pleasures was to shop there, pottering through the famous Food Halls and the toy department with his shopping basket. Whenever he entered Harrods, Mr al Fayed was invariably around to greet him. In due course, Mr al Fayed invited Johnnie and Raine to lunch with him at his sumptuous residence at Oxted so that they could meet his family. In return he visited them at Althorp.

Along with the changes Raine imposed on Althorp went the sense that, as one neighbour put it, she had somehow 'stolen Althorp from the county'. She is a profoundly urban creature, and the local gentry increasingly resented – or pretended to despise on grounds of taste or snobbery – what was happening as Raine organised weekend house parties for her friends from London.

But the greatest damage caused by what was happening was not to the house or the collections, but to the family. For while it seemed that Raine had now secured total victory, neither Diana nor her brother, Charles, surrendered. Their fight went on, and it would be many years before Diana would forgive her stepmother for having taken over Althorp and her father. Within the family, Diana had learned to fight a very bitter battle, and all the anger and resentment which she felt against this older woman stayed bottled up within her. At the same time, Johnnie was perfectly aware of how much his father would have hated what he had done at Althorp, and the old Earl's angry ghost was said to have been seen haunting desecrated Althorp. (Efficient as ever, Raine asked the Vicar of Northampton to exorcise it.)

In the past there had always been two solutions when the Spencers were in trouble – an influential marriage, or involvement with the court. Whether subconsciously or not, Johnnie now began to pin his hopes on both these sources of salvation.

Although the family was in such disarray, the younger generation had been re-establishing close connections with the court. In 1978

Johnnie's second daughter, Jane, had married Robert Fellowes, assistant private secretary to the Queen. They had been friends since childhood – Robert's father, Sir William Fellowes, having been the land agent at Sandringham. And while this marriage helped to re-establish contact between the Spencers and the court, Sarah too had become a friend of the Prince of Wales, who had been kind to her after the break-up of her romance with the future Duke of Westminster had left her unhappy and suffering from anorexia.

This fresh involvement with the court seems to have caused Johnnie, as a former courtier himself, to become obsessed with the idea of at least one of his daughters marrying royalty. Marriage with the royal House of Windsor would reverse the downward spiral of the Spencer family and simultaneously enhance its prestige. He seems to have hoped that Sarah might have married Prince Charles, leaving Diana as the perfect bride for Prince Andrew. But Diana had her own ideas. She had been closely following her sister Sarah's friendship with Prince Charles, and had formed a girlish crush on him herself.

It was after meeting him with Sarah that she asked the mother of a friend how she could get Prince Charles to notice *her*.

'Become a blonde,' she was told.

And so Diana did.

CHAPTER 16

A Royal Fairy Story

When Prince Charles proposed to Diana Spencer in Windsor Castle in February 1981, he did not know her very well. She did not ride or hunt, she did not sparkle socially and, in contrast with other young women he knew, she was virginal and unsophisticated. She seemed very young and inexperienced and, while she was undoubtedly in love with him, we now know he was not in love with her. So why did he propose?

The unromantic answer is that at thirty-two Charles knew he had to marry someone. For the last ten years his surprisingly tolerant parents had permitted him his sexual freedom, which as a freelance prince he had made the most of. But now the time had come for the most important act the heir to the throne is called upon to perform for the monarchy – select himself a wife to bear the royal children and one day to become queen herself.

This was overdue, and his family was getting nervous that he might follow the example of his great-uncle David, (later Edward VIII, then Duke of Windsor) who also had his mistresses and waited far too long to marry, ending up at forty abdicating his throne in order to wed the love of his life, the American divorcee, Mrs Ernest Simpson.

The precedent particularly worried the Queen Mother, who deeply disapproved of everything to do with the Duke of Windsor, and who was particularly close to her eldest grandson. He discussed almost everything with her, and she sometimes talked about young Diana Spencer. Although the royal matriarch was rising eighty, she was still as well informed as anyone at court, and thought she knew all there was to know about the girl.

After all, Diana was granddaughter of two of her own ladies in waiting, the late Lady Cynthia Spencer, and her special friend, Lady Fermoy, who had mentioned that her granddaughter seemed to be in love with the Prince. Perhaps he should think seriously about Diana. She was eminently suitable. Breeding counted in such matters, and as an aristocrat coming from a family of courtiers, Diana would know by instinct what was expected of her. The Queen Mother remembered seeing her as a child at Sandringham, and from all she had heard about her since, she was absolutely charming – as one would expect of a grandchild of Cynthia Spencer.

At around this time there were strong vibrations in Diana's favour coming from other members of the Royal Family. Ever since King George V had, from necessity, made it permissible for royalty to marry commoners – rather than the by now virtually non-existent European royal spouses once insisted on by Queen Victoria – they had chosen them from aristocratic families with courtier connections, like the Lascelleses, the Strathmores and the Airlies.

The Spencers were similar, but had closer past connections with the court than any of them, and, since the family was popular with both the Queen and the Queen Mother, Charles knew that if he married Diana Spencer he would be doing so with full parental approval, which was something he had always wanted. He was already acquainted with Diana as the shy teenage sister of his friend, her sister, Sarah. Compared with his other girl friends, Diana cannot have seemed particularly exciting, but the more he thought about her, the more it seemed that she would make an admirable queen. She would also have some less obvious advantages which for the Prince weighed strongly in her favour.

During the previous four years he had become deeply and, as it is now known, irrevocably involved with Camilla, wife of his polo-playing friend, Colonel (now Brigadier) Andrew Parker-Bowles. The affair had actually started ten years earlier when

Camilla, proud of her descent from King Edward VII's mistress, Alice Keppel, is said to have made him the irresistible invitation – 'My great-grandmother was the mistress of your great-great grandfather. How's about it, sir?' The resultant affair had ended when the Prince went off to command his frigate, HMS *Minerva*, and Camilla married the womanising Parker-Bowles. It began again some six years and two children later.

Since then the affair had grown in intensity, until it was fairly common knowledge at the Palace, which must have made the Prince's parents more anxious still to see him safely married. None of them knew, as we do now, that Mrs Parker-Bowles would be the one enduring love of the Prince's life, whose presence, as he put it later, would never be 'negotiable'. But already she was appearing in the guise of that most perilous of figures in the lives of princes from the House of Windsor, a quietly determined older married woman; and the Prince's dependence on her was arousing understandable concern.

By strict royal standards theirs had to be a hopeless love. Since he was future King and Head of the Church of England and she was someone else's wife, the Prince could never think of marrying Camilla. But he had to marry someone, even if it broke his heart, and he genuinely believed that it would break his heart if his marriage meant giving up this woman that he loved, for ever.

He and Camilla had undoubtedly discussed the situation, and whilst both accepted the fact that it was Charles's duty to marry, Camilla felt it was equally her duty to be there for him when he needed her, just as her great-grandmother had always been there for King Edward. If Charles could make his sacrifice for the monarchy, so could she, and with love and patience everything could work out in the end.

Clearly much was going to depend on the character of the girl he chose to be his wife. Ideally she should be another Alexandra to Camilla's Mrs Keppel, someone who, with time and understanding, could be led to tolerate and finally accept the situation, which after all, was something kings and princes had been indulging in since the world began.

Who better for this role than innocent Diana? She seemed to possess almost all the qualities that had made Queen Alexandra so beloved by her children – and so invaluable to her husband and his mistresses. Even Diana's innocence seemed in her favour, and the Prince presumably believed that this gentle, unformed, girl could easily be led towards the role that he envisaged. She had been working in a kindergarten and loved children. She also loved the Prince. Once she was Princess of Wales and mother of the royal children, she would have far too much to lose to make trouble over her husband's friendship with Camilla, which need never threaten her or endanger her position as future Queen of England.

Ironically, it was Diana's apparent perfection for the role of royal bride that caused such endless trouble later. For she seemed to offer such irresistible advantages to almost everyone concerned that this led to what would prove to be a fatal misunderstanding over the very nature of the marriage. For her it was all quite simple. At nineteen, she was still as romantic as ever and eagerly in search of love. She had had a teenage crush on the Prince even before her sister Sarah started going out with him, and when he proposed to her she genuinely believed he was in love with her. As far as she was concerned, she was embarking on a lifelong royal love match.

But for the others involved, and especially Prince Charles, the marriage was nothing of the sort. For them it was essentially an old-style royal marriage of convenience, the 'convenience' being that the union was intended to suit all concerned, the Spencers, the Royal Family, the Prince and Camilla, and the international media, especially the TV networks with however many millions of eager viewers round the world. But Diana's feelings were totally ignored.

Had she been older, more experienced, and of a colder and more calculating nature, this sort of royal marriage might still have suited her as well. Once married, she would be envied, fêted, and endlessly deferred to, with the prospect of becoming Queen of England and mother of the royal children. She would also bring much needed fresh prestige and honour to the Spencers by linking them directly with the Royal Family.

All that was lacking was the one thing that not unnaturally concerned her. What she wanted from the Prince was his undivided love, but he was very much in love with someone else.

Later, Diana would claim that almost from the start she had her doubts about the Prince's feelings and that even as he proposed: 'a voice within me said, "You won't be Queen."'

Whether this was true or not, it didn't stop her accepting his proposal and enjoying the intense media attention, along with her flat-mates' envy, her father's happiness and the quiet pleasure of upstaging her stepmother, Raine Spencer.

Someone should have made the nature of the marriage clear to her from the beginning. But who? And how? Prince Charles could not very well explain the situation, and no one else could risk derailing the marriage of the decade. The one person who did apparently utter a few heavily veiled words of warning was her grandmother, Lady Fermoy, who told her: 'Darling, you must understand that their sense of humour and their life-style are different, and I don't think it will suit you.'

At this point, the position of Ruth Fermoy is all important, and the fact that she felt it necessary to say this to Diana shows something of the genuine dilemma she was facing. In theory, nothing should have pleased her more than the prospect of her own grand-daughter one day becoming Queen of England. Indeed, for someone so involved with royalty as Ruth Fermoy, it would have seemed the culmination of her wildest ambitions. Once Diana had given birth to a royal heir, Lady Fermoy would stand beside her friend and patron, the Queen Mother, as joint great-grandmother of the future monarch, and the Fermoys too would have gained their place within the bloodline of the monarchy.

But it was not that simple. As Diana's grandmother, she was the one influential courtier who really knew the Spencers, and what had been going on at Althorp. She also knew about the complexities of Diana's character, and that there was considerably more to her than the shy and loving young girl she appeared. Like everyone at court, she also knew about Prince Charles and Camilla, and was intelligent enough to realise that Diana was never going to accept a rival.

To speak, or not to speak – that was Ruth Fermoy's dilemma. When it came to it, she decided to say nothing, apart from the fairly harmless warning that she gave Diana. She knew her well enough to understand that it would not make her change her mind, but if anything did go wrong it meant that she could salve her conscience. Having warned her, she was covered.

There was one further reason which, although unspoken, must have lain behind Ruth Fermoy's obvious uneasiness about Diana entering the Royal House of Windsor. It was this. Better than any-one, she knew that Jack Spencer had been right and that there was a streak of nervous instability among the Fermoys. Her husband's unmarried twin brother, Frank Roche, had been a serious depress-ive. So was her own son and Diana's favourite uncle, Edmund, fifth Baron Fermoy, who was already showing symptoms of the depressive illness that would lead to his suicide three years later. As a devoted monarchist, Lady Fermoy must have had serious doubts about the wisdom of introducing this particular genetic streak of the Fermoys into the British Royal Family.

What makes the situation even stranger is that while Ruth Fermoy was facing her dilemma, Diana's own doubts about her marriage were growing. She was by now more or less convinced that Prince Charles was still in love with Camilla Parker Bowles. Just two days before the wedding, over lunch, a desperate Diana told her sisters that she could not go through with it. 'Well, bad luck, Duch,' one of them replied, 'your face is on the tea towels so you're too late to chicken out'. As of course she was. She was irrevocably cast in the starring role in one of the most impressive and at this point the most widely seen royal ceremonies in history.

Some eighty years before, after the death of Queen Victoria, when the Royal Family began to lose their old symbolic power over the largest empire in history, they had reinforced their popularity, like the Roman emperors before them, by entering the entertainment industry. In 1901, Lord Esher, the Cecil B. de Mille of royalty, was asked to devise much of the grandiose royal pageantry surrounding the Coronation of King Edward VII. Victoria's coronation had been considerably simpler and shorter, but henceforth the pageantry of the great ceremonies of state involving the monarch and his family became the bedrock upon which the soon to be renamed Royal House of Windsor would consolidate their popularity.

Again, as with the Romans, one legacy the British Empire had left its leaders was an unrivalled talent for the pageantry of state, and the Windsors and their courtiers would raise these great royal ceremonies to something of an art form. During the 1930s, when the totalitarian regimes of Europe were staging their robot-like massed rallies at Nuremburg and Moscow, our public ceremonies were already being choreographed around the lives and rites of passage of members of this apparently benevolent, infinitely famous Royal Family, in their coronations, marriages, jubilees and funerals.

It was a formula that served them well. The televised Coronation of the young Queen Elizabeth II in June 1953 brought a boost of patriotic fervour to a jaded nation, with hopes for a royal revival in a second great 'Elizabethan' age. It was not to last. By the end of the irreverent sixties the younger generation of Elizabeth's subjects was becoming bored with the New Elizabethans. Resourceful as ever, the Windsors ventured warily upon the thin ice of co-operation with the media by revealing what was called 'the human face of monarchy' in a TV film entitled 'Royal Family'. This offered their fascinated subjects the novel revelation that this Royal Family who enjoyed barbecues, had nick-names for each other and laughed at one another's jokes were quite ordinary people after all.

This, of course, was total nonsense. For while these members of the House of Windsor may have looked and sounded ordinary, in fact they were living the most privileged lives of anybody in the land. But the royal soap opera had begun. Through the media, people began to feel they knew them personally. They could love or hate them like familiar relations. Sometimes they identified with them and finally, of course, they judged them.

But this ceaseless press and public interest in the Royal Family brought problems, particularly when the taste for royal scandal became insatiable, as it did at the time of Princess Margaret's unprecedented divorce from Lord Snowdon in 1978. But while scandal upset the Royal Family, it undoubtedly fuelled public interest in the monarchy, which was steadily increasing.

Then, towards the late 1970s, a new affliction hit the House of Windsor – age. With the Queen and Prince Philip entering late middle age, the Royal Family lacked youth and glamour. Younger members of the family were needed, which in turn meant more royal marriages. As public ceremonies, the weddings of Princess Margaret and Princess Anne had been enormously successful for this new performing monarchy (despite the fact that neither marriage lasted). It is easy to see exactly why the court was attaching such importance to this marriage of the future King of England. This wedding of the royal heir had two further advantages over all previous nuptials in the royal house of Windsor. The first was live satellite colour television. The second was Diana.

She was Cinderella. She was a fairytale princess who might almost have been the girl next door, and the gentle, still girlish image had immediate appeal for every woman who as a child had ever dreamed of marrying a prince.

On that summer morning in 1981, viewing the procession on live television as it passed through the crowded streets of London was like watching some splendid royal occasion from the pages of the history books. Such was the impact of the ceremony, and so great the international involvement of this massive audience, that Diana instantly became the most famous bride the world had ever seen. By the end of that extraordinary day neither she, nor the Royal Family, would ever be the same again.

In his address, Archbishop Runcie informed the watching millions: 'Here is the stuff of which fairytales are made.' It was also the stuff of which an international royal superstar had been created.

And as the more sentimental viewers dried their tears, the world was taking it for granted that this fairy story must have a happy ending, as it would have done if Prince Charles had loved her.

On the newlyweds' return from their honeymoon, it cannot have taken the House of Windsor long to realise they had a serious problem on their hands. Their bland assumption that they knew Diana Spencer simply was not true. A Spencer she may have been, but she was not a gently nurtured aristocrat, with the courtly manners and the loyal discretion of her courtier aunts and grand-mothers.

Despite the extraordinary success of the wedding, there was some-thing seriously wrong between the couple from the start, with the Prince uneasy and his bride obviously unhappy, nervous, desperately thin while suffering from bulimia, and often bursting into tears.

Any family would find this hard to cope with, but it must have been particularly hard for the Windsors. Neither by training nor tradition are royalty accustomed or equipped to deal with anyone behaving badly. This makes it understandable that from the start Diana received so little sympathy or support from this strange family to which she now found herself irretrievably committed. As far as they were concerned, she was clearly being tiresome, and should have known better what was expected of her. They only hoped that, given time, she would settle down and come to her senses.

Meanwhile, the inevitable reaction in the Palace was, 'Oh, poor Charles!'

Total immersion in the Royal Family must have been a formidable ordeal for someone as inexperienced as Diana. Only recently, when thirty-two-year old Sophie Rhys Jones became engaged to the Queen's youngest son, Prince Edward, she was asked by a reporter whether she thought that she could cope with being a member of the Royal Family. She said she thought she could just about do so now, but she would certainly have been unable to five years earlier. In contrast, back in 1981, Diana was barely twenty, ignorant of the world and the reality of the court, and had virtually nobody to turn to when things went wrong.

In an ordinary family the unhappiness of a young, jealous bride would have been their own affair. But this was not an ordinary family. It was the British Royal Family, and the bride would one day be the Queen of England. She was already admired and loved by millions. Surely somebody at court must have seen the danger of making such a young girl so potentially powerful while leaving her so unhappy.

With the birth of Prince William in 1982, Diana had consolidated her position in the Royal Family. She had performed her most important duty to the House of Windsor, and whatever doubts its individual members may have had about her, as mother of the future king, she was now of central importance to the monarchy.

The infant prince formed the one real link between his parents and was a source of unaccustomed joy between them. Prince Charles told his friends, Hugh and Emilie van Cutsem that he was 'utterly elated'. 'I can't tell you how excited and proud I am,' he added. Diana felt the same, and from the start adored her son. But the birth of Prince William had left her in the grip of postnatal depression, and the misery continued.

By now it was probably too late for things to change. The worse Diana felt and the more difficult she became, the more sympathy Prince Charles apparently received from his family and friends. They now felt she was causing him unnecessary anxiety and, as royalty can never be at fault, the blame would always rest with her.

It was a time when everyone involved required sound advice on how to handle the situation. There was one obvious courtier who should have helped – Diana's grandmother, Ruth Fermoy.

One of the most important moments of the royal day was the Queen's morning telephone call to her mother. The Queen had long relied upon her mother's wisdom and advice, and among other things they discussed family matters, which of course included

Charles and Diana's problems. This meant that as the Queen Mother's close friend and confidante, Ruth Fermoy knew exactly what was happening and was the one person at court who could have genuinely helped her granddaughter.

It seems as if she did the opposite. Like all true courtiers, her loyalties lay exclusively with the Royal Family. Ever since the much publicised Spencer divorce, she had always disapproved of her daughter Frances. As she had once renounced her daughter, it seems she now did much the same with Diana. Since she invariably agreed with the Royal Family, now she inevitably sided with the Prince.

But knowing what she did about the mental stability of the Fermoys, she must have been in an intolerable position. Shortly before she died in 1993, she said she blamed herself for not having warned Prince Charles about Diana before the marriage. By now it was far too late.

A member of Lady Fermoy's own family once called her 'very beautiful and very cold', and one gets an idea of her attitude to life from the diaries of the biographer Hugo Vickers, whom met her at dinner in 1982. 'There was talk of the death sentence,' he wrote afterwards. 'Lady Fermoy was all for the cat and caning. She said, "The fear of being hurt is the great prevention." She was also, naturally, pro-hanging.' She was hardly the one to make allowances for an unhappy granddaughter.

Diana's postnatal depression lifted around the time she and Charles went on tour to Australia and New Zealand, taking their baby with them in spring 1983. This was the first time since their wedding that they both saw how enormously popular the Princess had become with ordinary people. In Sydney, a million turned out to greet them. Prince Charles had never experienced a crowd like it, but it was painfully clear to him that once again it was Diana that they wished to see. This continued throughout the six week tour. The photographs show them sitting determinedly apart and the Prince is rarely smiling. Diana said that she returned 'more grown up and mature', but that her husband had become increasingly put out by her popularity.

Everyone agrees that there seemed to be a brief period of happiness between them just before the birth of their second son, Prince Harry, in September 1984. But when the Prince was born, Charles's attitude had changed from the excitement he had shown at the birth of Prince William. Initially he was disappointed to have a second son, having longed for a daughter, and Diana was convinced by now that Prince Charles had returned to 'his lady'. So instead of this birth bringing the two of them together, the marriage now began to fall apart, and the biggest crisis to afflict the House of Windsor since the Abdication, started forming in the wreckage.

CHAPTER 17

Death of a Princess

It was not long before the Spencers themselves became disappointed by their lack of contact with the court and with their royal in-laws. The high hopes of Diana's marriage rescuing the family from decline and adding to its lustre and prestige were fading fast.

Not for the first time the Countess's commercial instincts had been causing trouble – in Japan she had been promoting sales of copies of Diana's wedding dress and licensing the name 'Royal Spencer' to golf clubs. Unsurprisingly this had been disapproved of by the court.

At the same time, difficulties in the Wales's marriage had not helped relations between Johnnie and his royal son-in-law. Prince Charles had annoyed him early in his marriage by his tactless remarks on the restorations of the newly decorated rooms at Althorp. In return Johnnie started referring to him as 'my Gordonstoun son-in-law' and saying that one of the reasons he had done so badly on the polo field was 'because he is too mean to buy himself a decent pony'.

But the real cause of trouble was, of course, Diana. Although she made a point of not discussing her problems with her father he was very much aware of what was happening. Around this time he revealed something of his real feelings on the subject when interviewed by the *Nova Scotia Chronicle* during a trip to Canada. He was more forthright than he would have been in England.

'Prince William will grow up close to the Spencer side of the family,' he said, 'and he will be influenced by them as much as by the royals. I know the royals can appear to swallow people up when others marry in, and the other family always looks as if it had been pushed out, but that could never happen with us. We can cope with the pressures. We have been brought up with royalty and there is no question of being pushed out. Diana would not permit it to happen, and she always gets her way.'

Certainly his own hopes of playing any real part in the lives of his royal grandchildren were already proving over-optimistic. He had bought three seaside houses in Raine's name at West Wittering near Bognor, on the south coast. He loved going there, and would often drive down from Althorp on his own while Raine stayed in London in the home he had also bought for her in Mayfair. His dream was that the young princes would come down to West Wittering during their summer holidays. But although Charles and Diana visited once, the infant princes never came at all.

Diana's brother, Charles Spencer, was at the same time finding his position as brother-in-law to his future monarch equally frustrating. With his loyalties divided between his parents and his battles with his stepmother, his adolescence had not been easy. He had little respect for his father and found it difficult to accept authority. He proved his intelligence when he went to Oxford and gained a good degree in history. But at twenty he was immature and could be arrogant and unreliable. It was a time in his life when personal publicity was the last thing he needed, but, as Diana's brother, anything he did was news and it needed only a few 'incidents' of the sort indulged in by most lively undergraduates to get him christened 'Champagne Charlie', which was neither fair nor helpful in his situation. He still resented Raine as much as ever and tried to avoid going to Althorp whenever she was there.

As a result of this situation he pleased himself and led a surprisingly independent life for one so young. Shortly before his twenty-first birthday he already had his own London establishment in the form of a £200,000 house in Notting Hill Gate, purchased with money from a family trust. In 1986, just down from Oxford, his role as brother of the Princess of Wales, far from causing him trouble, prompted the American NBC to offer him a contract as a TV reporter for another royal wedding – between Prince Andrew and Sarah Ferguson. The easy-going Viscount was fluent and relaxed in front of the cameras, and, however much he came to hate the media later, he spent five successful years in television.

By now, Raine was firmly in charge of double-glazed and tourist-friendly Althorp, where she had set up a shop in the stables, arranged a conference centre and invited Americans to 'Dine with Di's Dad', as the *Evening Standard* put it, for £360 a head. Raine very much aware of her role as the royal stepmother, was happy with the increase in visitors the royal connection brought to Althorp. She called the extra income this produced 'my Di money'.

One gets some idea of the style in which she and Johnnie lived by the lavish party which she gave to celebrate Johnnie's sixtieth birthday in 1984. Alan Clark described it in his diaries: 'A magnificent sight . . . Barbara Cartland in electric pink chiffon, with false eyelashes as thick as those caterpillars that give you a rash if you touch them . . . some mature ladies so encrustulated with jewellery that they could barely move . . . the Bishop of Southwark in a purple cassock . . . and the Princess of Wales looking absolutely radiantly beautiful and not wearing one single piece of jewellery.'

This glimpse of Diana shows that she had been learning fast. The unsophisticated bride had turned into a glamorous woman of the world, who knew exactly how to make her stepmother and her rich friends look like overdressed Christmas trees. What is also interesting is that she was able to look so beautiful at a time when she was so unhappy. As she said herself, 'I've got what my mother's got. However bloody you're feeling you can put on the most amazing show of happiness. My mother is an expert at that.' And so was she, for by now she was entering the worst years of her marriage.

The Windsors were playing an extremely dangerous game by treating her the way they did. Jealousy would make her dangerous

– misery would make her lethal. But not even the most pessimistic courtier could have imagined all the problems they were now creating for themselves in this beautiful, unhappy young princess.

During the months following Prince Harry's birth in September 1984 something snapped within the royal marriage, after which any hope of reconciliation was gone for ever.

This was the moment when Charles and Diana, had they been an ordinary couple, would have made contact with their lawyers, made arrangements for the custody of the children, submitted to the mundane misery of divorce, and hopefully got on with their separate lives. But the royal taboo against divorce remained as strong as ever, and Prince Charles was in the historic situation often faced by royalty in failed marriages of convenience, where the need to maintain appearances at court locks them into personal relationships of the profoundest misery.

One of the strangest features of this situation was the lack of authority shown by the monarch. It is always difficult to interfere in children's married lives, but what was happening with Charles and Diana was so crucial to the monarchy itself – and, as it soon turned out, would have such dire consequences for the institution and for everyone involved – that it seems extraordinary that there is so little evidence of any real direction from either the Queen or from Prince Philip.

Just as Diana was originally chosen to be future queen partly at least because she was a Spencer, so now it was almost certainly her Spencer blood that helped her to cope with her predicament. Most women of her age, finding themselves in such a situation, would have totally collapsed. Not so Diana, and it was now that she revealed extraordinary resources, many of which must have come from her heredity.

She was an extremely complex personality, with qualities that contradicted one another, as one might have expected in someone coming from a family so rich in history, with many powerful individuals who might have contributed to her genetic make-up. The saintly monk, Ignatius Spencer, and her grandmother, Cynthia, both had the qualities of caring and concern for others, which became the hallmark of Diana's work among the sick and needy. The depressive streak in the Fermoys may well have aggravated her sense of worthlessness, her bulimia, and the half-hearted suicide attempts which happened early in her marriage. But the most striking thing about the Spencers is that this has always been a family of immensely powerful women. There was the Duchess Georgiana, who was fashion queen of London. There was her mother, the gambling bluestocking, Georgiana Poyntz, first Countess Spencer. Above all, there was the indomitable, intolerable Sarah Marlborough.

One of Diana's close relations goes as far as to ascribe much of Diana's character to Sarah Marlborough's genes. Speaking from personal experience, she believes that 'the Jenyns strain persists with the Spencers. They are such great haters, and they positively thrive on dramas.'

In 1989 Diana's brother Charles, impetuous as ever, following a two month engagement, married twenty-three-year-old Victoria Lockwood, the young and pretty daughter of an airline executive. His aunt, Lady Margaret Douglas-Home, remembering her own unhappy marriage, had urged caution. 'Aunt Margaret,' he replied, 'this one is different. I *really* love her.'

At the wedding reception, Diana found herself standing next to Raine, and some years later told Andrew Morton what occurred. Raine had apparently ignored Diana's mother, Frances, so 'I told her what I thought about her, and I've never known such anger in me. I took it upon myself to air everyone's grievances in my family. I stuck up for mummy and she said it was the first time in twenty-two years anyone had ever stuck up for her. I said everything I possibly could. I remember really going for her gullet. I said, "I hate you so much. If only you knew how much we all hated you for what you've done, you've ruined the house, you spend Daddy's money, and what for?"'

This extraordinary outburst reveals how deeply and passionately Diana could nurse her sense of anger and revenge when her jealousy became involved. Her ongoing battle with her step-mother had taught her how to fight and convinced her that she had to win.

It was the Queen herself who called 1992 her *annus horribilis*. Charles and Diana must have felt the same. At the end of March Johnnie Spencer died. It was a sudden death, just a few days in hospital, pneumonia, a heart attack and he was gone.

Twenty-eight-year-old Charles Edward Maurice, now ninth Earl Spencer, took over Althorp, reclaiming the house for his family and insisting on removing every vestige and reminder of the person he already called 'my former stepmother'. Raine's clothes were packed into plastic black bin liners and, in a final symbolic gesture, were apparently kicked down the great Althorp staircase. Raine's portrait by Carlo Sanchez had already been removed from the head of the staircase, like the image of a hated ruler at the end of his reign. This must have made the Earl feel better, but it was actually a fairly futile gesture, for during those precious years following his stroke, Johnnie had provided for her future by ensuring that she left the marriage several million pounds richer than when she entered it.

Moving into Althorp with Victoria and their three young children, the new Earl already had great plans for the future. Almost at once he set about trying to return the interior of the house to what it had been like in the days of his grandfather. He also said that by setting up home there with his young family, he intended 'to fill this house with joy for the first time in its history'. This would not be an easy task, for although he was now undisputed owner of Althorp and an estate valued at £89 million, despite all Raine's endeavours to turn it into a paying proposition, it was still running at a heavy loss and costing over £450,000 a year to maintain.

Exactly as had happened with his own father Johnnie, Charles was now the father of three daughters – Kitty, born in 1990, and twin girls, Eliza and Katya, born two years later. It was not until 1994, in spite of his much publicised marital misdemeanours, that Victoria gave him the heir to Althorp and its title that he so badly wanted, but the birth of Louis Frederick John would bring only temporary happiness to an otherwise unhappy marriage. After Victoria had undergone a course of treatment for anorexia and drink and drug addiction, Charles would decide to buy two homes in South Africa, taking them away from the constant intrusion of the worldwide media.

Diana, like her brother, was becoming increasingly obsessed by the role of the media in her private life. Since the days of Queen Victoria, it had been an unspoken rule at court that the Royal Family was protected by a wall of silence and discretion. But this did not prevent Diana from using the media to her own advantage when it suited her, even if it meant breaking this royal rule. By 1992, with her marriage all but over, she decided that the time had come to have her story told.

If nothing else, the undercover operation Diana devised shows how manipulative life at court had made this once innocent princess. Having chosen the former royal reporter, Andrew Morton, to write her book, she made absolutely sure that she never met him, so that when her book was published she could deny any responsibility for it. Instead she answered his written questions on a tape recorder.

The book, *Diana, Her Own True Story*, was a damning indictment of Prince Charles, Camilla and the marriage, but Diana consistently denied any involvement in the affair, even when the Queen's private secretary, who was also her brother-in-law, Sir Robert Fellowes, asked her outright if she had assisted Morton. Few at court believed her, least of all her own grandmother, Lady Fermoy. For her, the shame of what she saw as her granddaughter's betrayal of the Royal Family was unforgivable. With Diana's story in the open, further pretence about her marriage was impossible. She and the Prince of Wales would separate officially just before Christmas 1992, and divorce would follow four years later.

The saga of Diana and her own family was far from over. After her official separation from the Prince, she was anxious to have somewhere to escape to from Kensington Palace, and she particularly wanted a home in the country where she could take her children in the school holidays. Early in the new year she discussed this with her brother Charles, who, without thinking of the consequences, offered her the elegant, early eighteenth-century Garden House, in the park at Althorp.

She was happy at the thought of having her own country home at last, and where better than in the grounds of her ancestral home close to the brother she had always loved? In her excitement she sought the advice of her friend, the interior decorator, Dudley Poplak, took the princes to see it, and started making plans and choosing furniture and decorations. It had to be done swiftly as she wanted the house to be ready for the Easter holidays in April. But before this could happen, her brother had second thoughts and changed his mind.

Charles Spencer was particularly worried by the problem of security for his own family, as well as the invasion of his privacy. But Diana, who had set her heart on the house, became distraught. In retrospect it does appear a great missed opportunity, for a home at Althorp would have helped her to rebuild her life in close contact with Charles and her family, thus giving her and the children the stability they badly needed. But it was not to be. Charles Spencer was obdurate and, despite her pleas, returned her angry letters unopened.

This was not a good time for Diana and the Spencers. With relations now strained between her and her brother, Diana more than ever felt the need for love and reassurance from her mother. But Frances, now divorced from Peter Shand Kydd, needed help herself after another failed love affair, and could not give Diana the support she wanted.

Feeling hurt and angry at being let down by both her brother and her mother, it was now that Diana did the one thing that she knew would upset them more than anything. It was Diana at her most manipulative, and it proved to be the greatest mistake of her life.

Early that July, Jean-François, Comte de Chambrun was a happy but puzzled man. He had just become the third husband of the briefly widowed Raine, former Countess Spencer, and had been reading press reports about Diana disowning her former step-mother, and telling reporters that they were no longer related now she had remarried. Feeling that these words gave a false impression, the Count wrote a letter to *The Times*.

'Sir,' he wrote. 'Certain newspapers this morning have published information which states that H.R.H. the Princess of Wales might have made disobliging comments about my wife, Raine, the former Countess Spencer.

'I feel obliged to say this cannot be the truth. I had the privilege of being invited by H.R.H. to Kensington Palace. This was an informal family lunch, with just H.R.H., Raine and myself. After the coffee, H.R.H. took Raine by the hand, and said to her as she was next to me, "Raine, thank you so much for the love you gave to my father over all those years."

'Raine and H.R.H. fell into each others' arms, and they kissed goodbye in the most affectionate way ... As a witness of the most charming and delicate manner in which H.R.H. spoke to and kissed Raine, I felt it would only be meet and proper to write you this letter.'

On reading this letter in *The Times*, Frances was incensed. To her it seemed inconceivable that Diana's feelings towards her stepmother could possibly have changed so quickly. She also learned that around the same time Diana had also seen fit to visit her grand-mother, Lady Fermoy, shortly before she died that summer.

When Frances asked Diana what she thought she was playing at, her daughter answered that if *she* could forgive these two former enemies, the rest of the family should do the same. Since the rest of the family had no intention of doing anything of the sort, the result of Diana's peace offensive actually increased the tensions within the family, especially when her reconciliation with Raine began to turn into a much publicised friendship.

Diana's life remained unresolved and fraught with problems. She still had no home other than Kensington Palace. Her marital battle dragged on, and after the Princess's television interview on 'Panorama' in 1995, the Queen herself urged the couple to end their marriage. There had been too much dirty linen washed in public and too much bitterness between them. There was no alternative to the divorce, which came in 1996.

After the divorce, with a £17 million settlement, Diana felt free for the first time since her marriage to the Prince. Even Camilla was no longer a threat. Her two sons were of the utmost importance to her now, and she tried to teach them that there was a world outside the rigid confines of the palace, a kinder, more human world where people genuinely cared about each other.

Having put the past behind her, she still felt she had an all-important role to play and tried to use her extraordinary position to the maximum effect, whether by focusing attention on the plight of refugees in Bosnia or arousing world opinion against the lethal scourge of land-mines. Her enthusiasm for these causes was contagious and appeared to give a new purpose to her life. But more than ever now she wanted to resolve the problem of her private life. She still had romantic dreams about her future, but was wary of committing herself. During this period, she had had a number of affairs which came to nothing. But she was not expecting to marry overnight. As she herself said: 'I haven't taken such a long time getting out of one poor marriage, to get into another.'

Since their reconciliation, Raine had become increasingly important in Diana's life. As a woman of the world she was always there with practical advice, and soon they were speaking daily on the telephone and lunching together almost every week, either at the Connaught Hotel or Claridges. Then, one fateful day, Raine took Diana for lunch at Harrods to meet her old friend, the Chairman, Mohammed al Fayed.

Over lunch al Fayed talked with pride about the close friendship he had always had with her father and with Raine. He told her, 'My old friend, Earl Spencer, was like a brother to me. On his deathbed he asked me to take care of his family.' This was a promise he would like to keep.

In fact it was the Spencers' involvement with the aristocracy and the Royal Family that had aroused the interest of al Fayed from the start. He had always had an obsession with the Royal Family, so much so that he even spent a vast sum of money buying the former Paris home of the Duke and Duchess of Windsor. After his ruthless battle for control of Harrods, al Fayed had become suspect in the eyes of the British Establishment. Both he and his brother were refused British citizenship, which offended them deeply, and his friendship with Raine and her royal step-daughter may have helped to heal the wounds of such a very public rejection.

Al Fayed could be immensely charming and was, of course, very, very rich. He made sure that any contact with Diana came through Raine, and whenever Diana visited Harrods, he was always there to greet her in person and to make a fuss of her, just as he had with Johnnie. He insisted that it was his privilege to do so. By now he had appointed Raine to a non-executive directorship of Harrods and he offered a similar position to Diana. She was tempted, but in the end reluctantly refused. But she did not refuse his offer in 1997 to spend a luxurious holiday with al Fayed and his family at his villa in the South of France. By accepting this invitation, Diana's fate was sealed.

It was a sign of improving relations between Diana and Prince Charles that he now raised no objections to his sons spending two weeks of their summer holidays with their mother at the Fayed villa outside San Tropez. By all accounts the holiday was a success, so successful that al Fayed, who was never one to miss a trick, suddenly saw the chance of a lifetime.

Although Diana had previously met his son Dodi when playing polo with Prince Charles, it was only now, in the romantic climate of the South of France, that she seemed to notice him. More than that, al Fayed saw at once that she was obviously attracted to him. Think what it would mean if the mother of the future king of England could be somehow persuaded to fall in love with his only son, Dodi. For any other father it might have been hard to arrange. For al Fayed anything was possible.

Diana and the two young princes returned to England at the end of the holiday, but by then she had already accepted an invitation for another holiday – without her children. She had two previously arranged engagements, one in support of the land-mine campaign in Bosnia, and the other a short Greek island holiday with her close friend, Rosa Monckton. For both trips al Fayed put a Harrods private jet at her disposal.

Diana was both vulnerable and valuable, just how valuable al Fayed showed by spending a reported $20 million simply to ensure the success of the romance. It went on the *Jonikal*, a 200-foot luxury yacht which he purchased specially for the occasion. At the same time he ordered Dodi to break with his American fiancée, the model Kelly Fisher, leaving him free to fall in love with Diana.

Once more, Diana's life, unknown to her, was being taken over. A few weeks later, aboard the *Jonikal*, Dodi fell in love with her and she with him, exactly as al Fayed intended. They seemed inseparable. However, the world press closed in on them, and so did the past when they returned to Paris.

Had Diana not made her peace with Raine, she would never have become involved with al Fayed, nor would she have been in Paris with his son. But now the circle was complete as she returned so unsuspectingly to the Ritz Hotel with Dodi on the evening of the 30 August. Of course there were elements that no one could have foreseen and which also became part of her fate – the hurried telephone call Dodi made to his father in Oxted for instructions leading to a change of plan, the jostling photographers gathered round the doors, and the arrival of the man who was to kill her, the depressive, alcoholic driver, Henri Paul, with the equivalent of six whiskies and twenty milligrams of Prozac in his bloodstream.

As Diana and Dodi went through the doors of the Paris Ritz on that August night in 1997, who would have thought that the close friendship Johnnie and Raine Spencer had struck up with Mohammed al Fayed at the same hotel in 1980 would end seventeen years later with the deaths of both of their children.

Epilogue

When Diana met her death in the Paris tunnel at the Place d'Alma shortly after midnight on 31 August 1997 it was a tragedy in the strict Greek meaning of the word – the inevitability of fate in the life and death of the great and famous. With Diana, one keeps noticing this inevitability in the sequence of events, some of them buried deep within the past, but all converging on her failed royal marriage, the manner of its break-up, its aftermath, and now her death.

There was much within her early life that had directed her towards her marriage – all those aunts and grandmothers with their places at court, the early childhood spent so close to the royal home at Sandringham, the fact that her brother was a godson of the Queen, and that her sister would marry the Queen's future private secretary. Above all, there was her father's fervent wish, as a former royal equerry himself, to advance the Spencers by linking them through marriage to the Royal Family. The Royal Family had also needed Diana Spencer – as mother of the royal heirs, as future queen, and to give glamour and excitement to an ageing court.

Part of the tragedy comes from the sense of loss for what might have been had the marriage worked. What is left is pity for Diana as a victim, caught between these two great families – the Spencers and the Windsors. Both needed her and both had used her.

Ours is a world that lives by stories and, thanks to the worldwide media, Diana's life became our most addictive story. It was the great televised ceremony of her marriage that had made her overnight the most famous woman in the world, and throughout the dramas and disasters that ensued, the interest of her public rarely wavered. For them, she was the fairytale princess who had been badly treated by her Prince and by his court, and it was this that caused such endless fascination.

But there remained one thing the story lacked – the happy-ever-after ending she was always seeking. She had never found it in her short, unsatisfactory love affairs, and her friends were wondering if she ever would. In the spring of 1997 Diana seemed caught between her role as mother of the two young Princes, the causes she believe in, and the excitements offered by the rich and famous, particularly in America where she was becoming very popular. Her future was still uncertain, even when the press and television showed a radiant Diana with Dodi al Fayed holidaying in the sun.

At this point no one knew that the romance had been stage-managed by Mohammed al Fayed. Again, the story was all that mattered, and the hope that Diana had found true love at last kept her worldwide audience enraptured.

Had Diana not died with her lover as she did, this affair would probably have ended like the others, if only because so much was stacked against it. There would have been al Fayed himself to contend with, and her role as mother of the royal heirs. There was also Dodi, playboy son of a dominating father. But at this stage of the story, the one thing that mattered seemed to be that Diana was in love.

Writing to the widow of Robert Louis Stevenson shortly after her husband died, Henry James said that few other deaths had been 'so romantically right' as his. In terms of her story, so was Diana's. Her death was so sudden and so shocking that it came like the death of a great Romantic heroine. It had all the classic elements – she was beautiful and young, she had suffered, and she seemed to be so much in love.

There were two great ceremonies in the life and death of Diana – her marriage which made her a megastar, and now her funeral which made her a legend. One had been a celebration of joy and hope. The other brought with it the finality of death – an even more powerful emotion. Due to the unexpectedness of Diana's death, all the other members of the Royal Family found themselves acting out the parts which death allotted them – the grieving sons, the heartbroken Spencers, and the Royal Family that had once rejected her.

Her funeral became the final retribution which Princess Diana brought upon the House of Windsor. For, by dying as she did, she had cast its members in the roles in which she saw them, and that was how the world now saw them too. They had no time to change their image. Prince Charles did his best by flying instantly to Paris with her sisters to bring her body back to England. But when his tortured face appeared on the television screens, was it guilt or was it grief that lay behind his suffering? Now divorced herself, Camilla Parker-Bowles was left with the most unenviable role of all.

The Queen had originally wanted Diana to have a private funeral, but ended by agreeing to a full royal funeral at Westminster Abbey. For the people's expectations and the story, continued to dictate what had to happen – the two young Princes walking between their father and their uncle, following the gun carriage which bore the coffin of their mother, the vast and silent crowd of mourners, the royal women standing grim faced and isolated from the people as the funeral cortège passed Buckingham Palace.

In death it was Diana who was finally triumphant, and it seemed dramatically right that at her funeral her brother, Charles, Earl Spencer, should have the most important part of all to play. It is not given to many men to have the chance to rebuke the monarch from the pulpit of Westminster Abbey in front of millions. But Charles Spencer seized the moment and, speaking on his sister's behalf, promised to maintain the Spencer influence in the lives of the two young Princes. By speaking as he did, he said what everybody wished to hear, and the unprecedented rumble of applause that filled the Abbey at the end of his address will haunt the Royal Family for ever.

When the funeral was over, it was Diana's brother who reclaimed her body and took her home to Althorp. This was an importan decision for the Earl's own future and for that of Althorp. It is for burying her there that he will be remembered, for his decision has set his mark upon the house for ever.

Diana's secret grave on an island in the middle of the lake at Althorp is the perfect resting place for a legend, and her presence there is inescapable. The lake is surrounded by enormous lime trees, and for sixty days at the height of summer, people come from around the world to remember her. They cannot see where she is buried, but they know that she is there. It is a place with a magic of its own. A memorial urn stands on the edge of the water, and the island has been planted with two hundred white rambling roses.

Ironically, Johnnie Spencer's plans for the salvation of his family have worked, although in a sad and awful way. Through the death of his favourite daughter Althorp's future has been totally assured, together with the future of the Spencers. Diana has also done what was expected of her by the House of Windsor, by leaving them the two Princes. The fact that Prince William bears a strong physical resemblance to his mother, and shares something of her legend, may prove the brightest hope for the future of the monarchy.

After his funeral speech, Charles Spencer became immensely popular, but such popularity rarely lasts. He could never take Diana's place, and his own divorce proceedings, coming so shortly afterwards, with their revelations of his marital infidelities, negated any claim he might have had as a moral guardian of the two young Princes. But in spite of this the influence of Althorp and the Spencer family on the royal children will continue as they grow older. Charles Spencer, unlike the Windsors, had always loved Diana so that as royal uncle he will inevitably be the most important link they have with their mother. In the same way, William and Harry will always be drawn to Northamptonshire to visit their mother's island grave, and visit their uncle and their Spencer cousins. The main influence in the boys' lives will obviously come from the Windsors. But the Princes have the Spencer blood. They too belong to Althorp.

Acknowledgements

I must thank Her Majesty the Queen for access to papers in the Royal Archives relating to the career of the sixth Earl Spencer as Lord Chamberlain, and permission to quote from his letters, together with references to the sixth Earl in the diaries of King George V. I must also thank the Registrar of the Royal Archives, Lady de Bellaigue, for her invaluable help and also for her advice over the Earl's role as Lord Chamberlain.

The splendid Northamptonshire Record Office made available the domestic papers of the Spencer family, the Library of the University of Leeds helped me with the correspondence between the sixth Earl Spencer and Edmund Gosse, and the John Rylands Library at Manchester University gave me details of the great library of the second Earl Spencer.

As a number of the individuals I spoke to on the recent history of the Spencers asked me to preserve their privacy, I feel it safest if I give my general if extremely warm thanks to all who helped me with their recollections in this area. At the same time I must thank the following for their encouragement and advice: David Barrie, Sarah Bradford, David Cannadine, Michael Cole, Fr. H. Condron CP, the Duke and Duchess of Devonshire, Michael Holroyd, Lewis Jebb, Angela Levin, James Macdonald Buchanan, Richard Milward, Andrew Morton, Ben Pimlot, Jane Rick, Kenneth Rose, William Sitwell, Richard Stanley, Sir Roy Strong, Hugo Vickers and Philip Ziegler.

I am most grateful to Mary Roche for permission to reproduce photographs of her family. Edda Tasiemka, of the unique Tasiemka Archive, was an invaluable source of information of the press. Janice Behrend was indefatigable in unearthing details of the American saga of the Fermoys. And while Paul Hopkins gave me shrewd and tireless help over research, I must emphasise that any errors of omission or commission in this book are mine alone. I must thank Val Hudson, kindest of publishers, and Andrea Henry, calmest and most practical of editors. Ted Green was staunch as ever. And my wife Lynette was worldly, wonderful and wise. Without her help this book would not have been possible, but then, nor would much else.

Sources

Introduction

The two general books on the Spencers which are drawn on in the Introduction are: *The Spencers of Althorp*, Georgiana Battiscombe (London: Constable, 1984); and Charles Spencer's *Althorp, the Story* (Harmondsworth: Penguin, 1998).

CHAPTER 1: *The Rise and Rise of the Spencers*

Julia Cartwright, *Sacharissa* (London: Seeley, 1893). Gives details of Waller's muse, the first Countess Sunderland.

T. F. Dibdin in *Aedes Althorpianae* (London: Shakespeare Press: 1822). An account of the mansion, books and pictures at Althorp House.

M.E. Finch, *Five Northamptonshire Families* (Northamptonshire Record Society, l956). An invaluable source for the social and financial rise of the Spencers at Althorp in the sixteenth and early seventeenth centuries.

Harold Nicolson, *Good Behaviour* (London: Constable, 1956). For details on Sir Philip Sidney's death and funeral.

Nikolas Pevsner, *The Buildings of Northamptonshire* (Harmondsworth: Penguin, 1961). Provides details on Althorp and the Spencer tombs in Great Brington Church.

J.H. Round, *Studies in the English Peerage* (London: Constable, 1901). Describes the Spencer family's invented connections with the medieval Despensers.

Lawrence Stone, *An Open Elite England, 1540–1880* (Oxford: Oxford University Press, 1986). Has a useful section on Northamptonshire families.

G.M. Trevelyan, *English Social History* (London: Collins, 1945). Covers sheep farming, Tudor enclosures and the Tudor wool trade.

Peerage of England (London: Collins, 1779). Describes the first Sir John Spencer, and gives details of his will.

Edward Hyell, Lord Clarendon, *History of of the Rebellion and Civil Wars of England* (Oxford: Oxford University Press, 1967). Describes the character and death of Henry Spencer, first Earl of Sunderland.

C.V. Wedgewood, *The King's Peace* (London: Collins, 1955). Account of Sunderland's attitude to the Civil War.

The King's War (London: Collins, 1958). Circumstances surrounding the death of Henry Spencer, first Earl of Sunderland.

CHAPTER 2: *Shameless Sunderland*

G.N. Clark, *The Later Stuarts, 1660–1714* (Oxford: Oxford University Press, 1949).

John Evelyn, *Diaries*, ed. William Bray (Bell, 1908) and *The Journeys of Celia Fiennes* (Cresset Press, 1947). Both provide the contemporary sources on Althorp and Sunderland himself.

Charles James Fox, *History of the Early Reign – James II* (London: Millar, 1808). On Sunderland and Louise de Keroualle.

H.C. Foxcroft, *The Character of a Trimmer* (Cambridge: Cambridge University Press, 1946) includes a strongly hostile view of Sunderland.

J.P. Kenyon, *Robert Spencer – Earl of Sunderland* (London: Batsford, 1958) is the main source on this enigmatic character, also Kenyon, *The Stuarts* (London: Batsford, 1960).

Daniela Mignani, *Le Ville Medicee* (Arnaud, 1980). Gives an account of the court of Grand Duke Cosimo III of Tuscany at the time when Sunderland visited it.

Nigel Nicolson, *Great Houses of Britain* (London: Weidenfeld & Nicolson, 1978). For details of seventeenth-century Althorp.

Christopher Simon Sykes, *Black Sheep* (London: Chatto & Windus, 1982) devotes a chapter to the Sunderland's own black sheep son, Lord Robert Spencer.

CHAPTER 3: *The Great Inheritance*

Winston Churchill, *Marlborough His Life and Times* (Edinburgh: Harrap, 1956). A powerful and strongly supportive picture of Marlborough and his times.

G.N. Clark, *The Later Stuarts, 1660–1714* (Oxford: Oxford University Press, 1949).

Frances Harris, *A Passion for Government: The Life of Sarah, Duchess of Marlborough* (Oxford: Clarendon Press, 1991). An invaluable source on Charles Spencer, third Earl of Sunderland and the Marlborough inheritance.

Louis Kronenberger, *Marlborough's Duchess* (London: Weidenfeld & Nicolson, 1958).

J.H. Plumb, *Life of Sir Robert Walpole* (Cresset Press, 1956). Gives a generally favourable view of the third Earl of Sunderland.

A.L. Rowse, *The Early Churchills* (London: Macmillan, 1956). Rowse gives the best overview of the Spencers and the Churchills.

Gladys Scott Thomson, ed., *Letters of a Grandmother* (London: Jonathan Cape, 1993). From Sarah Marlborough to her favourite granddaughter, Diana 'Lady Dye' Spencer, later Duchess of Bedford.

Marjorie Villiers, *The Grand Whiggery* (London: John Murray, 1939).

CHAPTER 4: *A Liberated Woman*

Frances Harris, *A Passion for Government: The Life of Sarah, Duchess of Marlborough* (Oxford: Clarendon Press, 1991). Continues the story of the great inheritance up to and beyond her death.

Horace Walpole, *Diaries*, ed. W.S. Lewis (CT: Yale University Press, 1937–84). Describes the attempted marriage of Lady Diana Spencer and the Prince of Wales.

CHAPTER 5: *The Divide*

A.L. Rowse, *The Early Churchills* (London: Macmillan, 1956). Covers this episode and offers interesting views on the health of the eighteenth-century Spencers.

Lord Rosebery, *Life of Chatham* (London: A.L. Humphrey, 1910). Deals with question of the Spencer legacy.

Horace Walpole, *Diaries*, decribes the character and death of John Spencer.

CHAPTER 6: *The First Earl*

Joseph Friedman, *Spencer House: Chronicle of a Great London Mansion* (London: Zwemmer, 1993). Describes the building and subsequent redecoration and restoration of Spencer House.

CHAPTER 7: *'A Wild and Scrambling Life'*

Earl of Bessborough, ed., *Georgiana* (London: John Murray, 1955). Extracts from the correspondence of Georgiana, Duchess of Devonshire.

Amanda Foreman, *Georgiana, Duchess of Devonshire* (London: HarperCollins*Publishers*, 1998). The most scholarly account of the Duchess's life.

Iris Leveson Gower, *The Face Without a Frown* (London: Muller, 1944).

Brian Masters, *Georgiana, Duchess of Devonshire* (London: Hamish Hamilton, 1981) is also useful.

CHAPTER 8: *The Great Library*

Flora Fraser, *Lady Hamilton* (London: Secker and Warburg, 1996). For details of relations of Nelson, the Spencers and the Hamiltons.

Anthony Hobson, *Great Libraries* (1970).

Anthony Lister, *The Althorp Library of the Second Earl Spencer* (Bulletin of the John Rylands University Library of Manchester, vol. 71, no. 2, 1989).

Lady Sarah Lyttleton, *Correspondence* (London: John Murray, 1912).

Richard Milward, *The Spencers in Wimbledon, 1744–1994* (The Milward Press, 1996). Gives a detailed picture of the second Earl's life and times at Wimbledon.

G.M. Trevelyan, *George III and Charles Fox* (London: Longmans, 1929). Includes an account of the second Earl at the Admiralty.

CHAPTER 9: *Reform and After*

Walter Bagehot, *Biographical Studies* (London: Longmans, 1895). Lord Althorp and the Reform Act. A dissenting nineteenth-century view of Althorp.

Michael Brock, *The Great Reform Act* (London: Hutchinson, 1973).

Thomas Creevey, *The Creevey Papers*, ed. John Gore (London: John Murray, 1948); *Captain Gronow's Reminiscences*, ed. C. Hibbert (London: Kyle Cathie, 1991). Both describe Althorp in Parliament.

Abraham B. Kriegel, ed., *The Holland House Diaries* (London: Routledge & Kegan Paul, 1977).

Sir Denis Le Marchant, *A Memoir of John Charles, Viscount Althorp, Third Earl Spencer* (London: Bentley, 1876). The nineteenth-century official life.

Guy Paget, *The History of Althorp and the Pytchley Hunt* (London: Collins, 1977).

Ellis Archer Wasson, *Lord Althorp and the Whig Renaissance* (New York: Garland, 1987). A primary source on Althorp and the Reform Act.

CHAPTER 10: *The Holy Tramp*

Father Pius (Devine), *The Life of Father Ignatius of St Paul* (Dublin: Duffy, 1866). Although something of a work of hagiography, written by a fellow Passionist monk, this remains the standard work on the subject. It includes much of Ignatius's own journals, from which the account of his visit to Lord John Russell is taken.

Josef Vanden Bussche, *Ignatius (George) Spencer, Passionist* (Leuven: Leuven University Press, 1991). Provides a more measured view of Ignatius's life and takes account of modern reseach.

Father Ignatius. His diaries are in the possession of the Order of Passionists. The letters to and from his mother, Lavinia, Countess Spencer, are in the Northamptonshire Record Office.

Jerome Vereb, *Ignatius Spencer, Apostle of Christian Unity* (CTS Publications, 1992). Particular notice is made of his role as an apostle of ecumenicalism.

CHAPTER 11: *The Red Earl*

David Cannadine, *The Decline and Fall of the English Aristocracy* (CT: Yale University Press, 1991). Fascinating on the overall aristocratic decline of the period.

Virginia Cowles, *Edward VII and his Circle* (London: Hamish Hamilton, 1956).

Joseph Friedman, *Spencer House: Chronicle of a Great London Mansion* (London: Zwemmer, 1993). Account of renovations to the house by the fifth Earl.

Peter Gordon, ed., *The Papers of the Fifth Earl Spencer* (Northampton: Northamptonshire Record Society, 1981). In the absence of a full-scale biography of the Red Earl, Peter Gordon's introductions to the two volumes are businesslike and illuminating on the details of his life.

Joan Hassell, *The Lonely Empress. Elizabeth of Austria* (London: Weidenfeld & Nicolson, 1963). Details of the Empress hunting and at Althorp.

Sir Sydney Lee, *King Edward VII* (London: Macmillan, 1925).

Christopher Sykes, *Four Studies on Loyalty* (London: Collins, 1948) for an account of Sir Tatton Sykes's ordeal.

CHAPTER 12: *'Dearest Boy'*

King George V. The letters from Spencer to King Edward VII and George V and the description of Althorp from the diary are at Windsor Castle and are quoted by gracious permission of H.M. the Queen.

Christopher Hassall, *Edward Marsh* (London: Longmans, 1959). Gives an account of the sixth Earl at Althorp.

John Johnson, *The Lord Chamberlain's Blue Pencil* (London: Hodder & Stoughton, 1990).

Michaela Reid, *Ask Sir James* (London: Hodder & Stoughton, 1987). Describes the death of Margaret Spencer.

Charles Robert, sixth Earl Spencer. Correspondence to and from his mother is in the Northamptonshire Record Office.

Anne Thwaites, *Edmund Gosse* (London: Secker and Warburg, 1984). Tells of Lord Spencer's friendship with the author of *Father and Son*; Spencer's letters to Gosse are in the Library of the University of Leeds.

CHAPTER 13: *'Jolly Jack'*

Sir Alan Lascelles, *End of an Era* (London: Hamish Hamilton, 1986). Gives details of Jack Spencer at Cambridge.

Christopher Hassall, *Edward Marsh* (London: Longmans, 1959).
S.N. Behrman, *Duveen* (London: Random House, 1957).

CHAPTER 14: *The Fermoys*
New York Times, 30 September 1900.

CHAPTER 15: *Raine's War*
Angela Levin, *Raine and Johnnie* (London: Weidenfeld & Nicolson, 1993).

Notes

The enclosure movement

The enclosure movement is the name given to the conversion by landlords of open fields into those surrounded by hedges and fences in an attempt to maximise farming yields. The process, which began in the late Middle Ages with sheep farming, reached its peak in the mid-eighteenth century in response to new methods of arable farming. Enclosure often led to the loss of rights over common land and accordingly provoked social discontent.

The woollen industry in the sixteenth century

Wool was one of the most important industries in medieval and Tudor England. It was produced both for export in its natural state to the Continent and as the raw material for the manufacture of cloth in cities such as Norwich. The export trade was monopolised by the Merchant Adventurers Company, who had headquarters or Staples in Antwerp and later Hamburg. The slow decline of the broadcloth industry in the sixteenth and seventeenth centuries created severe economic problems.

James I and the inflation of honours

The accession of James I in 1603 brought a marked liberality to the distribution of favours and aristocratic titles, which his predecessor Elizabeth had granted only sparingly. James's natural extravagance, together with his consequent need for money, led to a corrupt market in honours. The peerage almost doubled in number during his reign, an absurd inflation that reduced both its own standing and that of the monarchy.

Sir Philip Sidney (1554–86)

Soldier, statesman and poet whose early death in battle at Zutphen led to his being admired as the epitome of Elizabethan chivalry. His literary circle, who were influenced by the new Protestant and humanist ideas, included Edmund Spenser. None of his writing, including the prose romance *Arcadia* (1590) was published until after his death.

Charles I and the Civil War (1642–49)

The Civil War was very broadly a conflict between those who sought to limit the scope of the King's powers and those who supported him. The latter, known as the Royalists, were based at Oxford, while the former, known as the Parliamentary party, were based at Westminster. The forces of Parliament, commanded by Oliver Cromwell, eventually prevailed and captured Charles, who was executed in 1649 after refusing all attempts at reform. The country was then ruled by Cromwell until his death in 1658. The monarchy was restored in 1660.

Protestants and Catholics

Anti-Catholicism was one of the dominant characteristics of life in England in the two centuries that followed the death of Queen Mary in 1558. Roman Catholicism was associated by the State with such threats to the nation as the Armada, the Gunpowder Plot and rebellion in Ireland, and Catholics became a discreet, gentry-led minority of the population, their religion often a bar to social advancement. Under the Stuart kings, Catholicism was more openly tolerated, especially at court itself.

Early Whigs and Tories

Whigs and Tories were the pejorative names given to each other by the two political parties that emerged in the late seventeenth century. The Whigs were often merchants favouring liberal ideas, while many of the Tories were more conservative country landowners. The Tories were favoured by Charles II and, after his death in 1685, some Whigs placed their faith in his illegitimate son, the Duke of Monmouth, who began a rebellion in the West Country in the hope of deposing his uncle, James II. Monmouth was speedily defeated at Sedgemoor and executed.

The Tories retained the upper hand in Government until the succession of George I in 1714, when they became tainted by the support of some of their number for the Stuart line. For the next fifty years, public life was dominated by the Whigs, who became the party trusted by the monarchy. They purged the Army, Church, Law and local government of Tories, who did not emerge from the wilderness until the advent of Pitt the Younger in the 1780s.

The Glorious Revolution

James II, who had been a Roman Catholic since 1660, devoted much of his short reign to advancing Catholicism's fortunes in Britain. He promoted

Catholics to key posts in the Army and Government, reviving Protestant fears of persecution. The birth of his heir in 1688 prompted several politicians to invite the staunchly Protestant William of Orange (who was married to James's daughter Mary) to invade England. James II fled and was succeeded by William and Mary, who ruled jointly until her death in 1694. William was succeeded in 1702 by Mary's sister, Anne.

Jacobites

There were a number of attempts to restore to the throne the exiled Stuarts, whose supporters were known as Jacobites, from the Latin for James (Jacobus). The two most substantial risings took place in 1715 and 1745; on the latter occasion the troops of James II's grandson ('Bonnie Prince Charlie') reached Derby. Both revolts attracted support from Scots (as an expression of nationalism) and, more discreetly, from Tories.

Marlborough and the War of Spanish Succession

The death of the childless Charles II of Spain provoked a contest for the throne between Louis XIV's grandson Philip and Charles, son of the Austrian Emperor. A grand alliance was formed by Britain, the Dutch Republic and several other European states against France, and between 1704 and 1709 the Allied forces under the Duke of Marlborough won a stunning series of victories at Blenheim, Ramillies, Oudenarde and Malplaquet. But Marlborough was replaced in 1711 after the Tories, who were opposed to the war, came to power, and peace was made at Utrecht in 1713.

Prime Ministers before Walpole

Robert Walpole (1676–1745) is regarded as Britain's first true Prime Minster (originally a term of abuse), partly because of the length of his ascendancy (from 1722 to 1742) and partly because he drew his power from the Commons, refusing (unlike his predecessors) to move up to the Lords. But there had been obvious chief ministers before him, among them the second Earl of Sunderland (who held power under James II) and Anne's principal advisers, Sidney Godolphin and Robert Harley. Walpole's precedessors, however, had to rely far more than he on fickle royal favour.

The New Whigs

The accession of George III in 1760 brought an end to the exclusion of Tories from Government. The cohesion of the Whig party was then shattered when one of their number, Lord North, agreed to serve the King on his own terms. Britain's defeat by the American revolutionaries brought to power the so-called New Whigs, who proclaimed themselves the true heirs of the party's traditions of liberty and reform. They were supported by many of the great noble families, but despite the talents of their leader, Charles James Fox, George blamed them for the fall of North, and they were eventually dismissed in favour of Pitt the Younger.

The French Revolution and the Whigs

The central event of the eighteenth century, the overthrow of the French monarchy in 1789, caused deep divisions within the Whig party. Fear of the consequences of radicalism led to a schism in 1794, with many of the most aristocratic Whigs throwing in their lot with Pitt's ministry. Another group remained in opposition under Fox, whose stance against the harsh measures brought in by Pitt to curb the threat of revolution in Britain helped to ensure that the Whigs continued to be identified with personal liberty.

The Ministry of All the Talents (1806–7)

The death of Pitt in 1806, while the country was at war with Napoleon, left no obvious figure in the ascendant. Lord Grenville became Prime Minister and forced George to accept his ally Fox as Foreign Secretary, while the former Prime Minister Henry Addington was also brought in to broaden the coalition. The ministry's great success was the abolition of the slave trade in 1807, but otherwise its individual members had differing views on every important issue. Fox's death in September 1806 further weakened it, and it was dismissed after falling out with George over its desire to extend Catholic emancipation.

Charles, second Earl Grey (1764–1845)

Prime Minister from 1830 until 1834. He first came to notice as a founder of the Society of the Friends of the People, whose radical ideas on parliamentary reform helped cause the schism among the Whigs in 1794. He succeeded Fox as Foreign Secretary in the Ministry of All the Talents, and then from 1807–30 was in opposition. As Prime Minister, he eventually secured the passage of the first Reform Act in 1832, which began to extend voting rights to the population at large. The tea is named after his son.

Later Dukes of Marlborough

The Marlboroughs are one of the great noble families in England, but have rarely played the national role they might have expected, devoting most of their energies instead to the upkeep of Blenheim. It was the fourth Duke who had Capability Brown landscape the palace's grounds, but he ended his life as a recluse. The fifth Duke changed the family name to

Spencer-Churchill, but otherwise did little beyond running up debts. The seventh Duke was Lord Lieutenant of Ireland in the 1870s; his younger son, Lord Randolph Churchill, became Chancellor of the Exchequer before rashly resigning, ending his political career at thirty-seven. His son was Winston Churchill.

Navarino (20 October 1827)

Naval engagement during the Greek War of Independence. A combined fleet of British, French and Russian ships, commanded by Vice Admiral Codrington, sought out and destroyed the Turkish-Egyptian fleet, which was anchored off the Greek coast. The victory made Greek independence certain, although Codrington was subsequently censured for having acted on his own initiative. The battle, in which Frederick Spencer captained *Talbot*, was the last action fought entirely under sail.

Index